A

B O O K

The Philip E. Lilienthal imprint honors special books
in commemoration of a man whose work
at the University of California Press from 1954 to 1979
was marked by dedication to young authors
and to high standards in the field of Asian Studies.
Friends, family, authors, and foundations
have together endowed the Lilienthal Fund,
which enables the Press to publish under this imprint
selected books in a way that reflects the taste and judgment
of a great and beloved editor.

The publisher gratefully acknowledges the generous contribution to this book provided by the Philip E. Lilienthal Asian Studies Endowment Fund of the University of California Press Foundation, which is supported by a major gift from Sally Lilienthal.

THE TOO-GOOD WIFE

ETHNOGRAPHIC STUDIES IN SUBJECTIVITY

Tanya Luhrmann and Steven Parish, Editors

1. *Forget Colonialism? Sacrifice and the Art of Memory in Madagascar,*
   by Jennifer Cole

2. *Sensory Biographies: Lives and Deaths among Nepal's Yolmo Buddhists,*
   by Robert Desjarlais

3. *Culture and the Senses: Bodily Ways of Knowing in an African Community,*
   by Kathryn Linn Geurts

4. *Becoming Sinners: Christianity and Moral Torment in a Papua New Guinea Society,*
   by Joel Robbins

5. *Jesus in Our Wombs: Embodying Modernity in a Mexican Convent,*
   by Rebecca J. Lester

6. *The Too-Good Wife: Alcohol, Codependency, and the Politics of Nurturance in Postwar Japan,*
   by Amy Borovoy

THE TOO-GOOD WIFE

Alcohol, Codependency, and the Politics of Nurturance in Postwar Japan

Amy Borovoy

University of California Press   Berkeley   Los Angeles   London

University of California Press, one of the most distinguished university presses in the United States, enriches lives around the world by advancing scholarship in the humanities, social sciences, and natural sciences. Its activities are supported by the UC Press Foundation and by philanthropic contributions from individuals and institutions. For more information, visit www.ucpress.edu.

University of California Press
Berkeley and Los Angeles, California

University of California Press, Ltd.
London, England

Library of Congress Cataloging-in-Publication Data

Borovoy, Amy Beth.
    The too-good wife : alcohol, codependency, and the politics of nurturance in postwar Japan / Amy Borovoy.
        p.   cm. — (Ethnographic studies in subjectivity ; 6)
    Includes bibliographical references and index.
    ISBN 0-520-24451-6 (cloth : alk. paper)—ISBN 0-520-24452-4 (pbk. : alk. paper)
    1. Alcoholics—Japan—Tokyo—Family relationships.   2. Alcoholics' spouses—Japan—Tokyo.   3. Parents of narcotic addicts—Japan—Tokyo.   4. Codependency—Japan—Tokyo.   5. Social work with women—Japan—Tokyo.   6. Sex role—Japan—Tokyo.   7. Wives—Japan—Tokyo.   I. Title.   II. Series.
HV5132.B67   2005
362.29′13′0952135—dc22   2004029705

Manufactured in the United States of America

14 13 12 11 10 09 08 07 06 05
10 9 8 7 6 5 4 3 2 1

This book is printed on New Leaf EcoBook 60, containing 60% post-consumer waste, processed chlorine free; 30% de-inked recycled fiber, elemental chlorine free; and 10% FSC-certified virgin fiber, totally chlorine free. EcoBook 60 is acid-free and meets the minimum requirements of ANSI/ASTM D5634–01 (*Permanence of Paper*).

CONTENTS

Preface   vii

Acknowledgments   xv

Introduction: "Dirty Lukewarm Water"   1

1. Alcoholism and Codependency: New Vocabularies for Unspeakable Problems   42

2. Motherhood, Nurturance, and "Total Care" in Postwar National Ideology   67

3. Good Wives: Negotiating Marital Relationships   86

4. A Success Story   115

5. The Inescapable Discourse of Motherhood   137

Conclusion: The Home as a Feminist Dilemma   161

Notes   177

References   201

Index   219

This book follows conversations held in Tokyo among a group of middle-class women. The women were brought together by their struggles with family members—husbands who drank too much or children with substance abuse problems. The severity of their struggles makes the women unusual, but the issues they confronted in making sense of their lives and creating order out of conflict are of a piece with issues and tensions confronted by "normal" Japanese families. The conversations took place each week at "the Center," a clinic offering both inpatient and outpatient mental health care in central Tokyo. I observed the meetings for one year.[1]

My presence at the weekly family meetings and the privilege of hearing the rather intimate stories collected here are the result of overlapping histories. On a personal level, they include my encounters with Japan in college and before, and my family's encounters with Japan in the 1960s. In turn, these experiences were framed, inescapably, by a historical moment in which Japan became an object of fascination to many Americans. Between the mid-1960s, when I was born, and the mid-1980s, when I went to college, Japan emerged from its recovery from the almost total ruin brought about by its defeat in World War II to become the second-largest economic power in the world. Living in Northern California in what later came to be known as Silicon Valley, my parents followed closely Japan's remarkable transformation in the late 1960s and 1970s, and Japan's accomplishments were part of our dinner-table conversations.

My father had been involved in the early licensing of American transistor and integrated circuit technologies to NEC, one of Japan's largest electronics makers, and he often marveled at how that industry had taken off. During his travels to Japan in the 1960s, the factories had seemed crude, and he, along with many other American observers, confident in American technology and capital, wondered how the Japanese would manage to compete in a global context. Yet he also noticed that the work was done carefully. While American companies had focused on checking their output to weed out the defective transistors on each chip, the Japanese had invested in making each more carefully, thereby producing a higher yield of usable circuits per chip. By the late 1960s, Japan's output of transistors and integrated circuit chips equaled that of the United States, and by the late 1970s it far surpassed it.

To me now, these reflections seem almost clichés of a very particular era. The fascination with Japan's economic success in the 1980s, alternating with a xenophobic kind of hysteria, was, in retrospect, in part a product of American provincialism—the sheer disbelief that a nation so different culturally from the United States could display such achievements. The language of the time, which described Japan's growth as a "miracle" (Johnson 1982), and Japanese society and politics as "an enigma" (van Wolferen 1989) betrayed this sense of wonder. There appeared a fixation on cultural difference as the key to unlocking Japan's success, as the "international business" sections of bookstores filled with popular books on "the Japanese mind," and business school students turned to medieval treatises on swordplay, such as Miyamoto Musashi's *The Book of Five Rings,* as guides to managerial ethics.

The question that animated the scholarship of the 1980s, and to a considerable degree still does, is how Japanese citizens mobilized behind agendas of rapid economic growth despite the enormous social sacrifices entailed. While the popular imagination produced only simplistic theories of "conformity" and "group orientation," those who looked more carefully saw something different: the Japanese state and its constituent institutions (schools, companies, neighborhood associations) had structured an environment that drew citizens into these social commitments. People felt "cared for." If there was a group orientation, scholars argued, it arose out of the ability of the contemporary Japanese state, firms, and families to solicit citizens' participation and to persuade them of the importance of these various social institutions—not from deeply rooted or intrinsic qualities of people (see, for example, Plath 1980; Rohlen 1989; Allison 1991).

Whether this participation should be considered enfranchisement or cooptation is a continuing subject of debate, but the question of how people were drawn into disciplined regimens of work, community, and education—and at what cost—fascinated me and ultimately motivated me to examine more carefully the family in Japan.

Upon graduation from college in 1986, I moved to Japan, alone, with the hope of learning some Japanese and finding out more about the culture, while supporting myself by teaching English. My inspiration was in part, no doubt, shaped by the fascination with Japan I'd grown up with. And during my stay, I grew quite close to a family that my parents had come to know in the context of the 1960s and 1970s, a young engineer and his wife, Shigeo and Katsuko Yamamoto.

The Yamamotos were, in many respects, a typical young couple of their generation: they had grown up during the impoverished years of World War II and the subsequent U.S. occupation and, in many respects, had been socialized into two quite different worlds: the prewar nationalism that had mobilized Japanese citizens to make extraordinary sacrifices for Japan's imperialistic and anti-Western war, and the postwar world of democratization, America-centrism, and internationalization. Yet they were also unusual. They welcomed my parents into their tiny Tokyo apartment, and gradually the two families became friends. The Yamamotos made many subsequent trips to the United States and to our home, and their accommodations to American ideas were significant: they often socialized as a couple with American couples (something rare among this generation), they learned a considerable amount of English, and they were at times outspoken about their political views and ideas. But what was also clear was their absolute commitment to family and productivity. Although, later on, they welcomed my prolonged studies in Japan and applauded my adventurousness, they raised their own daughters to be housewives and to stay close to home, caring for children and extended family.

The single year I had intended to spend in Japan became three. And as I studied, worked, and grew more involved in family life, my sense of the importance of the home sphere was heightened.

The Yamamotos lived an hour south of Tokyo, in a bustling city on the beach. Most people in their community seemed to regard them as an "ideal family." Katsuko made her home a warm and welcoming place not only for me but also for her family—so much so that both her daughters had chosen to marry men from the same town and lived only a few minutes away by bicycle. The daughters, Azusa and Chigusa, were frequent visitors and called or came over at the slightest provocation: they were on a walk, they weren't feeling well, one of their children had passed a developmental milestone (a new word, for example) or wasn't feeling well, and so forth. In each case Katsuko provided encouragement and validation and seemed to assume the pleasures of her daughters' lives as her own. I also observed the ways she ministered to her husband, Shigeo, each day handing him his briefcase and wheeling his bike from the back shed to the front door for his ride to the station. She also managed all the financial transactions, including filing the yearly taxes, which she learned to do at the local ward office.

During the course of the initial three years that I spent in Japan, I came to see the profound concessions that Katsuko had made to family life. Not long after they had married, Shigeo's parents moved in with them, and the four began a life together in very close quarters. Sami-san, Shigeo's mother, believed that idleness led to quarreling, so once the children began attending school, she insisted on teaching Katsuko to sew. Though Katsuko had little interest and, she felt, no particular talent, she agreed in order to keep the peace. Each day for six hours a day they sat together in a small room upstairs; Sami-san would bring home piecework from the local cleaners, teaching by carefully drawing pictures as they went. She was a stern taskmaster but also a good teacher, Katsuko recounted, and Katsuko gradually accommodated herself to the new life. She also made other adjustments. Katsuko's parents were Christian and Shigeo's parents followed Shinto practices. Upon their engagement, Katsuko's family had opposed the idea of a traditional Shinto wedding (it is sacrilegious for Christians to bow down before an idol), and at last the two sides agreed upon a civil ceremony. But the negotiations left bad feelings on the part of the Yamamotos. Later in married life, when Katsuko began to find the time for church, she made sure to complete all the morning's chores and prepare the grandparents' lunch, leaving it sitting on the table ready for reheating, before leaving for church. "Older people like to eat right at noon," she once told me, "or else they get cranky." During the three years I lived in Tokyo, both of Shigeo's parents died of cancer. Katsuko cared for them, largely at home and with little help, until their deaths. In between, Katsuko was diagnosed with ulcerative colitis, an incurable inflammation of the large intestine often exacerbated by stress. She eventually spent three months in the hospital, culminating in a surgery that removed much of her large intestine.

Eventually, Katsuko recovered and seemed to enter what appeared in many ways to be the prime of her life. With no parents to care for and her two daughters grown now with children of their own, she used her spare time to become more active in church activities, volunteer at the local senior center, and become more involved with her grandchildren. She also began teaching kimono-making professionally, earning some money on the side. In many ways it seemed that she had turned her hardships and setbacks into strengths—resources that she was now drawing on. Shigeo complained that she was often not home to answer the phone when he called during the day needing a phone number or a favor. But both knew that she had earned this freedom. In thinking about her experience, I often wondered how someone who seemed so canny and determined had never put her foot down in some way. It wasn't until many years later that I saw that it was her early years of endurance that ultimately conferred on her a later sense of entitlement. Coping, patience, endurance—the kinds of behaviors that I would have considered equivocations or concessions to an unjust system—were viable, even strategic, choices.

By the time I entered graduate school in 1989 at Stanford University, the image of "Japan Inc.," a smoothly functioning machine and a thoroughly integrated society, was undergoing intense criticism. Scholars were interrogating the historical conditions that had shaped American scholarship on Japan. Was our fascination with Japan as a "problem" in need of explanation in part the product of our own assumption that American-style free-market capitalism and individualism are the necessary endpoints of civilization? Had we fallen into a trap created by our own narrow constructions of modernity? Japan was not as cohesive as imagined. The very notion of culture as that which could explain national histories was being called into question (Ivy 1995; Sakai 1989). More broadly, the field of cultural anthropology and the concept of culture were undergoing profound changes. The notion of culture as whole, integrated, and shared by all members of a society—the "one society one culture" model that had animated earlier studies of "primitive" societies—was being replaced by an increasing focus on cultural fissures, social conflict, and historical processes. Culture was no longer a stagnant body of beliefs, rites, or received wisdom (Rosaldo 1989). To understand Japan, it became imperative to understand the specific processes, ideological and institutional, that seemed to hold the society together—despite internal conflicts and tensions—and to understand at what costs.

I increasingly focused on women as a nexus of the social worlds that served as the society's "glue." Important research was being done on women's status in Japan and on the 1986 passage of the Equal Employment Opportunities Law. Of particular interest was Margaret Lock's research on "housewife syndrome" and the medicalization (and depoliticization) of Japanese women's frustration (1987, 1988, 1990). Lock showed how women were being silenced: they took their complaints to doctors in the form of stress-related medical symptoms, whereupon physicians who recognized their problems (labeling them "child-rearing neurosis" and "kitchen syndrome") advised them to put their feelings aside and reintegrate into the home environment. Lock's work called attention to the dearth of venues women had to talk about their problems, and to the political stakes involved. Yet Japanese women had a history of civic participation and grassroots networking, and this prompted me to explore what else might be going on in the world of women's consciousness-raising.

I approached the heads of a number of feminist therapy and consciousness-raising groups in the hope of learning what kinds of conversations were emerging and what difference, if any, they were making. I secured funding for a summer of preliminary research and interviewed a range of women, including social workers in charge of various counseling programs at city-funded health-care centers. One such center agreed to let me observe and participate on a regular basis. By the time I returned for a full year of research, a new support group had been started for families of substance abusers, and this group became my main focus.

While affiliated with the Center, I also attended a wide range of women's activist and support groups, some explicitly feminist and others oriented toward mainstream housewives, some nonprofit private enterprises and others state-funded. The sites I visited, some more regularly than others, included the Tokyo Feminist Therapy Center, the Yokohama Women's Forum (funded by the prefectural government), Feminist Therapy *Mado,* a variety of grassroots consciousness-raising and encounter groups ("Zigzag," "Dakara," and "Kinari"), the Divorce with a Smile Bureau *(Niko Niko Rikon Sho),* Tokyo Lifeline *(Inochi no Denwa,* a telephone hotline supported by the city of Tokyo), and the Medical Social Casework Department at St. Luke's Hospital, a large, private, internationally oriented hospital. Each of these groups revealed to me, in its own way, aspects of feminist and women's politics in Japan.

The Social Casework Department was particularly important. This department offered counseling to patients who were visiting the hospital for a variety of reasons. It was the only department in the hospital that offered any kind of "talking therapy" or extended counseling. Many of the clients were women. And here, perhaps more than at the Center, I was introduced to the broad range of dilemmas that face the middle-class housewife of this generation. Patients were referred to Social Casework by other departments, including Psychiatry, Pediatrics, Obstetrics and Gynecology, and Dermatology. Once a week, I observed an entire day of appointments, witnessing women struggling to come to terms with philandering husbands, the ennui of their jobs, caring for the elderly, apathy toward child-rearing, difficult mothers-in-law, or gambling husbands. I have not included accounts of most of these encounters in this book, but they form an important context for my understanding of the dilemmas that face this generation of women.

In particular, the senior social worker in the department at the time, Dr. Fukazawa Satoko, was an important mentor to me. A woman then in her late fifties who had never married (she once told me that she could not abide the traditional role of the wife in Japan because she had come from a family of matriarchs), she both appreciated the deeply rooted historical realities of family life and simultaneously chafed against them. She once told me that behind the apparently modern, nuclear family of postwar Japan lies the thinly veiled reality of the traditional Japanese *ie,* or household—where support for the elder generations is imperative and the project of raising the next generation is paramount. These dualities revealed themselves to me on a daily basis, and I came to see the wisdom of her comment.

In one particularly telling piece of writing that she shared with me, Fukazawa describes a summer stay in Cambridge, Massachusetts, with a colleague, and her observations of the results of American feminism:

> As I rode to work on the subway, I would cast my eyes on many young women, those who were avidly reading the morning paper, women who seemingly paid no mind to such Japanese notions as "appropriate marital age" *[kekkon no tekireiki]* but were instead students in graduate school or young

professors whose activities took them all over the world. These women were determined to make the most of their intelligence. I was struck by the realization that "women's lib," which blew through Japan like a passing fashion, had had an indisputably powerful influence on American society.

. . . In fact, many of the social workers I met had experienced divorce and remarriage. Strong as they were on the outside, working right alongside men, I suspected that inside they struggled with isolation and loneliness. And as I got to know them better, I realized that these struggles were even larger than I had imagined.

In the shadows of the celebrated American virtue of independence *[doku-ritsu]* can be seen the silhouette of solitude *[hitori bocchi]*. For example, on a day when everyone is wearing short sleeves, a person walking around in a heavy coat will scarcely merit a glance; "I'm me and you're you" *[Tanin wa tanin, watashi wa watashi]*—so no one shows any concern. In a society composed of individuals *[ko no shūdan]*, unless you actively seek out this kind of a connection, no one will pay you any attention.

As someone who has lived my life subscribing to particular Japanese notions of femininity *[onnarashisa]*, believing that sauciness *[namaikisa]* was something to be suppressed and always attending to "the eyes of society" *[sekentei]*, I found this eastern university town a wholly pleasant place to be.

Yet since then, two years have passed and I am once again surrounded by a social world that requires obedience to "worldly appearances." Japanese society, which demands a certain attentiveness *[kikubari]* of its members, has its burdensome *[wazurawashii]* aspects, but I've come to think that for human beings it is a source of happiness. To the extent that we actually welcome this burden, I wonder if we sense that the shadow of loneliness steals near our personal lives.[2]

This essay, which I've read over again many times since she initially handed it to me, captures what I imagine to be the ambivalence that many Japanese women associate with American individualism, American marriage, and American feminism—accompanied by the simultaneous recognition of the toll that their own system has taken. It is this ambivalence which I explore in greater depth in this book.

ACKNOWLEDGMENTS

This book has accompanied me through a series of life phases and intellectual shifts. As a result, it reflects the inspiration and companionship of a broad range of colleagues, friends, and family members.

During my years as a graduate student at Stanford, the mentoring I received from my committee—Harumi Befu, Jane Collier, Carol Delaney, and Sylvia Yanagisako—was invaluable. As chair, Harumi Befu offered a great deal of guidance and support. The radical questions being raised about gender and kinship in the Stanford department at that time created an important environment and got me thinking about the contradictions entailed in American constructions of gender and femininity—in particular, the difficulty of being both "a good woman" and "a good person" (as Jane Collier once put it) when personhood is defined as independence. Also important was Renato Rosaldo, whose enthusiasm for Weber conveyed to me that there was a place for thinking about the importance of individual subjectivities in understanding cultural shifts more broadly. Tom Rohlen was also a central interlocutor during that time. His ideas on socialization and social order in Japan shed light on the trade-offs of Japanese institutions, such as companies and schools: their seductive powers of enfranchisement and paternalism and yet their squelching rigidity. His ideas helped me continue to make sense of Japan's social cohesion without relying on simple notions of conformity or the group. The companionship and advice of my fellow graduate students, particularly Bill Maurer and Diane Nelson, were also important.

At Princeton, I have benefited from continuing conversations with Sheldon Garon, whose history of the close relationship between the housewife and the Japanese state forms an important context for this material, and who turned my attention to the fine line the state perpetually traverses between protectiveness and repression. Sue Naquin, my department chair, offered thoughtful comments in the latter stages of revision and guided me through the process of submitting the manuscript.

Many others contributed ideas and inspiration; they include Vincanne Adams, Anne Allison, Jane Bachnik, Judith Barker, Gay Becker, Ted Bestor, Isabelle Clark-Deces, Tom Gill, Peter Hegarty, Marilyn Ivy, Sharon Kaufman, Jim Ketelaar, Arthur Kleinman, Sarah Lamb, Robin LeBlanc, Rena Lederman, Margaret Lock, Emily Martin, Ray McDermott, Brian McVeigh, Linda Mitteness, Laura Miller, Laura Nelson, Heather Paxson, Greg Pflugfelder, Louisa Schein, Ueno Chizuko, Merry White, and Tomiko Yoda. My Princeton colleagues, Betsy Armstrong, Sarah Curran, and Carolyn Rouse, read the entire manuscript and offered unending insight and support. My uncle Richard Gordon, a psychologist at Bard College, and my aunt Patti Hill Gordon, have supported and informed the project from the beginning. And in the final stages Bill Kelly and the students in his graduate seminar offered a wonderful discussion of the book in the context of key themes of contemporary Japanology.

Tanya Luhrmann, the series editor at University of California Press, helped thoughtfully shape the book and encouraged me to think about the women's stories in the context of broader human dilemmas. I would also like to thank my editor, Stan Holwitz, the two anonymous reviewers for the press for their thoughtful comments, and the others at UC Press who edited and produced the book, including Randy Heyman, Elizabeth Berg, and Jacqueline Volin.

The women in the weekly meetings at the Center in Tokyo, who shared their stories with me, are the biggest contributors to this project. I have tried to convey the importance of their insights in ways they would recognize, although the conversations I am engaging in (with Western feminism, for example) were not the primary focus of their concern. The fine-tuned observations about gender and marriage in Japan are in large part owed to the insight and perception of the women themselves.

The research depended upon the cooperation and enthusiasm of the staff of the Center, especially Tamura Misao, who has been a partner in study. Together we have kept in touch with the women in the group and formed a post-hoc source of support. At Saint Luke's International Hospital, my working relationship with Fukazawa Satoko has been a continual inspiration. In addition, conversations with Dr. Saitō Satoru, Hayakawa Kazuko, Nishida Chikako, and Professor Ehara Yumiko, my mentor at Tokyo Metropolitan University, were especially productive. David Slater and his colleagues in the Department of Comparative Culture at Sophia University in Tokyo provided helpful feedback during my year there as an Abe Fellow.

My husband, Jonathan Morduch, has been my intellectual companion throughout; he saw what was special in the women's stories early on, and his pleasure in the work kept me going. Sharing this work with him has been one of life's great pleasures.

The book is dedicated to my families, the Borovoys and the Yamamotos, for their love, generosity, and support. I hope that I can repay some small part.

Support for fieldwork was generously provided by IIE Fulbright, the National Science Foundation (Anthropological and Geographical Sciences #9209871), and the Stanford University Center for East Asian Studies grant for the study of "women in Asia." The writing process was assisted by a grant from the Joint Committee on Japan Studies of the Social Science Research Council and the American Council of Learned Societies with funds provided by the Andrew W. Mellon Foundation, and also by a National Institute of Aging Postdoctoral Training Grant, no. T32AG0045, Linda S. Mitteness, director.

INTRODUCTION

"Dirty Lukewarm Water"

Each week a group of housewives gathered at "the Center," a public mental health facility in a middle-class district of Tokyo, to participate in what was called a "family meeting." The meeting was, in fact, a support group for families of substance abusers. Despite the inclusion of *family* in the title, the group attracted only women: either wives of alcoholics or mothers of teenagers abusing drugs—usually inhalers of paint thinner, an extremely destructive type of hallucinogen. In 1992, when I first considered doing a year of research at the Center *(Sentā)*, the support group for families of substance abusers was new but had already become a key program. I had not at first set out to study alcoholism, families of alcoholics, or "codependency," but a social worker at the Center strongly encouraged me to attend the meetings as an observer. When she told me that Japanese men had problems with alcoholism and Japanese women had problems with codependency—and that the group offered a powerful form of therapy for the latter—I was startled by her word choice. Men's drinking and women's total care for them had always seemed so much a part of the given landscape of urban Japan, a taken-for-granted aspect of family, work, and social life. The very language of codependency seemed oddly out of place in its pathologization of what had long been considered an everyday fact of life. Yet the social worker stressed that the women were able to make great strides toward managing their codependency, and that there was a general sense of excitement about the group.

The group seemed to be an excellent window into some of the central tensions that have animated postwar Japanese society: the heavy toll of the work ethic, the corporate-sponsored drinking to relieve stress and promote collegiality, the alignment of family behind the needs of the corporation, and the rigidly gendered division of labor that continued to be taken for granted. Here was a group of women addressing these issues not as if they were natural and normal, but as problematic. Naturally, the women were motivated to do so by a tremendous problem, an impasse, in their everyday functioning, namely their husbands' alcoholism or their children's drug abuse. And perhaps they would not have considered these situations "unhealthy" otherwise. But in Japan in the early 1990s, such questions were beginning to be asked, and observing the support group seemed to offer me a window into how this process was unfolding. That this discussion was being raised through the awkward, transplanted vocabulary of American popular psychology was also important, and hardly coincidental.

After each official meeting, the women of the Center gathered for lunch and tea, to have what they called a "second round." While the tenor of the meetings at the Center was formal, tea took place down the street at a smoke-filled coffee shop against the ever-present background of loud rock music. The women's anonymity was assured, since the coffee shop was near the Center and not in their own neighborhoods, and they seemed to have forged a tacit understanding with the waitress: once, she had asked what their connection to the neighborhood was; when they answered that they were engaged in "research," she never pursued it, though they felt sure she must have guessed their affiliation with the nearby mental health center. A group of ten or so boisterous middle-aged housewives in a coffee shop in the midafternoon is an unusual sight in Tokyo, and the women joked that the staff there missed them when they did not appear for a week or two.

One day toward the end of my year participating in the weekly meetings, when I joined the women for their afternoon tea, they began reflecting on their experiences during the most trying times of their husbands' drinking. Abe-san, whose husband had stopped drinking several months before, announced, "I feel as though I've been in the middle of a dark cloud, but at long last I've managed to poke my head out and catch a glimpse of the sunny blue sky.[1] Hata-san said, "I have the sensation of sitting on top of a prickly mountain precipice, and I'd like to fall off." Her husband and son were still heavy drinkers. Considering her dilemma, Hoshi-san chose her words carefully: "During my husband's worst stage, I felt like I was soaking in dirty lukewarm water. It was dirty—but still I wasn't able to get out." In Japanese, a "lukewarm water situation" *(nurumayū jōtai)* refers to a situation that, because of its moderate and comfortable climate, invites complacency. Hoshi-san's image of "dirty" lukewarm water is a vivid image of the kind of situation in which these women found themselves: a situation that had the markings of a warm, intimate family environment and was thus difficult to leave—and yet that was ultimately untenable. The metaphor captures the sometimes fine line between situations that are acceptable, even idealized, in Japanese constructions of gender and family, and situations that have become uncomfortable, exploitative, or even abusive.

In confronting family members' substance abuse, these women (and many like them) face a profound cultural dilemma: when does the nurturing behavior that is ordinarily expected of a good wife and mother become part of a destructive pattern? When does it become exploitative? And, most importantly, how does society (through historically shaped constructions of family and community) affirm or even demand this kind of behavior? Social workers told me that women often wait ten or more years before seeking help for a family member's substance abuse problem, in part because managing family problems through attentive care and sheer endurance is explicitly considered the role of a wife and mother.

How these women came to view long-held notions of family and community as problematic (as problems that needed to solved) rather than simply as the accepted state of things is the subject of this book. As they confronted the question of what it meant to distance themselves from their husbands and children and to stop being the good wife and mother, their conversations turned from coping with alcohol or drug abuse to formulating a discourse of social criticism; questioning the role of good wife and mother ultimately meant criticizing "the normal."

The program at the clinic was designed to help women cope with family members' alcoholism and substance abuse, but ultimately it became a space for conversations about marital relations, mother-child relations, and even postwar notions of "Japaneseness." Thus this book reaches beyond the problem of alcoholism itself to examine the women's process of self-reflection and social criticism, and the deeper fissures and social asymmetries that lurk beneath the surface of the Japanese social order.

WHEN WILL JAPANESE WOMEN BE "LIBERATED"?

In the mid-1980s, when Japan was at the height of its economic influence and prosperity, a considerable degree of attention was being paid to Japanese women. From the outside, Japan displayed all the markers of capitalist modernity—prosperity, urbanization, hyperproductivity, and world-class levels of literacy and education. And yet it appeared to have failed in its feminist revolution. Japanese middle-class women, though increasingly urban and well educated, continued to inhabit the world of the home, viewing family and housekeeping as their central occupations. In the mid-1980s, long after Japan's postwar economic growth had peaked and dramatic social reforms had been completed, few women occupied positions in the upper echelons of Japanese government, business, or corporations. Bowing "office ladies" served tea, greeted guests, and were hired to create a "warm" atmosphere at large Japanese corporations. While, in the United States, the latter half of the twentieth century witnessed a dramatic decline in the number of full-time housewives, in Japan the proportion of full-time housewives continued to increase through the 1970s, reaching its peak in the mid-1970s (Yamada 2001).[2] To a surprising degree, Japan remained a "culture of separate spheres," in the words of one scholar, with women occupying different worlds than men, continuing to take full responsibility for housekeeping and child-rearing while men filled the role of economic provider (White 1992).

Japanese women's seemingly "traditional" orientation captured the attention of the American public. In 1984, "Japanese women" were featured in a photographic essay in *National Geographic* (positioned just before an article on vanishing wildlife) that highlighted the coexistence of modern values with women's traditional ethic of "three steps behind." The problem that Japanese women posed to the wider American audience was the nature of modernity itself, and the tacit expectation that sooner or later all nations would converge on a similar endpoint: the valuation of absolute gender equality, autonomy, and self-determination. To most Americans, Japanese women did not seem fully modern.

The early 1990s, when I began my research, were a particularly interesting time. The 1986 passage of the Equal Employment Opportunity Law (EEOL) in Japan seemed to herald the dawning of a new age: the law enacted a number of changes, long delayed in Japan, that prohibited discrimination in hiring and promotion based on gender. In addition, in the 1980s and 1990s, lawsuits over gender-based wage discrimination and sexual harassment resulted in several high-profile victories, and the absolute numbers of women working continued to grow.

Yet the bigger picture for both working-class and middle-class women over the past thirty years has been one of surprising stability rather than dramatic change. The EEOL did not bring about the momentous changes expected, in part because it contained no measures to punish employers who violated it.[3] Although greater numbers of women have been entering the workforce since the late 1970s, the nature of women's working trajectories and the kinds of labor they perform are radically different from men's working patterns. Still, today Japanese women earn on average less than two-thirds of what men earn in their lives—the lowest among the G7 nations.[4] And despite increasing numbers of women in the workforce, many middle-class women still see their commitment to family as centrally important, even those who work throughout their lives (see Kondo 1990).[5]

More importantly, though, middle-class women of the generation that facilitated Japan's prodigious economic growth seem to perceive the meaning of motherhood and domesticity very differently than their predecessors did: as a public service and not merely as a private or "emotional" enterprise. Even as recently as the early 1990s, when I was embarking on my research, it was difficult not to be struck by these differences. Housewives are a major presence in middle-class urban neighborhoods, and they were the main people I engaged with in my daily life. When I rented an apartment from the family next door, the wife managed all the legal and financial transactions; I hardly met the husband. Each day as I left for work or went about errands, it was the wives who populated the neighborhood landscape, whom I greeted, with whom I exchanged small gifts and objects (sweets, persimmons from a cousin's tree in southern Japan, garden gloves, etc.), and whom I came to know. Furthermore, the women not only populated the neighborhood, they managed and policed it. They were members of the "early risers group" *(asaokikai)* who picked up trash once a month, the PTA, and the local neighborhood associations—women whom Robin LeBlanc has referred to as "bicycle citizens," in contrast to male "taxi citizens," who bypass these community obligations as they commute to work (1999: 2–5). In one memorable incident, I noticed a drunken man who was not from the local community (and possibly transient) passed out on the sidewalk near my home. Within a minute after I had reached home, one of the local women knocked on my door to tell me to be careful: the women had already begun putting out the word. In another episode, while I was at home studying, a commercial truck, struggling to negotiate the narrow streets, backed into my outside fence and then quickly drove away. I heard the crunch and came out to see what had happened; already two neighboring housewives were surveying the damage. One handed me a piece of paper on which she had noted the truck's license plate and the name of the business written on the side. The sense of commitment these women brought to the home and the evident links between the betterment of the home and the betterment of the community made an impression on me and continued to inform my research.

After I returned from my initial summer of research, I organized a reading group at the local Japanese cultural center with a group of Japanese housewives who had been temporarily transferred to the United States with their husbands. I was eager to talk with the women about how they felt about their status and considered putting Betty Friedan's *The Feminine Mystique* (1963) on the reading list. However, as an earnest young anthropologist, I was hesitant to impose the values of Western feminism onto women from an entirely different cultural context. After consulting with an adviser who was more seasoned (and seemed to feel that Japanese women could do with a bit of consciousness-raising), I decided to recommend several chapters from the book. To my surprise, the following week many of the women, at first hesitantly but then more stridently, expressed the view that it was not particularly relevant to Japanese women's lives. In her analysis of the values of the American housewife, Friedan wrote:

> The image of women that emerges from this big, pretty magazine [McCall's] is young and frivolous, almost childlike; fluffy and feminine; passive; gaily content in a world of bedroom and kitchen, sex, babies and home. In the magazine image, women do no work except housework and work to keep their bodies beautiful and to get and keep a man.
>
> This was the image of the American woman in the year Castro led a revolution in Cuba and men were trained to travel into outer space; the year that

the African continent brought forth new nations, and a plane whose speed is greater than the speed of sound broke up a Summit Conference . . . but this magazine, published for over 5,000,000 American women, almost all of whom have been through high school and nearly half to college, contained almost no mention of the world beyond the home. In the second half of the twentieth century in America, woman's world was confined to her own body and beauty, the charming of man, the bearing of babies, and the physical care and serving of husband, children, and home. (Friedan 1963: 36–37)

The image of the American middle-class housewife as chiefly concerned with home decor and looking pretty for her husband did not resonate as closely for Japanese housewives as it did for Americans in the 1960s and 1970s. They saw their work as mothers and members of the community as taking precedence over their role as an object of desire to their husbands. The work of homemaking, including garbage disposal and recycling, managing the family budget, and purchasing household products that were ecologically sound, linked them to broader social concerns; and loving and caring for children was a source of pleasure and a social contribution. In fact, *The Feminine Mystique,* translated into Japanese in 1965 (as *Atarashii Josei no Sōzō*), did not cause the same widespread excitement in Japan, even among the middle-class women who were the book's target audience in the United States, and never became a bestseller. In contrast to American housewives of the 1950s and 1960s, many Japanese housewives of the same period were able to consider themselves productive citizens and to define their experience as both valuable and satisfying despite radically separated spheres of activity. In an important 1987 essay, "The Virtue of Japanese Mothers: Cultural Definitions of Women's Lives," Merry White wrote, "Rarely do you hear a Japanese woman say, 'I'm *just* a housewife'" (1987: 153; see also Vogel 1978, 1988; Imamura 1987; Lebra 1984; Marra 1996; and Lewis 1978).[6]

Historically, the family has been the basis of women's social participation; it is through women's role as housewives that they have lobbied for social legitimacy and political entitlement, including the right to vote, the right to an education, and broad participation in community activism and local politics. Women have enjoyed a great deal of freedom, stability, and support for being housewives—a situation considerably different from that of their American counterparts. And women's pride and pleasure in child-rearing have been more legitimated in Japanese society than in the United States.

Whereas in the United States (and to a lesser extent in Western Europe), the efforts of the state in the latter part of the twentieth century have largely been directed toward prodding women into the workforce rather than supporting them as wives and mothers, the Japanese state, by contrast, has at once sanctioned and exploited women's stay-at-home work, subsidizing the family wage and explicitly defining the role of the housewife as key to economic productivity and modernization. In the years of rapid economic growth following the war, the state, together with Japanese corporate enterprise, viewed the home as a kind of "satellite sphere" of Japanese industry—a place that supported and nourished the central project of economic growth and prosperity (see, for example, Gordon 1997). Women's work as housewives came to constitute the backbone of the regime of rapid economic growth and its constituent spheres, such as school and company. Large-scale corporations encouraged and supported the stay-at-home wife and the single wage-earner model by offering a comprehensive family wage, including pension benefits for nonworking women and housing and marriage subsidies.

The endorsement of the home and the housewife has made the formation of a feminist politics in postwar Japan a complex and contested project. While many women wish to move beyond the home, it seems ill advised to do so by diminishing the home and jeopardizing all the resources that come with it. The exploitative dimensions of women's work, so clear to the Western feminist eye, have proven unexpectedly difficult to name, and to resist. This history, which I elaborate further in chapters 2 and 3, forms an important backdrop for the women's conversations at the Center as they sought to change their responses to their families' demands.

In the early 1990s, in the wake of the passage of the Equal Employment Opportunity Law, it became increasingly clear that legal change, while a step toward implementing gender equality and equal opportunity, would not be sufficient to change deeply held notions of home and family with important historical foundations (see Gelb 1991; Machiko Matsui 1990; Mackie 1988). It was at this juncture that I began my research into feminist consciousness-raising and support groups, with particular interest in the growing number of counseling bureaus and clinical spaces that managed women's issues. In response to a sense that legal changes alone would be insufficient to bring about social equality in Japan, grassroots feminist groups, counseling, and "consciousness-raising" movements blossomed in the early 1990s, and I decided to learn more about their politics.

After an initial summer of observing groups and interviewing women from an array of publicly funded counseling programs (often located in city-funded women's centers), private "feminist therapy" groups, and grassroots activist groups, I was impressed by the fact that women's activism was often closely associated with women's work as wives and mothers: a large number of groups were mobilizing around environmental issues, consumer and nutritional issues, neighborhood cleanliness, and effective homemaking. Women who were working by choice (rather than because they needed to help support their families) often said that their ambition was to do socially "beneficial" kinds of work *(Yūeki rōdō)*, such as opening a macrobiotic lunchbox shop or training women to use computers so that they could find higher-paid jobs. The Group for the Promotion of Co-education in Home Economics *(Kateika no Danjo Kyōshū o Susumeru Kai)* was lobbying the Ministry of Education, schoolteachers, and deans to promote training for boys as well as girls in cooking and child-rearing in the context of home economics courses. Even groups that had explicitly adopted American therapeutic ideas, such as assertiveness training *(jiko shuchō)*, self-expression *(jiko hyōgen)*, and self-determination *(jiko kettei)*, tended to advise their clients not to lightly abandon their central base of support, the home (see Borovoy 2001a).

While a major thrust of the American feminist movement in the 1970s had been to urge middle-class and upper-middle-class women out of the home and into the workplace to achieve financial independence, in Japan this call was more muted, coming largely from the quarters of academic feminism or from women's lib activists who, though highly visible, failed to mobilize the large numbers of middle- and upper middle-class women who had responded to American feminism of the 1960s and 1970s.

AL-ANON AND THE AMERICAN
GENEALOGY OF CODEPENDENCY

In this historical context, the American notion of "codependency" was a highly unlikely set of ideas for Japanese women to embrace. The idea of codependency, first known as "co-alcoholism," emerged as an insight of the wives of American alcoholics who first convened in the 1950s as their husbands attended Alcoholics Anonymous meetings. Through sharing stories, these women concluded that by intervening and protecting the alcoholic—lying to his boss, cleaning up his messes, paying unpaid bills, and otherwise compensating for his forfeit of responsibility—they inadvertently "enabled" the alcoholic to sustain his addictive and destructive behavior (Haaken 1993: 329). Gradually these groups of women organized into a grassroots organization for families of alcoholics, known as Al-Anon, based on the enormously successful model of Alcoholics Anonymous. They began meeting regularly with other wives of alcoholics to share stories.

Al-Anon, which originally named the phenomenon of "enabling," discourages family members from intervening on behalf of the drinker (for example, procuring the money to cover a bounced check) under that theory that such a gesture "increases the alcoholic's sense of failure and guilt, and increases the family's sense of hostility and condemnation of the alcoholic. Thereby the alcoholic is doubly injured." The Al-Anon literature goes on to state, "The writing of the bad check and the redemption of it by the family are but two sides of the same problem" (Al-Anon 1977, 7–10).

Crucial to the Al-Anon literature is the notion that the family's behavior results from a systemic dynamic between the drinker and the family. The Al-Anon literature plainly states that "no wife ever made her husband an alcoholic." Yet "by lack of knowledge [a wife] may allow the illness to go unnoticed. By lack of adequate understanding and courage she may acquiesce in the development of the disease" (Al-Anon, "A Guide for the Family of the Alcoholic").

In the 1980s, the Al-Anon concept of enabling came under the influence of professional therapists and psychodynamic perspectives, and the vocabulary of codependency emerged (Haaken 1990: 396–97). In these newer discourses, codependency is no longer viewed as a body of coping mechanisms resulting from a particular social dynamic but rather as a psychological profile that itself causes particular behaviors. In this view, codependency does not result from engaging with substance abusers; rather codependents *choose* to associate with substance abusers (Beattie 1987: 30). Melody Beattie, author of the best-selling treatise on the syndrome, *Codependent No More,* quotes "Ellen," an Al-Anon member: "When I say I'm codependent, I don't mean I'm a *little* bit codependent. I mean I'm really codependent. I don't marry men who stop for a few beers after work. I marry men who won't work" (1987: 17, original italics). In the context of this new definition, groups such as "Co-Dependents Anonymous" (CoDA) were formed explicitly for those who have no relation to substance abusers and yet who identify as codependent.

Codependency theory of the 1980s saw codependency as a pathology with psychodynamic roots, specifically the result of a problematic upbringing or a "wounded self" (Rice 1996: 76–84). Codependency is described in terms of maladjustment, and pathologizing language peppers the lists of traits that define the codependent personality: obsessiveness, low self-worth, repression, denial, and self-loathing (Beattie 1987:37–44). Beattie writes: "Most co-dependents suffer from that vague but penetrating affliction, low self-worth. We don't feel good about ourselves, we don't like ourselves, and we wouldn't consider loving ourselves. . . . As co-dependents, we frequently dislike ourselves so much that we believe it's wrong to take ourselves into account, in other words, to appear selfish. Putting ourselves first is out of the question" (109–11). Beattie's text describes even basic features of human relationships as characteristics of codependency; codependents are those who "think and feel responsible for other people," who anticipate other people's needs (30), and who "let another person's behavior affect him or her" (31).

In retrospect, the popular codependency discourse of the 1980s distorted and oversimplified a complex tension. By describing the tendency to care for another as always bordering on the pathological, the popular discourse leaves little room for the conceptualization of healthy or necessary forms of interdependence, which, though asymmetrical, unequal, and confining in some moments, must also comprise some part of social relationships and social participation. In texts such as *Codependent No More*, all social practices that compromise individual rights, autonomy, and absolute equality are regarded as suspect—with little means of explaining why individuals would voluntarily enter into such relations except through self-sacrifice, "self-hate," or a troubled family background.[7] Janice Haaken articulates this tension: "The co-dependence label becomes a broad conceptual container into which myriad life difficulties and internal and external pressures are placed. The message is compelling because it seems to provide both the therapists who draw on the co-dependence literature and the individuals who identify with the 'disease' deliverance from the difficult task of separating out what is internal from what is external, and what is healthy and emotionally useful from what is pathological and emotionally destructive in worrisome, conflictual, interpersonal relationships" (1990: 405).

As feminist therapists Jo-Ann Krestan and Claudia Bepko remark, the 1980s fascination with the codependency idea may well be a reflection of Americans' quest for "painless relatedness"—a world in which "a healthy relationship is one in which individual needs are always gratified but the self remains invulnerable from the effects of another's behavior. Relational 'health' would be represented by a curious cross between total autonomy and perfect need gratification. Recovered from codependency, one could magically achieve the paradoxical feat of being perfectly fulfilled in a relationship without ever focusing on the other person" (1991: 53–54).

Codependency discourse of the 1980s is the legacy of humanistic and "liberation psychotherapies" that first emerged in the context of the antiinstitutional, countercultural movements of the 1960s and 1970s in the United States—including the transactional, gestalt, and existential psychotherapies of R. D. Laing, Fritz Perls, Abraham Maslow, and Carl Rogers (Rice 1996). These therapies draw on dominant strands of social thought that see psychological development as a process of "self-actualization" and argue that the true self resides inside the individual from birth. Because childhood is celebrated as the truest and purest stage of personhood, integration into society (through family, education, and work) is seen as the source of human maladjustment (Rice 1996: 28–34). Many of these therapies view immersion in social life as an erosion of the inner self. Socialization and social institutions are seen as antithetical to the process of self-realization. In Carl Rogers's "person-centered therapy," which was a popular therapeutic model at the time, Rogers emphasized the importance of self-acceptance on the part of the client and "unconditional positive regard" on the part of the therapist: complete empathy and withholding of judgment.

These ideas are echoed in 1980s codependency discourse. According to Anne Wilson Schaef, a prominent writer on codependency, all addictions "are generated by our families *and* our schools, our churches, our political system, and our society as a whole" (cited in Rice 1996: 185, emphasis in original). Persons become codependent when they lose sight of their "true selves" through growing up and responding to society's demands. In this context, all forms of socialization (including education, child-rearing, and religious practice) are quickly equated with "shaming" and abuse (205).

The psychodynamic orientation of groups such as CoDA (Co-Dependents Anonymous) stands in sharp contrast to the approach of Alcoholics Anonymous and Al-Anon, which eschew attributing the ultimate cause of drinking behavior to personality style or emotional need (Mäkelä 1996: 229).[8] While the focus of AA had been on the wrongs done *by* the member (the alcoholic), CoDA and ACOA (Adult Children of Alcoholics) focus on the wrongs done *to* the member (Rice 1996). The twelve steps of the original twelve-step programs are directed toward reintegrating oneself into one's social environment by taking inventory of damage done to others and systematically making amends. The reverse is true in the new codependency groups.[9]

In the 1970s and 1980s, a number of commentators began to criticize what they called the American "therapeutic society" (see, for example, Bellah 1985), as the language and ethos of self-help increasingly permeated public discourse. These commentators criticized what they saw as a never-ending quest for "self-awareness" and "authenticity," which ultimately eclipsed or even replaced a concern for shared political causes and social commitments (Lasch 1978; see also Bellah 1985; Coles 1980; and Sennett 1978). Liberation psychotherapy grew to be more about the narrow goals of "self-actualization" and "self-expression" than it was about a politics of social involvement and social change (Coles 1980). In a critique of the new psychology published in 1980, Robert Coles remarked, "Is it making too brash a leap to say that there is a connection between, on the one hand, the insistent emphasis on the self, buttressed by a reductionist psychology as a secular, philosophical *raison d'être* . . . and on the other hand, the proliferation of single-issue political activity, whereby one gives one's all to what one feels most strongly about, and the devil with any notion of a larger personal, never mind social, responsibility?" (1980: 140).[10] While most of these critics tended to be conservative in their orientation (lamenting the passing of an age when Americans were more committed to nuclear families and community betterment, despite the often constraining nature of these institutions), the critique of the therapeutic society allows us to see its self-centric, antisocial orientation. This orientation makes the embrace of the codependency discourse in Japan of the early 1980s unexpected (Borovoy 2001b).

In the 1980s, the language of codependency, the CoDA "twelve steps," and a number of popular self-help books appeared in Japan. Alcoholics Anonymous has been in Japan since 1976 and Al-Anon since 1982, sowing the seeds for a new awareness of substance abuse and related social problems. Alcoholics Anonymous had spurred the founding of a Japanese adaptation, known as Danshukai, as well as a number of grassroots support groups. But the idea of codependency came into popular usage through the efforts of the chief psychiatrist at the Center, Dr. Saitō Satoru. Saitō, a public health doctor and self-proclaimed social advocate, had himself translated some of the American texts into Japanese. He found, in his own words, that the concept of codependency neatly described the behavior he associated with Japanese women married to alcoholics: they seemed to "blur" their husbands' needs with their own; they spoke about their husbands "as if they were speaking about themselves"; they had "impoverished" facial expressions.[11] By the time I arrived at the Center in 1992, the language of codependency was deeply rooted. While Saitō himself was controversial (I discuss his ideas further in chapter 1), and the notion of codependency was disputed, particularly in the bio-centric world of the Japanese medical community, the ideas were broadly accepted and promoted by alcohol specialists, nurses *(hokenshi),* and social workers who worked at the community level (in city-funded health clinics, or *hokenjo*), as well as a number of broad-based citizens' groups (such as ASK), which had taken up the concept and promoted it through magazines and web sites.[12]

The idea of codependency—the notion that it is possible to care too well for a family member (and, in the American view, caring quickly lapses into caring too much)—called to the fore central issues, not only in family life but in the language of national identity, that had permeated postwar culture. The contradictions that resulted from embracing this imported language were made clear to me almost as soon as I began my fieldwork. One social worker, by way of orientation, told me that codependency was a very important concept for understanding Japan, and that in fact "all Japanese" were codependent: Japan itself was a "culture of codependency," he explained, in which people were extraordinarily sensitive to one another and women considered themselves virtuous to the extent that they sacrificed their own needs in the service of others. In another conversation, the chief psychiatrist told me that Japanese people were "addicted to human relationships."

The notion of Japan as a "culture of codependency" suggests the overlap between forms of nurturance that have historically been considered normal, healthy, and even virtuous and what is increasingly seen, in the context of substance abuse treatment and discourse, as unhealthy behavior. In order to better understand this proximity, it is necessary to consider the way in which the work of the housewife is woven into the fabric of social life and, more broadly, into the discourse of postwar national ideologies that have created a shared sense of purpose in the endeavor to promote economic success and social cohesion.

NURTURANCE IN POSTWAR NATIONAL IDENTITY

As I listened to the women's conversations and went about my daily life in Japan, it became increasingly clear that the concept of women's codependency pointed to a much broader national dilemma, beyond a husband's alcoholism or a child's substance abuse, or even a wife's role. To wives and mothers, the idea of codependency closely resembled what was expected of Japanese housewives of the postwar generation as a matter of course.

There is an important history underlying these expectations. In the late nineteenth century, in the context of the government's heated attempt to "catch up" with the West and consolidate national mores, statesmen of the Meiji era (1868–1912) promoted the ideal of the "good wife and wise mother" *(ryōsai kenbo)*, proclaiming the importance of the work of wives and mothers to Japan's project of modernization and nation-building. The home was construed as a microcosm of Japanese nationhood, and women were explicitly delegated the task of creating better Japanese citizens through industriousness, homemaking, and education of their children. Although the *ryōsai kenbo* ideology did not encompass mainstream middle-class women (it largely affected an elite class of Meiji and Taishō housewives), the discourse continued to be available, and captured the various ways in which the state continued to support and enlist women as modernizers continuing into the postwar period (Uno 1993a: 304–12). In both prewar and postwar years, women were considered central to the crucial task of instilling national values and identity in their children, and a number of women's organizations took on the role of policing public morality regarding issues such as temperance, austerity, and frugality (Garon 1993, 1994, 1997: 130–34; Nolte and Hastings 1991). Although women were forbidden by law from voting or formally participating in political life, the state welcomed women's participation in social reform and community activism through their roles as wives and mothers.[13]

Sharon Nolte and Sally Ann Hastings juxtapose the model of the Japanese "good wife and wise mother" with the contemporary European figure of the Victorian housewife, corseted and frail, who was meant to shelter the virtues of domesticity from the encroaching values of market competition and personal gains and profits. In contrast to this "cult of domesticity," which saw the home as, ideally, secluded from market values and industrial productivity, the Japanese "cult of productivity" celebrated a woman who is "modest, courageous, frugal, literate, hardworking, and productive" (Nolte and Hastings 1991: 172).

In an explicitly patriarchal family system in which authority, individual rights, and entitlements were granted only to men, women as household managers carved their own spheres of authority, spurred on by the agenda of the state. Even today, "the Meiji woman" *(Meiji no onna)* is popularly remembered as a strong and competent woman, the "pillar of the family" *(kazoku no shin),* who supported other family members while concealing her own role in their success, who offered "inside support" for public endeavors *(naijo no kō),* and who quietly made her husband look important in the eyes of others *(tateru,* literally to "prop up") by publicly deferring to him.

In particular, the *ryōsai kenbo* ideal emphasized the importance of child-rearing as key to the cultivation of moral values and sensibilities in the future citizens of Japan (Nolte and Hastings 1991: 171; Tamanoi 1991; Uno 1993b).[14] In a journal that contained the thoughts of intellectuals and statesmen on the nature of Japan's new modernity, one leading statesman wrote:

> Once a woman takes a husband and manages a household, her responsibilities are not light. Moreover, it may also be said that her obligations are really heavy and difficult when she becomes a mother and instructs her children. . . . Since children respond to their mother just like a reflection in a mirror, if the mother's disposition is not pure, then the children, reflect-

ing this, also cannot be pure. If we desire children of fine character and disposition, therefore, then their mother by all means should also attain similar perfection. (Arinori, cited in Braisted 1976: 252)

The complicated mixture of servitude and pride, or sacrifice and entitlement, that is the legacy of Meiji articulations of gender and family has been one of the key tensions of women's lives and feminist politics in Japan, and has continued to resonate in contemporary times. Indeed, this phenomenon has been treated in numerous popular television dramas and films. The notion of strength deriving from sacrifice, faith, endurance, and frugality continues to evoke nostalgia and national pride among women, as evidenced by the dramatic popularity of the serialized television drama *Oshin,* broadcast in 1983–84. *Oshin,* broadcast in fifteen-minute segments each morning by Japan's national broadcasting corporation, recounts one woman's life, beginning at the end of the Meiji era and ending in the present day. In doing so, it celebrates women's endurance and sacrifice for family along with women's capacity for strength, self-sufficiency, and economic success (Harvey 1995: 75–76). In brief, Oshin is born in 1901, the daughter of a tenant farmer who is forced to sell her into service to a timber merchant after a bad harvest. Oshin survives cruel treatment at the hands of the timber merchant and eventually escapes with the help of an army deserter and returns home. She marries into a moderately wealthy family that owns a textile business, but the business is destroyed in the 1924 Tokyo earthquake and the couple is forced to join the husband's family, where Oshin is treated cruelly by her mother-in-law, so much so that her second child dies shortly after birth. Eventually she flees and her husband joins her. Her husband sympathizes increasingly with Japan's militarization of the 1930s, supporting Japan's expansion, and her first son dies tragically in the war (from starvation and fatigue). At the close of the war, her husband commits suicide. In the postwar section of the drama, Oshin reunites with a man who had resisted the war and builds a prosperous supermarket chain.

The show received the highest ratings in the history of NHK (Japan's largest public broadcasting station): roughly 52 percent of viewers each morning. As Harvey points out, it was both written and produced by women, who, in the words of the screenwriter, saw it as a "requiem for our mothers born in the Meiji period" *(Oshin NHK Dorama Gaido,* cited in Harvey 1995: 87). At the same time as the show laments Oshin's hardship, it also celebrates her determination, endurance, and resourcefulness—all of which culminate in her eventual economic success. The show analogizes Oshin's upwardly mobile economic trajectory to that of postwar Japan and, by dramatizing the hardships endured, acknowledges the role of women in Japan's postwar economic growth (Harvey 1995: 88, 107–108). As one young fan of the show's incessant reruns observes on her web site, "She has [a] strong belief to stand on her skill without any man's help and [a] strong own opinion. That's similar to my character."

The ambivalence surrounding the theme of the Meiji woman and women's self-sacrifice for nation and family has also appeared frequently in fiction by women writers. One of the most famous novels to deal with the issue, *Onnazaka* by Fumiko Enchi (1961), begins with Tomo, the young wife of a wealthy Kyushu government official, traveling to Tokyo to seek a mistress for her husband, Yukitomo, a self-absorbed and greedy man. In some sense the mission symbolizes the great gulf between the role of wife as sexual partner to her husband and as household manager. In the ensuing years, family relationships grow quite complicated, as Tomo and Yukitomo's no-good son, Michimasa, returns home to live with them, and Michimasa's second wife, Miya, unhappy in her marriage, begins an affair with Yukitomo and conceives children. Eventually Michimasa's son from his first marriage returns home and takes an interest in one of his half-sisters, whom Tomo quickly arranges to have married off. Toward the end of the novel, Tomo attempts to care for an impoverished young woman, Kayo, who gave birth to an illegitimate child fathered by one of Miya's children. Through these relationships, the novel shows Tomo holding the family together by working behind the scenes, managing the various crises that arise from the irresponsibility of the men in the family, particularly her husband and son. In a climactic scene, Tomo, now weakened by a fatal disease, returns home from a visit to Kayo, slowly making her way up the hill that leads to her mansion. Tomo reflects on what her life has meant:

> Everything that she had suffered for, worked for, and won within the restricted sphere of a life whose key she had for decades past entrusted to her wayward husband Yukitomo lay within the confines of that unfeeling, hard, and unassailable fortress summed up by the one word "fam-

ily." . . . No doubt, she had held her own in that small world. In a sense, all the strength of her life had gone into doing just that; but now in the light of the lamps of these small houses that so cheerlessly lined one side of the street she had suddenly seen the futility of that somehow artificial life on which she had lavished so much energy and wisdom.

Was it possible, then, that everything she had lived for was vain and profitless? No: she shook her head in firm rejection of the idea. (1990: 189–90)

Literary critics have debated how we should interpret Enchi; some more conservative critics have argued that the notion of Tomo as a victim of the Japanese household system is too modern an interpretation, which reads our contemporary values into the situation of women of that time. Others see Tomo's plight as a masochistic path to which she is bound. Yet, despite Tomo's moment of awakening above, one sees within the structure of the novel the reasons that Tomo is drawn to her path, and indeed in the conclusion of the story she is somewhat vindicated, as the extent to which the fate of the Shirakawa family lay in her hands emerges into public consciousness. If Enchi's novel is meant to be an indictment of the patriarchal family system that forced women into misery, it is also a text that vividly portrays the seductiveness and importance of this role.

THE POSTWAR HOUSEWIFE
AS A LEGACY OF THE *RYŌSAI KENBO*

Although few women could, in reality, afford to become full-time house-wives in the early years of industrialization, women's involvement in public life continued, indeed intensified, in the wartime and postwar years (Garon 1997, 2000; Lewis 1978; LeBlanc 1999). The "professional house-wives" *(sengyō shufu)* who emerged in the late 1950s and 1960s, when large numbers of middle-class women were able to become full-time housewives for the first time, were the legacy of the prewar and Meiji good wife and wise mother: women who maintained close ties to the community and co-operated closely with agendas of the state (see Garon 1994, 1997; LeBlanc 1999). Women continued to use the home as a basis for claiming a voice in public affairs in the postwar period, mobilizing around consumer issues, environmental preservation, child care, and other issues that concerned them as housewives (see Lewis 1978; LeBlanc 1999). This phenomenon, known as "housewife feminism," speaks both to the conservative nature of mainstream Japanese feminism in this period and to the importance for women of the home as a platform from which to speak (for an excellent analysis, see Mackie 2003: 151–153).

Part of women's authority derived from the fact that the government, along with Japanese enterprises, came to view the professional housewife as integral to the postwar drive for economic growth. This was so much so that a number of prominent manufacturing corporations initiated programs (with sponsorship from the Ministries of Education and Welfare) to train housewives in their own homes to rationalize and modernize domestic work (through, for example, the purchase of household appliances, time-consciousness, and the democratization of kin relations) in order to create a more efficient and less stressful household environment and allow men to "devote [themselves] to production free from anxiety" *(Manejimento* 1955, cited in Gordon 1997: 247).[15] Andrew Gordon notes that the professionalization of the housewife was key both to the naturalization of gender roles and to what some postwar intellectuals came to call the "enterprise society": "A society where meeting the needs of the corporation is 'naturally' understood to be social common sense and to be congruent with meeting the needs of all society's inhabitants" (Gordon 1997: 247).

Middle-class women also became intimately involved in their children's education, facilitating the accomplishment of homework and the long push to pass a series of standardized exams, a struggle often jokingly referred to as a three-legged race binding mother and child. The race, ideally, leads to entrance in an elite university, the key credential for obtaining employment in a reputable, large-scale corporation (Vogel 1978; Allison 2000; White 1987).

The home became a kind of caregiving center in postwar society. Motherhood, rather than wifehood, became the dominant role of the postwar housewife. Sexual intimacy or "friendship" between spouses took a backseat to the efficient management of the home and the provision of a warm, supportive, nurturant atmosphere for husbands and children, attention to detail (such as snacks for a child preparing for exams), and the provision of what Takie Lebra (1984) has called "around the body care." (Chapter 4 explores these tensions in greater depth.) The housewife who wheels her husband's bicycle from the shed to the front door before seeing him off to work, who packs her husband's suitcase in preparation for his business trip, and who labors over her children's lunchboxes, packing items of pleasing colors and shapes as well as optimal nutrition (see Allison 1991) exemplifies the kind of loving care that came to be a key nexus between home and public regimes of productivity. For many women, these labors were also a source of pride.

In the 1960s and 1970s, social commentators began referring to Japan as a "maternal society" (Yoda 2000). "Motherhood" became a key metaphor for describing all Japanese social relationships. In a best-selling social science text in postwar Japan, *The Anatomy of Dependence* (*Amae no Kōzō;* 1973), which appeared in 1971 in Japan, the psychiatrist Doi Takeo describes *amae,* or "passive dependence," as an elemental Japanese emotion, deeply rooted in Japanese history and language. Doi describes the relationship of an infant to its mother as the prototypical *amae* relationship, characterized by total dependency and the capacity to be indulged, or "to presume on familiarity in order to behave in a self-indulgent manner" (1973: 74). He likens the experience of *amae* to a child's fulfillment at its mother's breast (even speculating that the etymology of the word *amae* may be related to the children's word indicating a request for the breast or food, "*uma-uma*" [72]).[16] In Doi's analysis, the *amae* relationship is the most desirable of all human relationships and the template for social relationships more broadly.

Doi discovered the centrality of *amae* in Japanese culture while training as a psychiatrist in the United States in the immediate postwar context. While there, he was struck by the American privileging of individual autonomy, which became the central problematic of his thought. He writes:

The "please help yourself" that Americans use so often had a rather unpleasant ring in my ears before I became used to English conversation. The meaning, of course, is simply "please take what you want without hesitation," but literally translated it has somehow a flavor of "nobody else will help you," and I could not see how it came to be an expression of good will. The Japanese sensibility would demand that, in entertaining, a host should show sensitivity in detecting what was required and should himself "help" his guests. To leave a guest unfamiliar with the house to "help himself" would seem excessively lacking in consideration. This increased still further my feeling that Americans were a people who did not show the same consideration and sensitivity towards others as the Japanese. As a result, my early days in America, which would have been lonely at any rate, so far from home, were made lonelier still. (Doi 1973: 13)

In the postwar years of the 1960s and 1970s, the language of *amae* became central to describing everyday relationships. Indeed, still today scarcely a day goes by without hearing the term used in numerous contexts. A mother who insufficiently disciplines her children or a boss who is not strict with his underlings is talked about as "*amai*"— "sweet," "soft," or indulging in wishful thinking (29). Japanese society itself is described as "*amai,*" a society where individuals are looked after by social organizations, such as families, companies, and the state.

In chapter 2, I suggest that the ideological success of the language of *amae* is linked to the way in which the word captured key elements of postwar social organization—specifically the way in which nurturance came to be an element (both ideological and real) of the way in which the state and its constituent institutions enfranchised and mobilized Japanese citizens. The notion of the Japanese company as a family was deployed by prominent Japanese managers such as Matsushita Konosuke to claim a unity of purpose among both workers and managers. Regimes of discipline in Japanese schools, which once relied heavily on authoritarianism and quasi-military measures, increasingly came to rely on socialization by peers (Rohlen 1989: 36). The "caring" quality of the state and its constituent institutions—and the intrusion or even coercion that often accompanies it—has been an important theme in postwar historical and anthropological analysis. In both prewar and postwar times, the Japanese state has remained invasively involved in the daily lives of citizens, in what some have referred to as "social management" (Garon 1997).

This "manageriality" is a constant feature of daily life in Japan. As a Japanese citizen (or visitor), one constantly feels "managed," prodded, and cajoled as one makes one's way through daily life. One is constantly "guided" by recorded voices at train station ticket machines or jaunty music accompanying traffic signals, indicating when it is safe to cross the street. Gum wrappers often contain the written exhortation, "Let's wrap our gum and throw it away!" Public pools commonly require swimmers to get out of the water for ten minutes at specified intervals in order to avoid catching a chill. In urban areas, where workers endure long commutes on crowded public transportation, passengers are continually guided. Recorded messages remind passengers at each stop, "Please be careful as you step off the train," "Please remember your belongings as you disembark," and, on a rainy day, "Please remember your umbrellas" or "Owing to the rain the platform has become quite slippery, so please be careful in stepping off the train." One can be critical of these incessant interventions, and certainly, as an American, I often found them badgering and intrusive. And yet many Japanese people seem to feel more ambivalent. One friend told me that Japanese people preferred being tended to *(kamatte morau)* to simply being "left alone" *(hotte okareru)*. Such ministrations are often linked with motherly nurturance in Japan and referred to as *boseishugi,* or "maternalism," explicitly linking the broader projects of state regulation to the home, women, and motherhood.

The idea of *amae* is in many respects a deeply compelling one. It depicts a world where social order is orchestrated and legitimized not through top-down commands but rather through intimate social relations and shared understanding; a society characterized by shared interests, in which trust is achieved through intimacy rather than contractuality. The notion that one need not "look out for oneself" but rather can achieve one's ends by presuming on the good graces of others suggests the possibility of harmonious human relationships that do not entail a curtailment of self-interest.

In the context of dominant American ideologies that fetishize individual rights and view social participation as a threat to self-development, there is little language for conceptualizing the necessary compromises in self-determination that sociality entails. Dependency relationships that compromise individual rights, autonomy, or absolute equality are readily classified as abusive or exploitative—with little means of explaining why individuals would voluntarily enter into such relations except through self-loathing, uncontrollable compulsion, or a troubled family background. In contrast, Japanese postwar cultural cosmologies describe a wide range of asymmetrical hierarchical relations as benevolent and mutualistic, making it difficult to draw a sharp line between those relationships that are "for one's own benefit" and those that veer into exploitation, systematic forms of inequality, or violations of dignity (Borovoy 2001b).

The language of codependency allowed women to express tensions in family and public life that had previously been difficult to articulate. What is the line between *amae* (an idealized conceptualization of social relations based on dominant constructions of family) and codependency—a set of behaviors that makes women complicit in an ultimately destructive and self-destructive pattern? How do the asymmetries that Doi views as richly rewarding (and fundamental to Japanese social relations) come to be exploitative? And how do they emerge from decisions women make self-consciously? I hope to show the fine line that exists for women between these sanctioned acts of nurturance and self-sacrifice, and something that could be called exploitation or abuse. The notion of codependency, for all its problems, helped shed light on this distinction.

FEMINISM OR FALSE CONSCIOUSNESS?

Inevitably I came away from each of the weekly meetings at the Center feeling inspired by the women's triumphs, the humor they brought to their predicaments, their capacity for self-reflection, and their strength. Yet when I presented the women's stories to scholarly and feminist audiences in the period following my initial year of research, I was faced with a problem: many members of the audience simply did not see what the women were accomplishing in the group. At one presentation, a scholar who had been trained in the 1960s and 1970s asked, "Don't these women realize that they are simply being duped by the treatment they are undergoing? They're participating in a therapy group when in fact they should be protesting gender inequality and demanding social change."

In responding to these questions I felt my values as a feminist and my values as an anthropologist coming into conflict. As a feminist I believed that women's issues were, at least in part, political issues—shaped by socially structured inequalities and best resolved by political mobilization and structural change. I also believed in the fundamental importance of gender equality, defined as equal access to employment, autonomy, and self-cultivation. To the extent that reproductive labor, household work, and child-rearing precluded women from attaining autonomy and independence, I could see this work as generative of women's oppression. And yet as an anthropologist, it seemed crucial to remember that the very meanings of family, domesticity, gender, and equality itself were deeply inflected by the history of Japanese family, nationhood, and modernity. I did not wish to depoliticize women's issues by simply arguing that Japanese women's roles were a matter of "culture" or were naïvely embraced by women; nor did I wish to argue that women's status could not be evaluated through the lens of Western feminism. And yet it seemed important to balance these two agendas, or at least to hold them in tension.

In fact, after a year of participating in the meetings and subsequent years of keeping in contact with the women, I did not at all believe that the women were being duped—that if someone could only explain to them the importance of an earned wage or the exploitative nature of housework, they would sit up and take note, realizing that in fact this had been the key to their subordination. Far from being victims of false consciousness, the women I came to know struck me as thoughtful, articulate subjects who made careful and strategic decisions. Nonetheless, most ultimately chose to operate within the confines of dominant gender roles. How to explain their decisions while showing that they were not simply victims of false consciousness became a guiding thread for making sense of their life stories.

In addressing these questions, I have been helped by theories of resistance, everyday politics, and the workings of power that became widely influential in American anthropology in the 1980s and which explicitly sought to question conventional (particularly conventional Marxist) models of political subordination and hence the process of political protest. While classical Marxian notions of political protest describe an overthrow of the dominant regime and a "laying bare" of reigning ideological belief systems (Williams 1997, cited in Dirks et al. 1994: 593), more recent theories emphasize the importance of gradual shifts in social consciousness. These theories emphasize that the workings of power are diffuse, embodied, consensual, and more deeply compelling than classical theories of ideology were willing to acknowledge (Gramsci 1971; Bourdieu 1977; Foucault 1965, 1979, 1990). Coming to terms with entrenched forms of social oppression is more than simply a matter of overthrowing those who control the distribution of knowledge; it is rather an internal and thoroughgoing battle of consciousness change, a wrestling with hegemonic forms of social power: the experiences, language, and practice of everyday life, which allow even systems of inequality or domination to appear reasonable or acceptable (Williams 1980: 38; Comaroff and Comaroff 1991; Gramsci 1971: 333).

Theories of resistance emerging in the 1980s shifted the focus from protest as political mobilization and confrontation (key markers of social change in the context of liberal and Marxist social theory) to protest that relies on shifts in consciousness and emphasizes the importance of everyday practices, private acts, and resistance to the dominant order that may be hidden, not explicitly political, not organized, and with no clear agenda for change (the "weapons of the weak" that James Scott noted in the historical records of Malay peasants [1987a, 1987b]).[17] These theorists are more likely to see a gradual coming to terms with the constraints of a system (even while working within it) as a meaningful form of social activism.

The 1980s were also a time in which a wider diversity of voices gained ground within Western academic feminism. Voices of feminists of color and third world feminists began to gain a broader audience. Anthropologists studying the worlds of non-Western women who subscribed to fundamentalist religious ideologies, such as Islamic fundamentalism, began to argue that such phenomena should not be viewed as evidence of women's passive submission, but rather as active, thoughtful, even necessary acts of self-cultivation (see, for example, Mani 1998; Mohanty 1991; Rouse 2004). Chandra Talpade Mohanty's influential article, "Under Western Eyes," argues that third world women have historically been viewed as passive victims of their societies, described primarily in terms of their "object status" (1991: 56–57). Western feminists assumed that these women's status as "religious" (read "not progressive"), "domestic" (read "backward"), and "family-oriented" (read "traditional") impaired their ability to make agentic choices and to control their own bodies and sexuality (72). The liberal view of freedom as rooted in autonomy and self-determination is at the root of these tendencies. The liberal view of human nature sees true agency only in those decisions that transpire outside the confines of social relationships, established beliefs, and material needs (Jaggar 1988). Women who are influenced by these constraints, in the context of either family or religious beliefs, are perceived to have sacrificed a crucial element of their humanity: the capacity for self-authorship.

In a thoughtful article on the contemporary Islamic fundamentalist revival among Egyptian women, Saba Mahmood (2001) argues that it is precisely this series of associations that must be questioned in order to appreciate the agency of contemporary Islamic women who are recommitting to the formal study of Islamic scripture and ethics of traditional comportment. The virtues of shyness and modesty, so central to this training, are easily read by Western feminists as evidence of women upholding male authority and complying with their own subjugation. Yet Mahmood argues that it is necessary to decouple the liberal notion of self-realization from the notion of "the autonomous will," and the notion of agency from the outcome of social change (208). "Agency," Mahmood argues, should be defined not as the overthrow of relations of domination but rather as a "capacity for action," shaped by social and historical conditions (210), that can take a variety of forms, including the pursuit of stability and the cultivation of inner strength through the capacity for endurance (217–23).

Central to this argument is the notion that the valuation of equality and autonomy (individual self-realization independent of social obligations) is so central to our liberal-humanist understanding of personhood that it is difficult to recognize the capacity for action or agency without it. We are left with the unsatisfactory conclusion that social movements that support women's strength and self-betterment through trajectories different from those of men are by definition systems of deception that can only serve to keep women in their place.

These arguments helped me see how different logics of gender and political economy create different paths to change and avenues of protest. For Japanese women of the high-growth generation, the resources of the home remained a considerable base of support despite broader social inequalities. As I explore the critical spaces made available to these women as they encountered discourses of addiction, it is clear that in coping with severe family problems, women do not take the steps we might expect; they rarely consider leaving their husbands, nor do they explicitly question or challenge a system that clearly deprives women of economic self-sufficiency, celebrates endurance and self-sacrifice, and holds up domesticity and motherhood as the key achievements to which they should aspire. Yet, far from being victims of false consciousness, the women who told their stories to me over the years reveal that even thoughtful, articulate subjects can choose to operate within the confines of dominant gender roles.[18]

Throughout my analysis I have struggled to balance my own feminist commitments to social equality and individual rights with what I see as the priorities of the women I encountered, without assuming that the women were simply naïve or content to be subordinated. My hope is to carve a path between arguing that women were "resisting" dominant gender role constructions in the ways that are most familiar to us and arguing they were simply victims of false consciousness, since neither argument is satisfactory.

ENGAGING WITH AMERICA: FORGING A LANGUAGE OF SOCIAL CRITICISM

The story of how women struggle to maintain the elements of familial nurturance and domesticity that are important to them while drawing lines between normality and exploitation is a small piece of a broader puzzle. How do women reconcile competing ideologies of modernity? What is a good woman? What is a good individual? To what extent should individuals depend on their families and other social institutions? Does equality mean the same thing for all cultures? The entry of the codependency discourse into Japanese therapeutic culture in the 1980s is one moment in a postwar history of Japanese attempts to grapple with the dilemmas of their own historically rooted cultural system using a language imposed by the West.

In the postwar era, the Japanese came increasingly under the influence of American notions of citizenship, selfhood, and gender. The ambitious agenda of the American occupation to "democratize" Japan went beyond rewriting the Japanese constitution and implementing institutional reform, to undertaking dramatic social reform and "social education." The transformation of Japan was seen by occupation officials as a testimony to the triumph and universality of American values (Pyle 1978: 153).

Yet the absorption of American values and ideas turned out to be a complicated and partial process. Despite the rewriting of the Japanese constitution, the massive reorganization of social institutions, and the influx of American culture, it became clear that the Japanese would not embrace American culture and institutions as they were. These themes have been explored by a number of anthropologists seeking to understand how the United States has been embraced and understood in postwar Japan. Karen Kelsky, in her ethnography of contemporary young "internationalist" Japanese women, *Women on the Verge: Japanese Women, Western Dreams,* explores the image of America as the land of individual liberties, self-expression, freedom, romance, and self-fulfillment, and shows how young ambitious Japanese women use this image to criticize Japan. In increasing numbers, young women, discouraged by the lack of professional opportunities in Japan, are learning English and seeking work abroad. She shows how these women use the West as a means to criticize aspects of Japanese society: hierarchical gender relations, the use of women primarily as temporary and low-skilled labor, and the idea of marriage as founded on a gendered division of labor. For internationalist women, the West appears to offer the possibility of total gender equality, personal freedom, artistic creativity, and romantic love. Simultaneously, they often reproduce stereotypical notions of Japan as feudalistic, confining, backward, or effeminate (Kelsky 2001). These women fetishize the white (and sometimes black) man as emblems of sexual potency, romance and passion, upward social mobility, and chivalry. In contrast, they view Japanese society as confining and Japanese men as infantile, tasteless, selfish, and poor lovers. In the words of one young woman: "Japanese men are the opposite of the Japanese GNP—they are the lowest in the world!" (17). For these young women, time in the United States provides weapons for social criticism of Japan.

Yet one of the problems implicitly posed by Kelsky's subjects is that these comparisons often reproduce stereotypical notions of both "Americanness" and "Japaneseness." Many of the young women, who are thoughtful and insightful informants, in the end find themselves unable to fully embrace life in America. Not surprisingly, their illusions of equality and endless romance are shattered, and they end up disillusioned with what they find in the United States. Their only recourse is to revert to revaluing their prior notions of Japan, yet neither of the two alternatives (American feminist self-determination or Japanese conformity) are attractive options. The grandiose views of "America," coupled with the strategy of leaving Japan, do little to lay the foundations for forging a critique from within.

Others who have attempted to make sense of American ideas and commodities coming into Japan have observed the process by which the Japanese adapt or domesticize American consumer goods to suit their own cultural predilections. The anthology *Re-Made in Japan,* edited by Joseph Tobin, describes the "re-contextualization" of American consumer goods in Japan—a process through which the Japanese are "engaged in an ongoing creative synthesis of the exotic with the familiar, the foreign with the domestic, the modern with the traditional, and the Western with the Japanese" (Tobin 1992b: 4). The argument reminds us that American goods are never appropriated "as is" and that globalization never entails the complete Americanization or homogenization of cultures. Following Arjun Appadurai's early observations on the nature of global transfers, global flows of media, information, knowledge, and, arguably, therapeutic practices allow subjects to imagine alternatives to their current situations, but they also produce abundant contradictions and disjunctures (Appadurai 1991). How individuals integrate these imaginings into their daily life and reconcile them with socially structured realities is a complex matter, particularly when the imported ideas challenge the existing ones. The "domesticization" paradigm is important but may not fully address the way in which the entry of American ideas can provoke intense negotiation—not merely the nativization of American categories.

The story I tell about the struggle of one generation of Japanese women to come to terms with the limitations of both Japanese discourses of family and nationhood and American discourses of individualism reduces to neither unilineal "modernization" (a total accommodation to the West) nor a determined return to "Japaneseness." Although American popular psychology offered women a window into exploitative aspects of Japanese discourses of gender, it is important to note that for the codependency concept to be useful to the women at the Center, it was first turned on its head: Japanese culture (not individuals) was codependent; codependent women were "good women"; codependency was understandable, "normal" within the confines of Japanese society, rather than evidence of maladjustment.

In making sense of cultural borrowing, it is easy to fall into one of two traps: either the receiving culture is seen as reacting to foreign influence through a defensive recourse to nativism or one accepts at face value the claims to "Americanization." Yet in some sense neither of these explanations, though each reflects certain aspects of cultural transfer from the United States to Japan, can fully account for the complexity of the situation that faces most Japanese citizens as they seek to reconcile their own historically rooted understandings of self and gender and the American ideas with which they are continually bombarded. In my observation, American popular psychology neither Americanizes Japan nor is seamlessly absorbed.[19] The stories that follow reveal the difficulty with which American ideas permeate other cultures in their original form.

What makes the clinic a particularly interesting place to study the practice of cultural appropriation is that, unlike many sites of cultural contact, the clinic is not a particularly "international" place. Nor are the clients particularly cosmopolitan in their outlook: they come to the Center not to seek out American therapies or develop a countercultural discourse but rather because they are looking for help with a private family matter. (In fact, as I learned, few of the women who attended the meetings had ever traveled abroad or even spoken at length with an American.) In seeking help for their problems, they do not explicitly position themselves outside of or in opposition to dominant cultural ideologies; nor do they set out to criticize the system in which they live. They are largely middle-aged, middle-class housewives who conceptualize themselves within the mainstream; yet, owing to unfortunate family problems, they confront a fundamental barrier to continuing to make dominant cultural assumptions work.

A similar story could be told of the counselors at the Center, who are trained neither in feminist theory nor in Western forms of psychotherapy. They are civil servants: college-educated women who passed the social welfare *(shakai fukushi)* section of the civil service exam. This means that they were trained within the mainstream discourse of the state-managed Japanese health-care system (accompanied by general training in psychology and social casework methods). Women who choose to enter the civil service often do so because it allows them to work while raising a family, since civil servants have more regulated working hours (less overtime) than workers in the private sector. It also offers women more opportunities for advancement. So the women stood out in that they were highly educated and ambitious, yet they were not particularly Westernized in their concerns. The tenets of Japanese academic feminism—for example, the view that gender roles are socially and historically produced, not innately determined—were not a part of the conversations at the Center. Counselors wanted women to draw more boundaries in the way they catered to their husbands and children, to know when they should stop; but they never questioned women's broader endeavor to strengthen their families, to keep their families together, and to be better wives and mothers if they could do that in a way that was not damaging.

There has been a tendency in recent anthropology to look for counterhegemonic discourses among marginalized groups, minorities, or others who position themselves outside of the cultural mainstream. In contrast, by examining the responses not of those who explicitly resist or criticize hegemonic frameworks but of the majority, who are compelled to undertake a critique of normalcy from within, it is possible to peer into the spectrum of possible social criticism within a given cultural sphere. As clients of the Center, women are pressed to reach beyond cultural truisms, yet they must do so while continuing to function within the confines of mainstream Japanese society. In doing this, they open up conversations that, while remaining highly personal, reveal tensions, possibilities, and constraints that face the Japanese (and in particular Japanese women) as they enter the twenty-first century.

My intention is to explore the range of ways in which women can be oppositional in Japan while remaining in the mainstream of Japanese life. The clinic offers a rare window into the social processes that shape daily social life in Japan. The question of whether women resist these dominant ideologies does not have a simple answer. Hegemonically constituted realities are rarely revealed starkly, like the diminutive figure of the Wizard of Oz behind the curtain. Jean and John Comaroff talk about emergent social criticism as occurring within "the liminal space of human experience in which people discern acts and facts but cannot or do not order them into narrative descriptions" (1991: 29). "It is from this realm," they write, "that silent signifiers and unmarked practices may rise to the level of explicit consciousness, of ideological assertion, and become the subject of overt political and social contestation—or from which they may recede into the hegemonic, to languish there unremarked for the time being" (29). It is precisely the more precarious, ambiguous shifts and challenges to hegemonically constituted realities in which I am interested here.[20]

METHODOLOGIES

This book focuses on a group of women born mostly between the late 1930s and the late 1940s. This generation, through supporting their children's education and their husbands' work, sustained the prodigious economic growth that defined the postwar era and in turn received a great deal of social support for their roles. The work of caregiving and nurturance was assumed among these women, and they received a considerable degree of validation as Japan prospered and Japanese society evidenced stability and cohesion. And yet the tensions and rifts in the system can be seen even among these women, particularly in the context of the Center, where they were grappling with social problems that were in part exacerbated by the demands of urbanization and economic productivity. As I discuss in chapter 6, these tensions are even more evident today in a younger generation of women who no longer derive the same sense of validation from domesticity (now frequently viewed as frivolous and separated from public concerns) and who increasingly desire the rewards of economic self-sufficiency and professional prestige. And yet, there is much evidence to suggest that even this younger generation experiences considerable ambivalence in deprioritizing the work of mothering and caregiving; and it remains unclear whether middle- and upper-middle-class Japanese women will in the end be willing to (or asked to) make the same kinds of compromises in family life that American professional women have made, however ambivalently.

The way in which these issues played out for women married to alcoholics and for mothers of substance-abusing teenagers was very different. Women coping with alcoholic husbands had to wrestle with the tacit assumptions of family and neighbors that a wife manages her husband totally and that a turbulent home reflects an inadequate wife. On the other hand, the lack of emphasis on romantic love and mutual attraction as the foundations of marriage appeared to offer women some leeway. Al-Anon discourse attempts to teach caregivers how to cultivate a healthy (but warm) distance between the caregiver and the drinker. These women, who did not experience pressure to reconnect or fall in love again with their husbands, were at least able to carve out some distance from their husbands without transgressing fundamental ideas about what constitutes a healthy marriage.

On the contrary, women who attended the meetings at the Center to cope with children's substance abuse faced an almost irresolvable impasse. The discourse of "tough love," imported from the United States, emphasizes the importance of the independence of the teenager as well as respecting the rights of the parent. The language of tough love as well as the language of codependency reflect complicated tensions between the need to make sacrifices in loving and caring for another, and the tendency to overstep boundaries by taking the problems of another (even one's own child) as one's own. U.S. substance abuse discourse relies heavily on the American language of rights and autonomy. Yet Japanese discourses of family and motherhood do not emphasize the independence of the child from the parents; neither do they grant the parents rights by which they may separate themselves off from the needs of the child. Mothers of teenagers experienced a considerable degree of pain and almost no social support for the tough love position, but despite this, some managed to carve out a stable life for themselves independent of their children, relinquishing responsibility for their children's problems.

As with many contemporary anthropologists, my methodology did not entail living with the people I was studying and participating in round-the-clock fieldwork. I lived an hour outside of Tokyo and commuted to work by train, attending the meetings once a week, joining the women for tea after the meetings, and interviewing several of them, by appointment, at greater length. Yet my attendance at these meetings afforded me a glimpse into family life and into a body of discourse that hardly would have been available to me had I been accompanying these women around town or in their daily life. The meetings and the Center were privileged spaces to these women, where they could be critical and reflective in ways that were prohibited in other contexts. Through the meetings and the borrowed language of alcoholism and codependency, the women shared private information and cultivated a language for thinking and talking about themselves and their families that belonged to that domain only. This weekly meeting, which occurred at a prescribed time and a prescribed location, was a very charged encounter, a window into the miseries—and the pleasures—of gender relations in Japan and women's capacities to reshape them.

The meetings at the Center were modeled after meetings of Alcoholics Anonymous and Al-Anon (for families of alcoholics) developed in the United States. Like AA meetings, they had no official leader. One staff member facilitated and kept time, and one took notes on the entire proceedings. Starting with the person seated next to the facilitator, each person introduced herself, stated why she was attending the meeting, and then spoke briefly, uninterrupted, about an event or thought she had had during the course of the week. When everyone had spoken, we went around the circle one more time, allowing women to comment on what they had heard, empathizing with various stories told or sharing related experiences.

The meetings took place in a drab seminar room with a chalkboard and a beige carpet. The tenor of the meetings was studious. For exactly an hour and a half, the approximately twenty women who usually attended the meetings sat in a large circle, their hands and legs crossed, their purses, jackets, and umbrellas neatly folded on their laps or tucked under their chairs. Many took out handkerchiefs to hold, nervously fondle, and dab at perspiration as they listened or spoke. Some closed their eyes as they listened, and few made eye contact, even when addressing each other. In general, women dressed neatly for the meetings, and many commuted distances of an hour or more. Women considered their words carefully, as if to make most effective use of this weekly forum, and they were encouraged by staff members to contribute thoughts that would be of broader use to those listening. (In order to participate in the group, clients were required to undergo a weekly educational seminar over six weeks on the nature of addiction and codependency.) Each spoke uninterrupted for anywhere between one and ten minutes; in general everyone was quite conscientious about dividing the time proportionately to make sure that each member had sufficient time to speak, and the meetings almost always ended exactly on time.

The stated purpose of the meeting was "to look within oneself" *(jibun o mitsumeru)*, and the women were very diligent. Many said that they contemplated what they would say earlier in the week or in the train on the way to the Center. The staff spoke of self-change through learning from others, citing the Japanese proverb "Observe others' folly and fix one's own" *(Hito no furi o mite jibun o naose)*. Women frequently began their narratives with phrases such as "Thanks to what I've learned here," "Thanks to sitting in this chair all these years . . ." or "Owing to everyone's support . . ." *(minna san no chikara o ete)*.[21] In the year in which I attended these meetings, there was very little outright drama. Women who cried suppressed their tears as they spoke, often nursing a single tissue with which they dabbed delicately at their noses and eyes as they folded it into smaller and smaller bits.

The women who attended the meetings at the Center were predominantly born in the late 1930s and 1940s, members of a generational cohort that had traversed two historical eras: they were socialized into the values of the prewar militarist-nationalist regime and came of age in the postwar era of American-imposed democracy. The contrasts were stark, despite the many continuities we now know to have existed under the surface. The prewar years had demanded a great deal of Japanese citizens, in the interest of establishing the Japanese empire. The state-imposed notion of the *ie,* or "household," defined the family, with the father as its authority and figurehead. The *ie,* in turn, was considered the smallest unit of the nation, and family life was very much tied to the purposes of nation-building. (I treat these ideas in greater depth in chapters 2 and 3.)

Upon returning to school following the summer of Japan's defeat and the beginning of the American occupation, the women were subjected to what seemed an entirely new set of standards. The passages in their textbooks that described the links between the ordinary Japanese family and the mythical lineage of the emperor were crossed out. The new, American-imposed constitution specified that men and women should be treated equally and that marriage, not the hierarchical line between parent and child, should be the foundation of the home. These women, and all Japanese citizens, were left to somehow reconcile these vast differences.

Women who traversed these two eras seem to have retained the influence of both. In her ethnography of middle-aged women and their experience of menopause, Margaret Lock writes that women born in the first decade of the Shōwa era (the era lasted from 1926 to 1989), are thought to retain traditional values. Lock cites a telling survey conducted by the Hakuhodo Life Institute (a large marketing research agency) which reports that women born in the early Shōwa years continue to feel out of step with postwar values:

> Political rights for women, [the respondents] agreed, were necessary. However, they still believe that wives should listen to their husbands and try to support their husbands in any way possible.
>
> Their married lives are characterized as adhering closely to traditional values: when their husbands returned home, sometimes around midnight, they made sure that the bath water was hot enough for their husbands to drain away the stresses and strains of the work day. They took out the kimono their husbands would wear while sipping hot sake and eating dinner.
>
> They understood their husbands might not want to talk. "If I worked as hard as my husband did at his place of work, I wouldn't want to talk much," they thought. . . .
>
> They did not bother their husbands with household affairs or the problems they faced each day in raising children. Those were their responsibilities as housewives and mothers. (Hakuhodo Institute of Life and Living 1984: 111, cited in Lock 1993a: 82–83)

Ultimately, this generation of Japanese citizens, often known as the "single-digit Shōwans" (*Shōwa hitoketa,* those born in the Shōwa era, 1926–89, the reign of Emperor Hirohito) emerged as the "company men" and "education mothers" who were central to the postwar project of rapid economic growth (Kelly 2002; Lock 1993a). In chapter 4, "A Success Story," I focus on the story of one woman, as told in her own words, growing up in the context of the American occupation of Japan (1945–52), her training as a young bride in her husband's house, and her eventual steps to cope with her husband's alcoholism while remaining true to her early socialization as a diligent young wife and citizen. She was widely regarded as a "success story" at the Center.

All the women who participated in the meetings could, by some definition, broadly be considered middle-class—some upper-middle, some lower-middle. Yet, there were significant differences. Hoshi-san's husband was a manager at Japan Steel, a major (initially state-subsidized) corporation. Fukuda-san's husband had at one time driven long-distance trucks and by most standards would be considered lower-middle class. Despite such differences, the vast majority of the women in the group, including Fukuda-san, did not work full-time, a marker of what might be considered middle-class status. They subsisted on their husbands' wages, a "family wage," although some (roughly half) contributed to household budgets through part-time work or piecework.

Because of the varying status among the women, it is difficult to talk about them all in one breath. The Japanese state has been extraordinarily successful at promoting a shared set of ideals concerning gender and family, what is often referred to in Japan as "middle-class consciousness" *(chūryū ishiki)* (Kelly 2002). Japanese schools instill these values through their curricula on morality *(dōtoku)* and home economics *(kateika)* and through their policing of students' lives outside the classroom (see LeTendre 2000; Rohlen 1983). Japanese companies also instill such values, through their family-wage structure and pressure on their employees to find suitable wives. This kind of socialization is everywhere apparent in Japanese social life. The ideology of postwar Japan as a "vast middle class" has been properly challenged (see, for example, Ishida 1993). And yet, while we can agree that the notion of homogeneity does not characterize postwar Japanese society, there is a vast body of postwar discourse on "the values of the Japanese" (a literature known as *Nihonjinron,* which I address further in chapter 2) that has shaped the popular imagination. As Kelly

(2002) has argued, although the notion of a vast, undifferentiated middle class is problematic, the discursive axes and institutions that characterized groups of individuals were widely disseminated and came to dominate public discourse—a set of ideas around generation, life-cycle, the education system, and so forth.

To the extent that discourses of family and gender were pervasive, I speak about the women's shared notions of the family. But the specificities of their class status are crucial. For example, Hoshi-san, whose husband, unrecovered, eventually lapsed into depression and total abdication of family responsibility, eventually separated from him, renting her own apartment and starting a new life. She was able to do that because her husband sent her money each month, and her grown children chipped in for her rent and appliances. Yet separation (or divorce) was simply not a possibility for most of the other women. Koike-san had a more unfortunate story. At the time that I knew her, she was single-handedly supporting her husband and two sons. Her husband, who was eventually diagnosed as a schizophrenic (beyond his problems with alcohol), had dropped entirely out of the workforce, after a series of failures and layoffs. While both she and her husband had been educated and socialized along middle-class trajectories, she now found herself living in public housing, a single-wage earner, and upon her husband's death, ultimately deprived of the benefits that she would have received had her husband continued to work in his later years. Her story reveals the class and gender inequalities that are an integral but often hidden part of the "company man," single wage-earner model that governed large enterprises. The Center's model of recovery was very much geared toward the middle-class housewife: they encouraged women to build on the strengths and privileges of being the household manager, including close connections to community, command of household finances, and so on. The assumptions were that women were being supported by their husbands, that their husbands had little incentive to leave (since they relied upon their wives' services), and that a woman's happiness was to be found as a wife and mother. In fact, it is noteworthy that Koike-san was the one member I knew who eventually grew disenchanted with the meetings and stopped attending. As I will explain later, she was somewhat more radicalized than the other women from an early age, and she grew to question the broader postwar system that accorded stay-at-home housewives so many privileges. Although Koike-san was unusual, her disillusionment shed light on the privileges of the middle-class house-wives who enjoyed a life of economic stability and relative independence, if not gender equality. In contrast, women who could be considered lower-middle or working class enjoyed neither of these.

RETURN VISITS

Each time I returned to Japan in the years following my fieldwork (sum-mers in 1998 and 2000 and a year-long stay in 2003), I visited the women. The group no longer met, and my visits became an excuse for the women to gather together. After the last meeting I attended during my initial year, the women presented me with a Hello Kitty address book in which they had recorded their names and addresses. (I noticed that no one had filled in the first page, as each must have felt it would be presumptuous.) I used the book to reunite everyone, working through the social worker, Takemura-san, who had been in charge of the program. The social worker reserved a large tea room with tatami mat floors *(zashiki)* at a teahouse near the Center, and determined that we would all gather and hold a "meeting," in the old format, in which each person would share her experiences and thoughts from the past years. On my first visit, I suspected that only a few women would show up, perhaps a few of the women I had known best. To my amazement, I found over thirty women, gathered at the turnstile of the station to greet me and one another. They clearly relished this op-portunity to reunite. In the tatami room at the teahouse, the women sat in a circle and talked about their life in the past years. When the meeting was over, several went on to another teahouse to continue the conversa-tion. Although most of the women had left the Center (they were en-couraged to "graduate" after a certain period of time), many participated in other self-help groups, often Al-Anon or Nar-Anon, or other support groups through the local health centers. These gatherings, along with the correspondence I carried on with several of the women, gave me a broader picture of what the women's lives were like after the time I was involved in the meetings.

I had become closer to the women over the years; occasionally I sent a photocopied letter or photograph, sharing with them the various events in my life (marriage, employment, the birth of my first child). In return I received letters with drawings, photographs, and pressed flower petals, describing what they had been doing and their daily lives. However, despite the fact that meetings were nominally convened in my honor, my presence was not in any way central to conducting the meeting or to these women's exchanges with one another. On my most recent visit, the social worker told me to entitle the event "A Talk with Amy" on the invitation, although the principal exchanges took place between the women themselves. I had become a legitimate reason to get together and to take time away from their families on a Saturday afternoon in order to talk with other women. In fact, the group that continued to gather over the years grew to include several women whom I hadn't known from my initial year at the Center but who had been invited to join by friends in the yearly (or biennial) reunions.

In the context of these meetings, I followed the women's progress in their lives as they grew older. Of the women married to alcoholics, few were ever able to really change the dynamics of their marriage or their husbands' behavior, though they grew more skillful at managing it and at carving out separate lives. Several women experienced the death of their husbands, and this became a source of grief for them but ultimately also a source of liberation. The mothers of teenagers also experienced dramatic changes. There were stories of tragedy (Katō's son ended up in prison, and she is currently out of touch with him) and also stories of recovery, in which troubled teenagers grew into educated, working adults. Some of these children had already started their own families. The mothers became grandmothers, and some were, perhaps not surprisingly, very involved with their grandchildren, in some cases living with their children and in other cases going over to the house to make meals, do laundry, and help with the housework. Yet many of the women placed limits on their involvement, a sharp break from the way in which they had previously conducted family relationships. Wada-san confiscated the house key from her son after he helped himself to a small amount of money without asking. Katō-san, who had been living with her daughter, decided to move out of the house when it was announced that a grandchild would be born. She did not want to take responsibility for caring for the child; she was older, her back hurt, and she felt she had done enough of that kind of work in her life.

I am often asked how I, as an American, was permitted to enter into such a confidential space. And yet it was, ironically, my very status as an American that made me eligible. I sincerely doubt that a Japanese student or "outsider" to the clinical community (such as I was) would have been granted permission to attend. The desire on the part of the clinicians to teach Americans about Japan, along with what I suspected was an assumption on the women's part that as an American I was open-minded and tolerant (perhaps with looser moral standards than those held by most Japanese), gained entrance for me. The women often commented on my Americanness (to which they attributed my bizarre status: I was almost thirty years old, living alone in Tokyo, pursuing a higher degree, unmarried, and without children). And it became an important text not only in how they perceived me but in how they described themselves.

Like the staff, I participated in the meetings during my year of research—sharing stories of my life in Japan, my own discoveries, and occasionally offering encouragement to the women. And my sense was that while I was by no means an "invisible" observer, my presence there did not affect the overall tenor of the meetings. In what follows, I share the conversations that transpired and the women's reflections on their lives. Some of the narratives are quite hopeful, as family problems slowly resolve themselves. Others are quite tragic. Yet all, I believe, reveal the ways in which women must cobble together the partial and often contradictory discourses that history and culture have offered them in order to make sense of their life predicaments.

Chapter 1 | ALCOHOLISM AND CODEPENDENCY

New Vocabularies for Unspeakable Problems

COPING WITH ALCOHOL

Fukuda-san's husband began to drink heavily when he was working as a long-distance truck driver delivering coal. At the end of a long day of hard labor, the workers regularly went out drinking to relax and enjoy some camaraderie. In 1970, when Japan cut back on its use of coal, he switched jobs and went to work for a painting business. The paint thinner weakened the effect of the alcohol, and he steadily increased his consumption. As Fukuda-san tells the story, "By 1980, he was completely addicted to alcohol, but at that time I didn't know anything about the disease of alcoholism. I just thought that, more than anything else, he really liked his alcohol [*Nani yori mo osake*]." Although by 1980 his drinking was causing major problems in both his work and his family life, three more years passed before he was diagnosed with alcoholism; throughout this period he continued to work. After nine more years, Fukuda-san was encouraged to visit the Center and seek support for her own difficulties. She described the events to me once over tea:

> In 1980 he started getting bad hangovers, and he'd take days off work. On Sundays he'd start drinking in the morning, and on Mondays he wouldn't be able to get up. So other people would have to cover his work for him, and they stopped being able to depend on him. The problem got worse and

worse. And I was always the one who had to call up and say he wouldn't be coming in that day. I couldn't say he had a hangover, so I'd say, "He isn't feeling quite well today. . . ." At first they understood that [sore de tsūjita], but after a while they didn't. "He's hungover, no doubt!" they said to me once.

One time he had to drive down to Kyoto, leaving in the evening. When he arrived, he passed out in the car—unconscious. He was taken to a hospital in Kyoto and they diagnosed it as a "liver problem." It was the first time he had ever been to a doctor. They told him he was basically healthy, and he stayed there for ten days while they treated his liver. I stayed with him, sleeping next to his bed. Then we came back to Tokyo. Not one single person told him to stop drinking! The doctor said, "If it's just a little, it shouldn't be a problem." I myself thought the cause was that he worked too hard. Anyway, he was drinking beer on the way home.

He started drinking heavily again. In 1983, I went to the local public health center [hokenjo] and for the first time I was told that the problem was an alcohol problem [arukōru no mondai]. They gave me an introduction to a hospital and I went for a consultation in secret. If I suggested to him directly that he had an alcohol problem, it would have been a terrible scene. But I knew something was wrong; he was a different person. If I said one thing he didn't like he'd turn over the plates, throw things, say crazy things—I thought he'd gone insane [nō miso ga okashikunatta].

I brought him home a pamphlet and tried to talk to him about it calmly. If I said, "Now Dad, your drinking habits are not normal anymore," he would start throwing things. Once he threw a fruit knife that stuck in the wall behind me. "What is this hospital?! Some kind of hospital for lunatics?! Are you trying to call me a lunatic?!" he'd yell. "I'm no drunkard!" [Nani kono byōin?! Kichigai no byōin janai ka?! Ore o kichigai ni suru ka?! Ore aruchū janai!]

He's a hectoring husband [teishu kanpaku], which meant that if I said "Don't drink," he would. And if he said, "Go buy me some sake [Osake o katte koi]," I did. I thought to myself, "So this is what living hell is like [Ikijigoku wa kō iu koto da na to omoimashita]." I was the perfect "service wife" [sewa nyōbō], picking up after him, changing his clothes, pulling up his pants when he came out of the toilet half-dressed.

One month after my visit to the health-care center, he himself suggested going to the hospital. They diagnosed it as cirrhosis of the liver and told him he needed to check in. But my husband resisted being admitted because he had delivered coal to mental hospitals before, so he had seen people behind bars. And the doctor said he *would* be put behind bars while he went through withdrawal. He argued with the doctor for an hour but refused to be admitted. I sat next to him saying over and over, "Doctor, please admit him, please make him check in," until finally the doctor got mad and threw me out of the room. My husband decided to commute as an outpatient. They prescribed antabuse and that was how he eventually stopped drinking.[1]

Fukuda-san's story reveals several common themes that appear in women's histories of coping with their husbands' alcoholism: the many years they endure before even seeking help or finding appropriate care; the way in which men's heavy drinking is tolerated and even normalized in the Japanese workplace; and the fact that a relatively small (though growing) number of doctors are educated about alcoholism and are prepared to make a distinction between heavy drinking and alcoholism as a disease requiring special forms of treatment. Her story also reveals the widespread public ignorance about the nature of alcoholism and addiction itself, and the association (which her husband shared) of alcoholism with insanity—rooted in part in the fact that historically alcoholics were confined to lock-down wards in mental hospitals and treatment was largely limited to behavioral management. The case histories of the women who arrived at the Center showed how women were often pushed to extremes before they even considered asking for help. Patience *(gaman)* and endurance *(nintai)* have historically been considered necessary virtues of married life. As Koike-san put it, "When my husband would return home after drinking, I'd feel disgusted, but in my case, he wasn't violent or verbally abusive when drunk, so I didn't have a strong sense of victimization. I felt that it was something that I simply had to endure *[gaman shinakya ikenai]*."

In my private conversations with women attending meetings at the Center, they shared stories of husbands' repeated hospitalizations and their years, even decades, of struggling single-handedly to hold the family together until their husbands' drinking was finally identified as the predominant problem. In Fukuda-san's case (and her case was unusual in that her husband eventually did stop drinking), her husband recovered without ever receiving outside professional care; Fukuda-san herself, with help from her son, facilitated the turbulent withdrawal process at home.

Drinking and alcohol are woven into the fabric of everyday life in Japan. Businessmen convene at bars and nightclubs after a day's work to conduct business more casually or simply to socialize. Students gather for *nomikai* (literally, "drinking gatherings") after sports events and club activities; college students drink with their professor after evening or afternoon seminars as part of the seminar experience. There is little enforced government regulation of alcohol consumption, advertising for alcohol, or age limits in Japan, with the exception of strict punishment for drunk driving. According to some estimates, one in every eleven minutes of television advertising is devoted to promoting alcohol. While the legal drinking age is twenty, the law does not require liquor stores or drinking establishments to check identification before serving or selling alcohol. The state benefits from taxes on alcohol consumption. Until quite recently, vending machines selling beer and sake were ubiquitous in public spaces such as train stations and in local neighborhoods. Alcohol consumption, including heavy drinking, is commonplace.

Consumption levels of alcohol have been gradually increasing in Japan over the past decade, while in the United States and Europe levels have steadily decreased. A World Health Organization survey of alcoholics per capita in fifty nations conducted in 1995 placed Japan roughly in the middle; however, most health-care workers in the field agree that due to the limited awareness of alcoholism as a chronic, addictive disease, the number of alcoholics is always underestimated. A government survey reported that there are 2.2 million alcoholics (Japan's total population is 123 million), but volunteer groups have argued that there are in fact as many as ten million (one in six adults) who drink to excess (*Japan Times,* Feb. 12, 1993). Both the number of heavy drinkers (defined by the World Health Organization as people who drink 150 milliliters of alcohol or more a day) and the cumulative amount of alcohol consumed more than doubled in Japan between 1965 and 1985, rising from 364,640 kiloliters to roughly 870,000 (National Cancer Center, *Cancer Statistics on Japan 2001*). In the United States and most Western European countries, it decreased by 15–30 percent between the years 1970 to 1972 and 1994 to 1996 (Global Status Report on Alcohol 1999: 13–15).

Beyond amounts consumed, Japan stands out for its surprising tolerance of drinking and public drunkenness. It is not unusual to see men in suits passed out on train platforms or street corners in after-hours commercial districts of Tokyo, or to see pools of vomit on train platforms and street corners, sights that strike many visitors as incongruous with the general level of safety and decorum in public spaces in Japan. A general level of public safety enables a businessman to sleep on a train platform without fear of being beaten up or robbed. In addition, the helplessness, infantilism, and loss of control associated with drinking do not seem to carry the same negative implications as they do elsewhere (Stephen Smith 1988). High school and college nurses report that students often innocently come to the infirmary seeking sympathy and remedies for hangovers after a night of drinking (Hashimoto 1995).

Alcohol is an integral part of working life in most Japanese companies, both large and small. Though white-collar organizations have historically been more extravagant in their drinking customs, truck drivers and construction workers also often drink together after a day's work, even if this means crouching on the sidewalk near the work site for an evening bottle of beer or shōchū (a harsher liquor than sake, made from potatoes). Large companies allocate funds for employees' drinking after work, and the kind of intimacy and relaxation that occur in these after-hours contexts is considered integral to work. In her analysis of a Japanese after-hours hostess club, Anne Allison has shown how businessmen are "taken care of " by young female hostesses, who tease, flatter, and flirt with them as they pour drinks and entertain them (Allison 1994). In this context, drinking facilitates the "humanization" of work through spiritual refurbishment, self-affirmation, nurturance, and social approval (101, 200). It is also an opportunity for men to "let their hair down" after a hard day's work, do business more informally, and engage in a more playful way with colleagues, often across hierarchical ranks. Through after-hours drinking, the meaning of work is broadened to include playfulness, relaxation, intimacy with colleagues and superiors, and even sensuality and sexuality. The after-hours space, Allison points out, works very much in the interests of the company. It draws workers away from life at home, fusing their identity as men not to their role as husbands and fathers but to their role as workers and masculinized consumers of leisure. Because the workplace comes to include not only work but also collegiality and play, it allows male workers to identify with their companies in a more total way, imagining themselves as "workers twenty-four hours a day" (198–200).

In popular culture, drinking is constructed as a vehicle for the expression of individuality and, particularly, masculinity. In a Tokyo Broadcasting Service television series investigating hidden facets of Japanese society (*Soko mo Shiritai* [1993]), a cameraman followed various characters on their late-night drinking routes. The show emphasized the personalized nature of men's drinking rituals. Clients frequent the same establishments, where bar owners (often women, who are referred to as "Mama" or "Mama-san") indulge their clients in a personal, even intimate way (Allison 1994). In one case, the customer of a small bar routinely slept in the bar after a night of drinking, meticulously sweeping a small spot on the floor at closing time and, with the help of the proprietor, carefully spreading a tarp, sheet, and sleeping bag, and then climbing in. The owner and bartender, who consented to the practice, quietly locked the door behind him. At the close of this scene, the TBS cameraman pokes his camera down into the man's sleeping bag. "How often do you do this?" the narrator asks.

"About four times a week."

"What does your wife think?"

"Well, we've agreed upon this system."

"What?"

"It's just a burden to her if I go home anyway *[Kaeru to nyōbō ni mei-waku kakeru]*. So she likes this better."

At the end of the episode, the male narrator concludes, "My impression is that a man is most manly *[otoko rashii]* when he's drinking. It's not that he doesn't love his wife, but he's truly *himself [jibun rashii]* when he is drinking among his friends" (TBS Broadcast, *Let's Find Out About [Soko mo Shiritai]*, 1993).

Although many men become adept at modulating their drinking so that they can be social but remain in control of themselves, others cannot. In one of many personal experiences that involved men's drunkenness, my husband, my son, and I were invited over to a friend's house to celebrate the New Year. New Year's is one of the most widely celebrated holidays in Japan, and many take a holiday from work for several days, relaxing at home, watching television, and enjoying special New Year's foods. We arrived at noon and were immediately offered special New Year's sake and a beautifully baked fish. As we sat on the tatami under a *kotatsu*, a low table with a heater under it, we made conversation with our friend's husband, a businessman in his late fifties, as she busied herself with meal preparations and work around the house.

He was a reserved man, but as he drank more and more cups of sake, he gradually began asking us about what we thought of Japan and expressing his opinion on matters of the world, the Japanese economy, foreign relations, and so forth. At each juncture, he poured himself another cup of sake, and after a while he stopped bothering to place the sake bottle back on the table in front of us, leaving it cozily within arm's reach on the tatami. Eventually his two daughters returned home from shopping, and we all moved to the bigger family table near the kitchen for the next course, a pot of sukiyaki. The father sat at the head of the table and dutifully manned the sukiyaki pot (traditionally a man's job), while we sat at the other end of the table chatting with the daughters. Shortly afterward, when I glanced at the other end of the table, I noticed that he had quietly gone to sleep, his head completely collapsed onto his chest with an arm still outstretched to the sukiyaki pot. I asked if he was all right, and the daughters giggled and gestured to ignore him. His wife delicately approached him and asked in a quiet voice if he would like to retire to his bedroom. Each time she asked, he abruptly revived himself, reaching out to add something else to the sukiyaki pot or take another bite, only to fall asleep again in mid-mouthful. Soon he was snoring and muttering to himself at the head of the table, and it grew increasingly difficult to ignore him and continue to make polite conversation, but this is precisely what the situation required us to do. Eventually, after much cajoling, he agreed to retire to his bedroom. At that point, he stood up, thanked us each formally for coming, and disappeared downstairs for the rest of the afternoon.

What struck me about this episode was the way a husband and father's drinking to the point of passing out was simply something to be managed within the context of daily family life. The fact that the husband had consumed enough alcohol to pass out was not seen as worrisome or unusual. Nor did it seem to create a major disruption. Without growing violent or obnoxious, he quietly drank himself into a stupor, while we were encouraged to ignore him and make light of the situation. Eventually the problem was managed by his wife, who deftly escorted him from the scene. The event also highlighted the husband's marginalization in the goings-on of the household. He appeared as a somewhat buffoonish presence to be tolerated and indulged.

THE INVISIBLE LABOR OF MANAGING ALCOHOL

Alcoholism in the United States calls attention to itself and attracts resources for treatment because of the destruction and waste of resources it causes: traffic accidents, violence, homelessness, public disruption, crime, and family breakups. Yet these effects have been largely contained or concealed in Japan. It is noteworthy that in the Japanese context, although heavy drinking is an almost obligatory aspect of working life for men (Stephen Smith 1988) and alcohol consumption has increased over the past ten years, Japan continues to be a highly productive society with high levels of social stability. Heavy drinkers are relatively protected in Japan. Although driving under the influence of alcohol is a problem in Japan, the fact that most workers commute by train, rather than car, protects the heavy drinker and allows him to drink on his way home from work. Because the streets are relatively safe, even passing out on the train or the train platform does not pose the same danger of theft or injury as it would in other urban environments.

But beyond the issue of safety, the story betrays an underground economy of labor by wives and mothers, police, train conductors, bar hostesses, and other blue-collar and "pink-collar" workers who work to mitigate, mediate, or conceal the otherwise destructive effects of alcoholism. Train conductors regularly wake sleeping men to alert them to their stop; they also pick up drunken businessmen from the train platform. Bar hostesses, too, graciously put drunken men into taxis. And wives undress their drunken husbands, put them to bed, and then wake them up the next morning, feeding them and sending them off to work again. The fact that alcohol consumption rose dramatically in Japan between 1965 and 1985, the period of Japan's dramatic economic growth and a period marked by widespread social stability, testifies to the way in which the social system mediates and contains the destruction typically associated with alcohol addiction. It also suggests that numerous problems associated with alcohol abuse are kept hidden in Japan, including child abuse and domestic violence. These abuses are only gradually becoming the focus of social service intervention and the object of popular discussion. Some estimate that 20 percent of child abuse is attributable to alcohol abuse; others say this is just the tip of the iceberg.

In Stephen Smith's 1988 study of drinking and alcoholism in Japan, he remarks that because the amount or frequency of alcohol consumed is not in itself considered a symptom of alcoholism, men's drinking is often diagnosed as a problem only when drunken behavior erupts into public conflict or disruption. According to Smith, "Most patients who are diagnosed as alcoholics have come to that situation because of disturbances in their social relations. They eventually exceed the ability or desire of families to make excuses for them" (185). Thus, as long as women (and others) continue to prevent this disruption, alcoholism goes unrecognized as a clinical and social problem. The educational program at the Center, too, while directed at families of alcoholics, emphasized posing a "burden" (meiwaku) to society as an important marker of alcoholism, and included films of police rescuing alcoholics and other dramatic situations. The films sent the message that posing a burden to society was one of the chief liabilities of being a heavy drinker.

Thus, men drinking heavily, even to the point of their being frequently incapacitated, was often not seen—in and of itself—as a major health problem requiring treatment. Women saw it as their job to keep their husbands' drinking from spilling over into public disruption, and physicians reinforced the message that women should simply "manage" their husbands better in response to their drinking. (In Fukuda-san's story above, one physician who had recognized the problem of alcoholism suggested that it was within a wife's power to persuade her husband to seek treatment.) Women were frequently told that their husbands would "get better" if they received good care from their wives. For example, Koike-san told me: "When he'd go to the hospital, come home, drink again, and return to the hospital, the doctor would just say, 'Take care of his general health and make good food so that he gets better.' I didn't realize that it was the drinking itself that was the first fundamental problem. Finally now I see that."

It is interesting to note that because women were committed to helping their husbands function despite their drinking and because heavy drinking alone was not recognized as a problem unless it created broader social disruption, it was often a husband's inability to continue working that finally marked a departure from normal social functioning and suggested a deeper problem. Koike-san, whose husband had not worked for several years and who had been supporting her family single-handedly, told me that during that time it had never occurred to her that alcoholism might be the problem.[2] Her husband's inability to work stood out as the most problematic of his actions:

> "How did my husband come to such a state?"—I didn't ask myself. I suppose I just wasn't thoughtful enough about it. All I knew was that he couldn't work like usual people. I figured he must have some defect in that regard. . . . All I could think was that he didn't have the power to face adversity [*Tada konnan ni tachimukau kiryoku ga nai shika omowanakatta*]. All I knew was that I couldn't expect him to work normally. If only he could find a job that suited him, I kept thinking. He couldn't last at any of his jobs. Two or three years and he'd want to quit. Three times the company he worked for went bankrupt. Then he tried to start his own business, but that didn't go well. Whatever he did didn't end up well. I thought maybe he was unlucky. And that he wasn't the kind of person who can surmount trying situations.

The gendered division of labor surrounding alcoholism explains why so little attention is paid to female alcoholics and male codependency. Codependency by definition seems a women's problem, and social workers report that men rarely if ever enter into support groups for families of substance abusers. Although the problem of female alcoholism of course exists (there are a very small number of hospital wards that admit female alcoholics), as does male codependency, the problems are less likely to be "named" or diagnosed. Women's alcoholism is more easily hidden, since women can cover up for their drinking in the privacy of their own home and are not expected to earn a living wage.[3] Similarly, men are less likely to fall into the role of dependent caregiver. The caregiver role is unfamiliar to them, and in the case of extreme dysfunctionality, a husband can always consider separation or divorce without losing the capacity to support himself.

ALCOHOLISM AS A DISEASE
AND CODEPENDENCY AS A PROBLEM

The disease model of alcoholism, which broke ground in the United States in the 1950s, claims that alcoholism should be considered a disease, a biochemical transformation, of which the chief symptom is a loss of control with respect to drinking. Heavy drinking alters the brain's chemistry, so that it comes to depend on alcohol to maintain its new homeostasis. Hence drinkers can no longer control their desire for alcohol, and alcoholism should not be considered a weakness of will. In the United States, the disease model redefined alcoholism as a disease rather than a moral failure, as it had previously been characterized, and prescribed specific kinds of treatment, such as attendance at AA meetings, predicated on the desire to stop drinking entirely.

The notion of alcoholism as an addictive disease that requires specific forms of intervention is gradually gaining recognition among physicians in Japan; however, many physicians who treat alcoholics in nonspecialized hospitals still treat patients' liver problems and, after a brief detoxification period, dismiss them with the advice that "a little" alcohol should not be a problem. In common parlance, the term describing the state of being severely drunk (*arukōru chūdoku,* literally, "alcohol poisoning") is the same term that describes the condition of alcoholism, or chronic drinking.

In recent years there has been a growing movement among physicians to educate the public and the medical world about the notion of alcoholism as an addictive disease. These physicians use the term *arukōru izonshō* (alcohol dependency syndrome) to describe alcoholism, rather than *arukōru chūdoku.*[4] The Center was centrally involved with attempting to institute this shift in consciousness. The notion of alcohol addiction constitutes a radically different construction of the problem of heavy drinking and its management. Under the old paradigm, women were encouraged to manage their husbands' drinking privately and often attempted to stop their husbands' drinking single-handedly by resorting to all kinds of covert means—pouring out their husbands' alcohol, consulting doctors secretly (as Fukuda-san did), or, an age-old tactic, pouring antabuse into their husbands' miso soup. Alcoholism was treated very much like a mental illness: families were encouraged to cope with the matter privately until this was no longer feasible, at which point the patient was likely to be forcibly committed to a mental hospital, where conditions were typically grim (Munakata 1986; Stephen Smith 1988). Women who could no longer take care of their husbands privately were forced to relinquish them to the care of a hospital, where they were often involuntarily incarcerated.

The disease model changed these dynamics. This model of alcoholism, which grew up in tandem with Alcoholics Anonymous spiritual support groups in the United States, emphasizes that no one can "make" the alcoholic stop drinking. Because alcoholism is characterized by a loss of control, stopping drinking requires a major commitment on the part of the drinker himself (or herself), and a profound psychological, even spiritual, transformation. Women who attempted to "put" their husbands into treatment found that they were turned away. A key concept in the AA construction of alcoholism is that an alcoholic must "want" to stop drinking, and must undergo an almost spiritual process of transformation in order to recover. In turn, a wife cannot "manage" her husband's recovery or "solve" the problem. A key element in the husband's recovery is that the wife withdraws from the role she has taken on, by necessity, of effectively managing the household and shutting her husband out.[5] She focuses on her own "recovery," which involves carving out her own world independent of her husband, even if he continues to drink, and finding ways to live her life, supporting a husband without attempting to "cure" him. A caretaker is also encouraged to examine her own tendency (or "need") to care for her husband and the validation she may derive from that caregiving.

Through the management of their husbands' drinking and the encounter with the discourse of alcoholism as an addiction, women embark on new regimes of self-exploration and self-expression as they encounter new vocabularies for describing social relationships. For most of the forty or so women whom I came to know over my year of participation, this process, as much as their husbands' struggle to obtain sobriety, became the focus of their recovery. In fact, few men were successful in becoming sober, and most never entered long-term treatment. The women were left to come to meetings and, along with other women, draw on new narratives, rooted in U.S. pop psychology, of marriage, self, and identity, to try to better their situation. For women who had become accustomed to entirely managing their husbands' problems, the diagnosis of alcoholism revealed new vistas, allowing them to stop feeling that they weren't being "good enough" wives and mothers and to start asking whether they had been "too good."

Before the meetings, few women would have considered their husbands' alcoholism an impetus for self-discovery. (In fact, most were referred to the Center not because they were seeking help for themselves, but because they were referred by their husbands' physicians.)[6] Most women accepted their referral to the Center reluctantly, assuming it was merely one more thing that they were being asked to do for their husbands—that coming to the Center would help cure their husbands. A central turning point for the women took place when they gave up the idea that they could "cure" their husbands and began coming to the Center "for themselves." The idea of women coming together to talk and share stories, speaking frankly about family problems, particularly with strangers, is somewhat unusual in Japan. The fact that the unfortunate situation of a husband's alcoholism was one of the few possible provocations for these women to convene and reflect on problems of Japanese marriage attests to the conservatism of Japanese society.

THE CENTER AS A SPACE FOR SOCIAL CRITICISM

The Tokyo Metropolitan Mental Health Care Center, where the meetings were held, was an institutional-looking building, a two-story, box-like white cement structure with large dark rectangles of glass. It was the largest of three city-funded outpatient mental health care services in Tokyo— part of a network of community health care facilities that provided telephone and outpatient counseling, as well as the weekly group meetings I attended. It seemed an unlikely place for women's consciousness-raising, but women often spoke about it as the only place where they could "really talk" about central issues in their lives. One of the older women, Fukuda-san, once told me that she considered it her "second home town" *(furusato)*: a place of rebirth.

In fact there are few spaces to talk openly about family or personal problems in daily social life in Japan, particularly for this generation of women. Often, family issues are not divulged to neighbors or even to extended family. In village life, women often used to hold "meetings around the well" *(idobata kaigi)* where they exchanged gossip and information; in the urbanized living spaces of the postwar period, however, neighbors have grown increasingly anonymous, and women's worlds have increasingly become confined to the home and to activities centered around the children. Whereas men gather over golf games and after-hours drinking to "vent" and talk over personal matters with friends and colleagues, there are few such opportunities for women. Middle- or upper-middle-class women may gather to do volunteer work, participate in child-rearing seminars or the PTA, or take cooking classes, but these gatherings often emphasize social betterment and community service, and are not conducive to confession or venting.

Margaret Lock has shown that in modern times Japanese women often vent their frustrations to physicians. The expansion of the medical sphere through the system of national health insurance, combined with the fact that there are few acceptable spaces for addressing social tension and conflict, has made the sphere of medicine one of the few sanctioned spaces for expression of social grievances (Lock 1987; Ohnuki-Tierney 1984). In a series of provocative articles exploring the phenomenon known in the Japanese mass media as the "housewife syndrome," Lock showed how women's social complaints were medicalized, given names such as "child-rearing neurosis," "high-rise neurosis," "marital overdose," and "kitchen sickness" (Lock 1986, 1987, 1988, 1990; see also Madoka 1982; Katsura 1983). She pointed to the conservative approach taken by many physicians, who viewed women's complaints as weaknesses to be surmounted and encouraged women to reintegrate themselves into their housewife roles.

The network of public centers, which included the Center (founded in 1985), was part of a broader city-government effort, begun in the 1960s, to change public attitudes toward mental health and to provide a space for consultation. The agenda was to promote the "rehabilitation of the mentally ill" and to promote "acceptance of those who have psychological problems." A key strategy was better outpatient and consultation services. (Report on Local Community Mental Health Committee of Tokyo 1981). Although the Center was not initially involved in alcoholism treatment, in the mid-1980s, as it became clear that alcohol was increasingly becoming a social problem, the Center implemented an alcohol treatment program. The categories in operation at such publicly funded institutions as the Center play a key role in Japanese social life, because such centers serve as a triage site: a place where people come when they don't know where else to go or even how to define the problem. For this reason, they shape the way people define and manage problems that arise in daily life.

The chief psychiatrist at the Center, Dr. Saitō Satoru, saw his promotion of the ideas of alcoholism and codependency as part of a broader mission of social criticism. He was particularly concerned with Japan's program of rapid economic growth and the toll it had taken on the people. In his widely read books on addiction and codependency, *Kazoku Izonshō* (Family Addiction, 1989) and *Kazoku no Yami* (The Dark Side of Families, 1998), Saitō describes alcoholism and substance abuse as centrally intertwined with the broader social system in Japan, especially the needs of the enterprise society, the demands placed on women as caregivers, and the importance placed on academic success in children's lives. He often uses the language of addiction as a metaphor for the Japanese system of middle-class advancement through education and productivity, describing Japanese parents as "addicted" to the school system or "workaholism" as Japan's biggest addiction. According to Saitō, society "makes" people into addicts in its relentless pressure for "social alignment" *(shakai teki dōchō)*.

In an early conversation, he told me, "It's women who are enabling workaholism. Women prepare food for men, wait up for them, ask them if they want a bath before they go to bed. This enables men to become pathologically dependent. We have to look at them as a pair—not just the husband. Overdevotion goes along with overwork. Most Japanese men don't even know where their own socks are kept!" (personal communication, October 30, 1992).

In an essay entitled "Two Types of Troubled Fathers," Saitō points out that alcoholism exists not only among day laborers in the slums, but also among the Japanese elite. These elite alcoholics epitomize for Saitō the hard worker and good husband:

> A typical man graduated from a top-tier university and works at a top-level bank. He has attained a high social status. When he gets drunk he gets violent. His wife contemplates divorce. At work people think of him as someone who does his job. But this kind of alcoholic hurts his family and hurts the next generation. The office only values efficiency and productivity. This kind of alcoholic actually thinks he has fulfilled his role. . . . He goes out drinking after work with his coworkers, his "pseudo-family," and relives his childhood, referring to the proprietor of the bar as "Mama. . . ." Gradually he gets pushed to the margins of family emotions. (Saitō 1989: 46)

Saitō's metaphorical use of *addiction* and his claims that "any family" could be an alcoholic family and that being a "good wife" itself is a form of addiction are overblown and serve the rhetorical purpose of making his work appeal to a broader audience. He pathologizes the work of the wife and mother in a way that makes many social workers and clients uncomfortable. And yet, through the language of pathology, Saitō has called attention to latent patterns in Japanese society that had not previously been described as problems.

Whereas most Japanese health-care practitioners were not interested in the problem of addiction in the 1970s, Saitō, influenced by the American recovery movement, took his ideas to nurses and social workers who worked in the trenches of public health care, many at local ward-funded health-care centers *(hokenjo)*. Focusing on one of the largest and most central wards in Tokyo, with a population of some 800,000 people and four public health centers, Saitō trained the local public health nurses to deal with addiction themselves rather than referring patients to nonspecialized hospitals. He initiated the first family meetings at these local centers. The ward in central Tokyo where the Center is located became a model for other districts. In 1983, he started one of the first alcohol treatment programs at a large public hospital in Tokyo, Matsuzawa Hospital, training the psychiatrist who managed it. By the early 1990s, he had trained the psychiatrists who managed several major alcohol treatment centers in Tokyo.

The success of Saitō's worldview shows the resistance of Japanese society and the women themselves to politicizing women's issues, and the tendency to talk about these issues as medical or psychological problems. Saitō viewed the reinterpretation of addiction as a means to social change and the medicalization of women's family problems as a step toward feminism. In explaining his rationale for starting the support groups, he once told me, "Why did the idea of codependency take off in Japan? I think it had to do with the fact that these problems had been around for a long time. People had some consciousness of it *[jikkan]* but there was just no word. Just as women were starting to feel discontented with the ethic of self-sacrifice for the sake of the family, the theory of codependency came along to medically validate their feelings" (personal communication, April 30, 1993). "I want to interpret so-called medical problems more broadly," he continued. "Serving one's husband to the point of losing one's own sense of self is not a medical problem—it's a way of life! That's why it should not be handled by doctors!" He viewed the meetings at the Center as a kind of grassroots feminism. Although Center and Al-Anon meetings are currently reserved for wives of alcoholics, he hoped eventually to establish a group that would be open to all women—a group he imagined would be called "Ladies

Anonymous." The idea revealed the simultaneous politicization and medicalization of women's issues. The very notion of "Ladies Anonymous" illustrates the dearth of vocabulary available to women to describe their discontent; alcoholism and codependency provided a language for them to talk about life problems (see also Lock 1987).[7]

The way the clinic functioned as a triage facility, and at times as a catchall for a variety of social problems, illustrated the shortage of spaces where women's problems could be addressed. In the absence of facilities to deal with this social problem, medical facilities stepped in. I observed this process in the context of the weekly case conferences, in which the clinic staff met with a psychologist and psychiatrist in order to triage new cases or assess the progress of ongoing cases. A central issue in new cases was domestic violence—a key problem in the context of alcoholism. Public discourse on domestic violence (increasingly known as "dv" in clinical circles) is limited in Japan, though growing, and there are as yet few publicly funded shelters for abused women, and little educational material.[8]

Interestingly, alcohol treatment facilities in hospitals often seemed to function as a quasi-shelter for women battered by their husbands. Alcohol treatment units often have "family inpatient units" *(kazoku nyūin)*—something rarely found in the United States—where family members of alcoholics can check themselves in to rest and recover. In one case presented at the case conference, a mother came in for counseling; her son was a habitual gambler who was violent at home and possibly schizophrenic. The father was an abusive alcoholic. The mother (the client) described herself as "mentally exhausted" *(seishin teki ni maite iru)*. The psychologist decided that the first step should be to admit the mother (seemingly the only sane member of the family) to the hospital. In this way, the hospital stepped in to provide shelter for the woman, while the more difficult task of luring the husband and son into treatment remained unresolved.

THE FAMILY MEETING

Though the tenor of the meetings was at times somber, as I described earlier, the meetings were a radical departure from many other alcoholism groups available to women: specifically, they aspired to be nonhierarchical (like the American AA model) and they encouraged women to speak freely about their feelings and thoughts. In contrast, the Japanese adaptation of Alcoholics Anonymous, Danshukai, one of the largest organizations for families recovering from alcoholism (it has forty-seven thousand members, in contrast with AA's five thousand in Japan), is a self-help group where families of alcoholics attend the same meetings as the alcoholics themselves. Danshukai has been self-consciously adapted to suit the needs of "Japanese culture."[9] In contrast with the meetings at the Center, which were seen as a chance for women to help themselves, men played the leading role at the Danshukai meetings and women were considered "auxiliary members," there to support their husbands (Stephen Smith 1988). While Danshukai shares the AA notion of social support and sobriety as means of recovery, it departs from the Al-Anon notion (which was taken very seriously at the Center) that family members cannot heal their families' illness, that alcoholism is the abuser's problem and not the family members', and that family members should attend meetings to learn to manage and to look after themselves rather than to "fix" the abuser. Instead Danshukai adheres more closely to conventional Japanese gender role constructions. At the end of the meeting, after men recite a "Sincerity Pledge" of sobriety, women recite a "Family Pledge" that includes these affirmations:

My husband/son joined Danshukai. Stopping drinking is truly hard.
My husband/son, who made the decision to abstain, is wonderful.
My husband's/son's drinking is an illness. Because it is an illness it must be cured. Furthermore, it can be cured.
My husband's/son's affliction is my affliction.
In order that my husband/son stops drinking I will suffer, too; I will be cured, too. (Stephen Smith 1988)

Many women who eventually came to the Center had been to Danshukai meetings. Several stopped going because their husbands refused to participate and they found little reason to continue attending on their own. Others reported that it was difficult to speak freely there. Koike-san, a regular member of the weekly meeting at the Center, complained that Danshukai replicated the subordinate role of women. She told me that at the end of Danshukai meetings, it was the women's responsibility to serve tea to everyone. Since they served two or three cups per person, this involved a considerable amount of work. "Doesn't this go against the philosophy of codependency?" she asked. When she suggested a system of "self-service," one of the members rejected the idea because other branches of Danshukai served tea the conventional way. Eventually she stopped attending these meetings.

The emphasis at the weekly meetings was on women learning to "talk about themselves" rather than focusing on their husbands' or their children's recovery. The very definition of recovery for caretakers entailed learning to disentangle their own lives from the lives of the substance abusers—letting the substance abusers make their own mistakes and allowing themselves to relinquish the caretaking role.

And yet the reality is that there are few precedents for women to publicly discuss their own feelings and private experiences, or for the idea that public sharing could have a therapeutic effect. Because of the stigma of mental illness and the view that families should take responsibility for managing it, outpatient treatment has been markedly limited in Japan and largely conducted in hospitals, where administering medication is the central aspect of treatment. Counseling clinics and private therapists' offices are notably few. In general, "talking therapies"—the notion of healing someone through conversation with a therapist—have not taken root in Japanese medical practice, and neither psychoanalysis nor any other psychodynamic psychotherapy has gained a broad following in Japan. The "indigenous" therapeutic practices in Japan, notably Morita and Naikan therapy, draw on Zen practices and other pursuits of self-cultivation to emphasize quiet self-reflection *(hansei)* and physical labor as means to spiritual healing. In particular, they emphasize reintegration into the social whole through appreciation of one's privileges and expressions of gratitude toward others. Even at the Center, the word *counseling* was used infrequently. Individual consultations were referred to as "interviews" *(mensetsu)* and support groups were called "meetings."

In the late 1980s, when Saitō began experimenting with group meetings for women married to alcoholics, there were few support groups in the context of Japanese psychiatry. "Group meetings" usually meant a collective case interview led by a physician, in which the doctor consults with each family sequentially, asking for information and then offering advice (see Stephen Smith 1988; Takemura Misao, personal communication, October 23, 1993). The patients hardly engage with one another. Saitō was fond of telling the story of how, in the early years of experimenting with the group therapy format at the local public health center, one of the social workers persisted in talking about her cat for over a year. Yet eventually the meetings at the Center achieved a reputation as a successful experiment; nurses and social workers from hospitals all over Japan came to train and observe. In particular, there was much excitement about the family meeting.

The women who had been coming to the meetings the longest often constructed their stories as a narrative: a dilemma posed by their family and then an insight they received from that dilemma—a strategy or a way of coping that they learned. The new arrivals at the group often talked in a rather desultory way about the scenes and antics of their husbands or teenage children, their own health problems, and their struggles to manage these problems. They focused on the details of their families' illnesses or incidents related to the problem rather than how they felt about it. Their distress often seemed to manifest itself in stress-related psychosomatic symptoms, such as fatigue or dizziness; they rarely talked about anger or sadness. At the first meeting Aoki-san attended, she described how her anger first emerged as physical disorientation, though finally she sought help:

> I'm Aoki. In my life I'd never experienced anger until the time my husband and I went in for a consultation at the hospital. On the way home I was so distracted that I was running red lights and so forth. When I got home my daughter noticed something was wrong and pulled out my futon. I got in but couldn't sleep. Suddenly I remembered there was the community healthcare center [hokenjo]. So I got up and went. I talked to someone there for two hours, pouring out my soul, until the place closed. I finally felt I had cleared my head [Kimochi ga sukkiri shita].

The staff considered an expressive narrative voice and "power of articulation" (hatsugen ryoku) important elements of women's "recovery." The most salient feature of narratives of recovery was the women's ability to speak about themselves (jibun o hanasu). Women who began their sentences with "my husband" or "my son" were regarded as not yet recovered. Japanese housewives frequently are known in their communities as "X's wife" or "Y's mother," and they often identify and introduce themselves that way. These women said that it took them a while to understand the concept of "talking about themselves" (jibun o hanasu).

Clinicians put particular emphasis on women's clarity in marking the subject of the sentence. Wives of alcoholics were known among clinicians to "leave out" the subjects of their sentences and to talk about their husbands as if they were talking about themselves *(otto no koto o jibun no koto no yō ni kataru)*. While omitting the subject of a sentence is not uncommon in Japanese grammar, clinicians interpreted the phenomenon as women forfeiting their identities to care for their husbands. The head of the alcohol treatment program at a large public hospital in Tokyo was quoted as saying, "As they take care of their husbands, they are overtaken by a sense of duty, believing that their husbands simply could not get by without them. They lose a sense of the boundary between themselves and their husbands and start to leave out the subjects of their sentences" *(Otto no mendō o mite iru uchi, watashi ga inakereba to iu gimu kan ni shihai sare, otto to jibun to no ryōkai ga nakunari, shugo ga nukeru) (Yomiuri Shinbun,* June 12, 1993).

In one meeting, for example, Ōta-san, an elderly participant whose adult son lived at home with her, said: "Ōta *desu* [I'm Ōta]. I'm here for my son's drug addiction. [He was] admitted to the hospital two times this year. [If he] didn't like it then he would just leave; [he has] no appreciation for money. [He] comes home and doesn't do a thing. Doesn't talk with my husband. I have to really hold myself together or else."

At another meeting, this same woman (Ōta-san) introduced herself in a way that caught the social workers' attention. Instead of repeating the conventional introduction, "I'm Ōta. I'm here because of my son's drug addiction," she elided the two sentences saying, "I'm drug addiction Ōta" *(Yakubutsu no Ōta desu),* transforming her son's sickness into an adjectival phrase modifying herself, a grammatically correct construction in Japanese. The staff commented on the elision after the meeting, citing it as symbolic of how "attached and identified" she was with her son.

Wetzel (1994) remarks that Japanese sentence structure deemphasizes the speaking subject as the fixed reference point of the sentence and that verbs are conjugated contextually, according to the relationship of the speaker to the interlocutor, rather than according to the personal pronoun itself, independent of its context. Bachnik and Quinn (1994) and Wetzel (1994) go further to argue that the construction of language is intertwined with cultural constructions of self. This sentiment is reflected in the importance placed on grammatical constructions by the Center's clinicians. The idea is a rather heavy-handed application of English grammatical structures as "normal" and "healthy"; one does not need to fully accept that language conditions notions of self in such a literal way to see that language may naturalize a slippage in boundaries, making this slippage difficult to problematize explicitly. In explicitly placing themselves at the center of their narratives, and in clearly distinguishing the "I" of the sentence, women attempted to overwrite implicit cultural assumptions coded into daily life through language. Nonetheless, the social workers' equation of Japanese grammatical forms with the deletion of self and their positioning of self-expression and self-assertion as antidotes left women to negotiate between two rather reductionistic discourses, neither offering a nuanced model of how to articulate one's own desires within the context of social expectations.

JAPAN'S RECEPTION
OF THE CODEPENDENCY PERSPECTIVE

In my early meetings at the Center, it became clear that while the codependency concept held considerable allure for women (particularly, the idea that it is possible to go too far with being "helpful" and that one can love while also drawing boundaries between self and other), the women had not embraced the wholesale pathologization of the concept of caregiving that was prevalent in the 1980s United States. Women often talked about their codependency in affectionate, almost proud, terms (particularly with respect to their children), telling stories of how they couldn't resist spoiling their children or lending them money, even when this occurred in the context of destructive behavior.

Nor did social workers view Japanese codependent women as deviating from rational behavior, succumbing to psychodynamic compulsions, or lacking self-control. In contrast with the American pop psychology language of self-loathing, there was little sense that the situation in which the women found themselves betrayed a self-destructiveness on their part. From the standpoint of social dictates, most Japanese codependent women had made all the "right" decisions and were, in fact, supremely in control of themselves and their surroundings. As one social worker explained it to me, in Japan, "the wives with the problems are seen as being the 'good wives' *[Mondai no tsuma wa 'ii tsuma' to sarete imasu]*." While the notion that some people are more codependent than others exists on the periphery, neither group discussions nor educational materials focused on members' upbringing or family environment as causal explanations for codependency. Nor was there a sense that the women had actively chosen alcoholic or otherwise troubled husbands owing to individual maladjustment. Although women were encouraged to talk about their feelings at each weekly meeting, they rarely discussed their upbringing or childhood environment as a causal explanation for their situation. Instead their conversations focused on the way in which society expects women to behave in codependent ways, the social expectations and belief systems that produce and even require codependent behavior. Codependency was read as being produced socially rather than psychodynamically.

In fact, most women arrived at the Center with a strong sense that they had been doing the best they could, and yet, despite this, they had remained unable to remedy the situation. Many women told me that it took them a very long time to accept the concept of enabling and the idea that their own behavior could be counterproductive. For example, Fukuda-san, a client at the Center, told me over tea:

> His relatives used to blame his drinking on me. "Just don't buy him sake! Don't give it to him! Just take it away!" they'd tell me. But frankly I could never imagine that I had done anything wrong. I had put myself out for my husband's every wish. I kept telling myself that at the time. I thought I was doing exactly what I was supposed to do: "serve" my husband [otto ni tsukusu], buy the sake, protect the family. But over the years of coming to the Center I've begun to see that I too had some responsibility. I helped create the kind of relationship environment where he could drink [nomu kankei o tsukutta].

Social workers at the Center often remarked that Japanese women seemed to see self-sacrifice as a virtue (jibun o gisei ni suru no ga bitoku to sarete iru). Yet in truth, the social and economic practices that crystallized in the postwar period supported and sustained this belief system. In many ways, women were expected to quietly support their husbands. But in truth, particularly beginning in the postwar decades of the 1950s and 1960s, as men began to work away from the home, women have largely been in charge of managing the home—and managing the husband. Women's efforts to cover up for their husbands' drinking and to continue to maintain appearances to the neighbors, the husband's boss, or the extended family was, to them, merely an extension of what they had been doing previously. The notion of women as the de facto manager of the home has coexisted with the symbolic notion of men as "the boss." This situation became extreme in the families of alcoholic men. An example of the explicit sanctioning of women's cover-ups, and the fine line between women's "quiet" support and actual management of the family, is revealed in the following advice from a Japanese psychiatrist that appeared in the "Life Guidance" advice column of the *Yomiuri Daily News* in 1985–86:

HUSBAND SOAKS IN DRINK EVERY NIGHT

I am a housewife in my thirties. I want to discuss a problem concerning my husband.

My husband is in his late forties. He has his own business, and I take care of the bookwork for him and help him run the company. The problem is with his drinking. He drinks about seven *go* [about three quarts] of alcohol each night. . . . After having observed him carefully over the sixteen years of our marriage, I can summarize my husband's strange behavior through the following description: (1) He soaks in alcohol every night, literally drinking until he passes out. (2) While drinking he forces me to sit down in front of him while he complains to me for two or three hours about all kinds of things around the house. (3) He makes decisions for the company and for the family without discussing them with anyone. (4) He is so jealous that I can't go anywhere without being questioned in a humiliating manner. (5) I can't remember him being at home without a drink in his hand.

I have never disobeyed him. When he criticizes me, he gradually starts screaming so the neighbors can hear every word he says. Sometimes he even throws things around. My daughter says that he doesn't possess a single fatherly trait. Do you think he can ever change?

The psychiatrist replied:

It would be somewhat hasty for me to make a judgment about your husband based merely on your letter. . . . One thing seems certain: . . . drinking has gotten the better of [your husband] and this should be tended to, through professional treatment if necessary.

. . . I don't know what kind of business you have, but why don't you quietly take steps to run more of the business yourself, while establishing him more as a figurehead. Judging from what you write, I have the feeling that you could do this.

A person like your husband may seem arrogant and demanding on the outside, but his basic nature is probably very dependent. Your daughter says that he doesn't act like a father. This is another reason for assuming more of the responsibilities of the business and enduring more of the hardships for him.

Compared to the adversity you suffer now, this [course] of action may actually lead to fulfillment. If you follow this advice, even though you say your husband doesn't listen to others, he can be influenced by virtue of his dependency to seek treatment for his drinking.

I offer this advice for the benefit of your family. (McKinstry and McKinstry 1991: 62–63)

This advice makes clear why women would have felt that sustaining their husbands by hiding their transgressions and taking over family matters was the right thing to do. The management of the family business is seen as a natural step from the usual "quiet support" *(naijo no ko)* a wife gives a husband. The advice strikes me as quite reasoned, considering contemporary constructions of marriage and family. Yet it is this advice that the clinicians at the Center and those involved more broadly with alcohol care seek to overturn.

In what follows, I suggest that, ironically, to the extent that codependency is seen as being surprisingly close to "the normal" in Japanese social life (and therefore less easy to pathologize), it may carry the potential to produce a somewhat more useful conversation in Japan than it has in the United States (in its popular rendition), allowing women to explore the often subtle distinctions between "healthy" and "destructive" interdependence.

Chapter 2 | MOTHERHOOD, NURTURANCE, AND "TOTAL CARE" IN POSTWAR NATIONAL IDEOLOGY

THE ANATOMY OF DEPENDENCE

In the 1960s and 1970s, large volumes of literature on "theories of Japaneseness," or *Nihonjinron,* filled the shelves of Japanese bookstores. A common theme uniting these texts was the importance of emotional intimacy, motherly nurturance, and person-to-person relations in holding together Japanese society and social institutions. Many of these texts were the efforts of self-appointed social commentators, capitalizing on Japanese readers' demand for such materials. Others were scholarly analyses by psychiatrists, anthropologists, and sociologists who attempted, based on carefully collected data, to articulate what it meant to be Japanese in the context of a historical moment in which prewar ideals of nationhood and community had been widely repudiated (Doi 1973; Nakane 1970; Kimura 1972; Minami 1974). In *The Anatomy of Dependence,* Doi Takeo described the intimate dependency of an infant on its mother as the Japanese ideal prototype for all social relationships (72–74). In *Japanese Society,* social anthropologist Nakane Chie argued that highly hierarchical and integrated Japanese companies were held together by an "accumulation of relationships between two individuals," not by a more abstract, universalized loyalty to the whole (1970: 42). Identification with the vertical group emerged, she argued, from these localized relationships and "the exceedingly high degree of . . . emotional involvement" that characterizes group alliances (4). Central to the work of Doi, Nakane, and others was the construction of the family as the sine qua non of Japanese cultural ethos and the primary unit of Japanese society: the template upon which other social institutions are modeled.

Of such texts, *The Anatomy of Dependence* (1973) became arguably the most influential on everyday discourses of Japanese culture in Japan. *The Anatomy of Dependence* is an exegesis on the sentiment of *amae,* which Doi defines as the basic emotional urge that has fashioned the Japanese for two thousand years. *Amae* is "the desire to be passively loved" and to presume on familiarity in order to behave in a self-indulgent manner. Doi arrived at the notion of *amae* while training as a psychiatrist in the United States shortly after the war.[1] While there, he was struck by the American privileging and reification of individual autonomy, which became the central problematic of his thought: why do Americans appear to celebrate the prospect of mutual autonomy while denying their dependence upon one another? Doi writes, "Even psychiatrists—specialists of the psyche— could not detect *amae,* the need for passive love" (22). In comparing Japanese human relations to the mother-child relationship, Doi focuses exclusively on the sentiments of the child, neglecting those of the mother. As he puts it, "The essence of the Japanese experience lies in the period of infancy" (83).

The ideological success of the notion of *amae* must be understood in the context of the ideological crisis the Japanese faced at the end of the World War II and their continuing attempt to grapple with the West (particularly "America") as a hegemon and prototype of modernity. The discourse of *amae,* couched in the language of Freud, offered a narrative of national identity that allowed Japanese citizens to locate themselves in Western discourses of modernity, while connecting them to a history of received ideas concerning family, community, and nationhood. Although Doi's agenda was in part to incite the Japanese to "grow up" and shed their dependence in order to become socially responsible adults, the text celebrated and romanticized *amae* as a pleasurable experience that Japanese people seek but Westerners are not likely to understand.

Central to Doi's analysis is the notion of family as rooted in the love between parent and child, this love in turn forming a kind of social contract that is generalizable to all social relations. In Doi's rendering, the love from parent to child is unquestioned and noncontractual, beautiful, and natural. In turn, the child is depicted as innocent, wholly dependent, and entitled to the care it gets from its parent. This notion of the family as a deeply intimate sphere, shaped by the landscape of parent-child relations and characterized by a selflessness and communalism that can then be translated to the outside world has historical roots in prewar discourses on the family and the nation. To understand the notion of dependency that is so commonly valued in everyday social life, it is necessary to consider some of the historical roots of this discourse and the reasons that its rehabilitation after the war might have been so deeply compelling.

The notion of the family as the template for all society has roots in late nineteenth-century and particularly prewar discourses on the national polity. Discourses of family had been central to Meiji period (1868–1912) and prewar visions of Japan's modernity and shared national culture. Incipient conceptualizations of the modern nation-state in the Meiji period specified the multigenerational household *(ie)* as the smallest unit of the national polity *(kokka);* prewar government-issued statements and tracts, such as *Kokutai no Hongi* (Cardinal Principles of the National Entity of Japan [1937]), described the state itself as a "national family" *(kazoku kokka)*—with the emperor as father. In this context, family was defined as a male-dominated space, a patriarchal household, in which inheritance and property were passed down through the eldest male descendent. All members of the family were beholden to the head of the household and risked being expelled should they disobey him (Yoshizumi 1995: 186–87).[2] Because the family registry *(koseki)* consisted not only of living family members but also of ancestors who had passed away, traced as many generations into the past as was known, the *ie* was also a symbolic entity, in which, at least in principle, all Japanese families could ultimately be traced to one ancestor (Kawamura 1989), allowing for the nationalist claim that all Japanese subjects were ultimately linked to the divine (the emperor) (Dower 1986; Weiner 1995; see also Hall 1949).

The particular notion of the family as a hierarchical sphere (prioritizing the relationship between parent and child rather than that between the spouses), and yet an affective one, has deeper roots in prewar national representations of the family as a prototype for national unity. In the face of Western imperialism and the Japanese project of "catching up with the West," scholars had hailed the family as a defining marker of Japaneseness that set Japan apart from the West, allowing it to modernize in its own distinctive way. Scholars such as the prominent philosopher Watsuji Tet-surō celebrated the Japanese family as the institution that shielded the Japanese from the "self-centeredness" of the West and allowed them to cultivate a sense of national oneness.

In his 1935 analysis (*Fūdo* [A Climate]) of the ways in which climatic patterns influence cultural values and social structures, Watsuji argued that the unpredictability of the Japanese monsoon-prone climate had promoted an emphasis on "the community of family life" (1961: 141). Watsuji defined the national spirit of Japan as embodied in the home, particularly the relationships of loyalty and affection between parent and child. He used his concept of the family to distinguish Japan from what he observed to be the selfishness and individualism of the West:

> What has been said of the specific character of Japanese love holds good in entirety for the family way of life. Here the point of enquiry is the relationship not between male and female but between husband and wife, parent and child, elder and younger brother or sister. This relationship is, above all, that of gentle affection, aiming at a completely frank union. The artless ancients, when speaking of quarrels between husband and wife or of jealously, already display this sense of warm and unreserved family affection. Again, the fine poem of Okura, the Manyo poet—"Silver or gold or jade, none are as precious as my child"—has long been regarded as entirely appropriate to the heart of the Japanese.
>
> . . . Through every age, the Japanese strove for the sacrifice of selfishness within the family. So there is a full realization of the concept of the fusion of self and other. . . . The most striking feature of Japanese history is this readiness to stake one's life for the sake of parent or child, or to cast away life for the house. (1961: 142–43)

Yet, Watsuji acknowledged, the family system is no longer as deeply rooted as it once was. Will Japanese individuals, as they are increasingly swayed by "modern European capitalism" (144), come to see the household as merely "an association of individuals" (144)? No, he argued, the very structure of the home, in which rooms are separated by rice paper screens *(shōji)* and sliding doors *(fusuma)*, itself reveals the deep-seated Japanese mentality. In contrast to the European vision of the individual as the primary unit of society, Watsuji argued, the Japanese see the home as the foundational unit. And within the home, individuals are not separated but instead are drawn together in mutual respect and self-sacrifice. "*Fusuma* and *shōji* have no power of resistance against anyone desiring to open them and their function as partitions . . . always depends on the trust of others and their respect of the expression of the wish for separation indicated by the simple fact that they are drawn. In other words, within the 'house,' the Japanese feels neither need of protection against others nor any desire for separation from the desires of others" (164). Watsuji described the concept of *aidagara,* or "relationality," as the centrally defining feature of Japanese national culture—a set of ideas that Doi Takeo would no doubt have been exposed in to in high school and college preparatory.[3]

What is particularly important about Watsuji's analysis—and what makes him particularly relevant to postwar thought—is his emphasis on the affective ties that underpinned the hierarchical and patriarchal families he was describing. In the 1930s, when Japan was fully embarked on an aggressive imperialistic war in the name of the emperor, Watsuji described the emperor as a benevolent and nurturing father figure for the national family of Japan—the "father of the nation" who is descended from the sun goddess and so shares her qualities of "gentle and emotional affection" (151; see also Morris-Suzuki 1998: 118). In *Cardinal Principles of the National Entity of Japan (Kokutai no Hongi),* a government-issued tract that Watsuji collaborated on (widely circulated in schools and read at public assemblies in the immediate prewar years), a section entitled "Love for the People" describes the emperor's "endless love and care for his subjects": he "loves and protects them as one would sucklings, and, depending upon their cooperation, diffuses his policies widely" (Hall 1949: 76). For Japanese subjects in the prewar period, familism and filial piety were celebrated not simply as a manifestation of the supposed divine origins of the Japanese people but of human relationality, modesty, and moral virtue in contrast with Western greed, materialism, and individualism.

The notion of loyal and devoted social relationships as being rooted in parental love is evident in the writings of Doi more than a generation later—although the family in evidence in Doi's writing in the postwar years of the 1960s and 1970s is dramatically different from the "family of gods and ancestors" that dominated the prewar period. On the cover of *Anatomy of Dependence* is a mother holding her child's hand—a considerably more intimate picture of a nuclear family guided by a nurturing, maternal presence rather than an authoritarian, paternal one. Similarly, while for Watsuji feelings of family unity and love had been inextricably bound up with feelings of love for the nation (family unity bled naturally into national unity),[4] Doi's postwar analysis links family to considerably more personalized attachments. He no longer evokes the family of the father's extended lineage but rather the nuclear family, rooted in maternalist images of indulgence, nurturance, sensitivity, and interdependence. There is a shift away from the patriarchal rhetoric of "obedience," "duty," and "discipline" and toward one of mutualism and interdependence. Simultaneously, the rhetoric of "nation" is replaced by a rhetoric of "culture." Yet the fundamental notion of Japanese society as undergirded by the loving relationships of family had already been laid by prewar thinkers such as Watsuji and was newly adapted in the postwar years.[5]

Indeed, one might argue that the ideological embrace of the notion of *amae* as an everyday sentiment in the postwar period can in part be attributed to Doi's success in accommodating and rearticulating these historically received ways of thinking about family and community. In some of the more strained passages of the book, one has a sense of Doi exculpating Japan's wartime leaders, including the emperor himself. Doi argues that hierarchical relationships of loyalty and obligation can, in retrospect, themselves be understood as manifestations of *amae* or a frustrated need for *amae* (84). Doi's ability to render these relationships, and all familial relationships, in deeply humanistic terms may in part account for the palatability of the language of *amae* (indeed the need for it) in the postwar period.

At the same time as the language of *amae* allowed accommodation of past realities, it obscured the logic of new ones. Although the notion of "benevolent paternalism" was evident in prewar national discourses of family and nation, obscuring the realities of exploitation and authoritarianism in families and elsewhere, the notion of the loving caregiver in the language of *amae* further obscures this exploitative dimension, describing nurturing relationships solely in the language of mutualism and pleasurable dependency. The difficulty of articulating the experience of exploitation in a relationship in which one's superior is constructed as a benevolent protector is evident in the relationships of postwar employees to their companies. Similarly, the beautification of the caregiver makes it difficult to articulate the labor and sacrifice entailed in child care, as many of the women at the Center found out. If *amae* can be understood as an articulation of a kind of implicit social contract in postwar institutions, in which caregivers (mothers, bosses, teachers, and so forth) care for their charges, and in turn the charges forfeit their autonomy and rights to self-determination in order to be coddled, then the stories of the women at the Center are the stories of a rupture in this contract and the absence of a language with which to fill the resulting gap.

The household system was officially dismantled in the wake of Japan's defeat, as it was seen by Allied powers to have undergirded the ideology that had fostered Japan's military authoritarianism. The official household registry, which previously traced the family's lineage patrilineally as far back as it was possible to go, could now officially list only two generations. The language of *katei,* or "family-home," evoking a warm, nuclear, domesticized home, emerged in the 1920s with the growing bourgeoisie and was used to describe a number of postwar democratic institutions, such as the "family court" *(katei saibansho)* and the science of "home economics" *(kateika),* in place of *ie* (Nishikawa 1995: 30–31).[6]

Beyond official reforms, dramatic changes shaped the landscape of family life beginning in the mid-1950s. After an initial postwar baby boom, total fertility declined rapidly in the early 1950s as women undertook family planning in an endeavor to invest more resources in fewer children (Japan Statistical Yearbook 1998: 59). In the context of Japan's economic growth, large numbers of citizens moved from the country to the city, and in the wake of industrial expansion, a growing middle class occupied vast suburbs around the cities. In 1956 the Japanese Public Housing Corporation began to construct large urban apartment complexes *(danchi)* that included modern amenities (such as flush toilets and dining areas), designed for the families of the increasing numbers of white-collar "salarymen" moving to the cities. These young families became known as the "apartment-house tribe" *(danchi-zoku)* and were the first generation to purchase, en masse, such household appliances as washing machines, refrigerators, toasters, televisions, and automobiles. An emerging focus on the family and the retreat into consumerist pleasures and private and emotional relationships (and away from political engagement) were later dubbed by the media *mai-hōmu shugi* (my home-ism) (White 2002: 78). Still, it is important not to portray the transformations in the family as a dramatic reversal. The centrality of parent-child relations as the backbone of the family and the link between home and community had been clearly forged in prewar discourse and during wartime itself. Because of women's association with maternal love and affection, the family became an obvious site for promoting peace, community, and the transformation to democracy.[7]

In contrast with the rural families and petty entrepreneurs that had constituted the middle class in the early years of industrialization (in which women also contributed to the family enterprise), the new middle class was characterized by an increasingly entrenched gendered division of labor. Men were increasingly absent from the home, commuting longer distances to work and working longer hours in the push to regenerate the country (Gordon 2000: 287, Ezra Vogel 1963: 34–35). And by the early 1960s, for the first time in history, large numbers of middle-class women could afford to become full-time housewives.[8] As women increasingly took over the home and the reproduction of labor and human capital associated with it, a culture of domesticity took root, akin to what had taken place in the United States in the 1950s, evidenced by a proliferation of women's magazines with information on cooking, educating, child-rearing, decorating, and saving money.[9]

Eventually, women's work as housewives came to constitute the backbone of postwar high growth, the pillar upon which all other institutions depended. This is partly because the state, along with big business, promoted this division of labor, maximizing profits and working hours by utilizing men differently from women.[10] The state, in conjunction with Japanese business, embarked on a program of active domesticization of women: subsidizing women's stay-at-home work through a system that some have referred to as "housewife welfare" *(shufu hogo seidō)* (Sechiyama 2000). Companies subsidized the family through a comprehensive family wage that, in larger companies, has included health care, housing subsidies, a "marriage bonus" for newly married employees, subsequent bonuses for each child, and more recently, pension coverage for nonworking women (Sechiyama 2000: 134–35; Rohlen 1974). (These allowances are given by about four-fifths of Japanese companies and are thus not limited to the largest enterprises. In many cases, the allowances stop if the spouse's income exceeds a certain amount [Higuchi 1997: 105].) In 1961 the government passed a spousal deduction law stating that spouses earning less than $10,000 per year could deduct this money from their taxable income; those who earned more than this amount must pay taxes according to the income bracket of their combined income with their husbands. In 1986, under the revised Pension Fund Law, housewives automatically became eligible for retirement benefits under their husbands' plans (without extra cost), even if they never personally contributed to the fund (104). The government and Japanese enterprises saw the full-time housewife as a necessary complement to the hardworking husband.

In addition, women grew increasingly consumed with the role of mothering. In the context of urbanization and the democratizing reforms that had taken place in the occupation and postoccupation era, children were increasingly viewed as investments rather than immediate sources of labor. The role of urban women increasingly revolved around mothering in a way that had not been the case in merchant or farming families. In the context of growing opportunities for upward mobility, children's exam preparation emerged as a central rite of passage and a key tool for upward mobility, and women became actively involved in the work of managing children's education (see Ezra Vogel 1963 for an excellent portrait of what this looked like in the late 1950s, when meritocracy was still a reality for many).

In an essay exploring the notion of Japan as a "maternalist society," Tomiko Yoda (2000) shows how the notion, which drew its inspiration from a nostalgia for an (imagined) agrarian, collectivist past, derived new support in the context of the postwar privatization of the home and the emergence of the enterprise society *(kigyō shakai)*. She calls attention to the construction of middle-class domesticity as a "personal" space of psyche and emotion, existing outside the relations of economic production, and as a "cozy" matricentric space. Popular movies on the family *(hōmu dorama)* of the 1950s and 1960s increasingly centered on tales of domesticity and the daily routines of home life (rather than on the difficulties of working-class life or class conflict); women were managers of this home life, and stories described relationships between mothers and children. In turn, fathers were portrayed as peripheral, even helpless figures within the home, who were supported and coddled by family members when things went awry at work but did little to support or sustain the family emotionally (Sakamoto 1997: 242; Yoda 2000: 877; see also Ezra Vogel 1963: 212).[11] Yoda points out that these movies reflected not only the feminization of the home but also the conflation of urban middle-class values with

"Japanese culture" itself: "The generalization of matricentric domesticity, thereby, mediated the national self-image emerging in the economic high-growth period: Japan as a country of vast homogeneous middle-stratum, defined by the shared pattern of consumption and the aspiration for educational and material betterment in life" (2000: 877).[12]

Doi's language of *amae* captured this notion of Japanese society as the embodiment of middle-class values, a closely knit, warm, intimate space. A key idea of Doi's text is the notion of a familial closeness that is almost intuitive: a Japanese family so tightly woven that it need not rely on verbal communication, a "world that need not rely on words" *(kotoba no iranai sekai)*. The idea is romanticized in Doi's *The Anatomy of Dependence,* in his description of Japanese hospitality as characterized by a host or hostess caring for his or her guests, rather than requiring them to "help themselves" (Doi 1973: 13). Japanese expressions such as *ishin denshin,* or "telepathy" (literally, "separate hearts communicating as one"), also capture this idea, and it is often said that close friends or even all Japanese people share this skill.

It is easy to see how such ideas were compelling in the context of the postwar years, when the family was viewed as a microcosm of the new democratic ethos. Yet the shift away from prewar authoritarian modes of patriarchy entailed a new set of obfuscations. The notion of *amae* naturalizes and beautifies the gendered division of labor. The language of nurturance and shared understanding makes the description of inequality and exploitation increasingly difficult.

Beyond the life of the family, what stands out in postwar cultural identity discourse is the emerging association of Japanese motherhood and "maternal" values of indulgence, protection, and nurturance with Japanese culture itself. Motherhood is described as both instinctual (in terms of *bosei,* maternal instinct) and as uniquely capturing the sensitivity, compassion, and intimacy rooted in Japanese culture. I encountered these ideas in numerous contexts in my fieldwork. A psychiatrist at a large, private Tokyo hospital told me: "Japanese are enormously sensitive to the powers of motherhood *[Haha ni taishite no kanjūsei ga tsuyoi].* They place a high value on 'skinship'—a Japanese tradition. *Amae* is something that just naturally emerges in daily conversation. That is the nature of the culture *[Amaeru (to iu koto wa) nichijō kaiwa ni shizen ni deru. So iu karuchā desu kara]*."

Shifting notions of motherhood were central to postwar theories of the Japanese cultural ethos. In the context of increased opportunity for upward mobility and the importance of children as valued human capital, home life increasingly centered on relationships between mothers and children, with woman's role as mother privileged over her role as wife. The importance of children as a resource in the family's upward trajectory meant that women were required to invest considerable resources in facilitating children's exam preparation and homework. Even with respect to husbands, women's work to provide a comfortable, efficient home was prioritized over her role as emotional companion and sexual partner.

In this context, a new fascination with child-rearing as a science emerged, producing discourses on child development that emphasized gentle socialization and the importance of motherly nurturance and love, including the importance of breast-feeding.[13] Child-rearing experts such as Matsuda Michio, often described as "Japan's Doctor Spock," offered women advice on gentler and subtler forms of discipline and socialization, in contrast to an earlier paternalistic reliance on corporal punishment. Like Dr. Spock, Matsuda published updated versions of his texts through the years, but his texts from the 1960s offer telling insights into this historical moment, in which constructions of motherly love started to focus on tender emotional nurturance and mothering began to be considered a full-time job. Although the books were addressed to new urban mothers, they reflect the historical belief that child-rearing was something one learned from experience or through consulting members of the extended family, rather than something one studied in books. The lessons of the book are never stated in the voice of the physician (as in Dr. Spock) but instead emerge through stories and characters, all in the voice of the child. In a typical scenario from *I Am Two Years Old (Watashi wa Nisai)*, a farm woman comes to sell her goods at an urban apartment complex *(danchi)*, and the young mother who answers the door (presented in sketches throughout the book as the modern housewife of the 1950s, with knee-length skirt, blouse, bun, and apron, while the farm woman wears traditional Japanese *mompei* and sandals) takes the opportunity to ask the farm woman for advice with a child-rearing dilemma (Matsuda 1961: 9). The question concerns whether one should punish one's children to make them obey. In response, the old woman (in a heavy rural dialect) tells the story of her own son. After they hit him at home as punishment, she and her husband were called into the principal's office because he was hitting other children. Hitting him only seemed to provoke him to hit others, she advised (9).

The advice points to a softening of disciplinary practices in child-rearing manuals (itself a new genre) in the immediate postwar ethos of democracy. In another chapter, the two-year-old wakes up before his parents and goes looking in his father's pockets. Eventually he finds a cigarette case and, wondering how his father opens it, pounds it open with a can-opener and then unwraps all the cigarettes. By the time his father wakes up, his mother has already removed him from the scene. When the father picks up the boy and spanks him, the boy cries and, according to Matsuda, wonders to himself, "Why did Daddy spank me? I didn't do anything. All I did was open the case. Bad Daddy. I hate Daddy." Later that day, the child finds a box of matches, lights one, and begins crying. When the mother swoops down and rescues the child, he tells her he "hates matches." When the father returns home from work later that evening, he asks whether the child behaved better after his chastisement. "No, no," the mother replies. "He didn't think anything about breaking the [cigarette] case. All he did was resent you. But he does learn when he comes close to hurting himself" (Matsuda 1961: 12). The story suggests that it is more effective for children to learn their lessons naturally, as they unfold in daily experience ["shizen genshō no yō ni"], rather than through forced punishment.

In the context of the growing role of the mother and the increasing identification of women with the role of primary caregiver, the ideal of motherhood and the "motherly instinct" (bosei) became increasingly fetishized. Writers such as Erik Erikson, Ashley Montague, and Dr. Spock appeared in translation. Beginning in the 1950s, mothers were increasingly described in terms of their intense intimacy with and "devotion" to their children; and this devotion was defined through metaphors of nurturing and intimacy, rather than in disciplinary terms. This discourse continues today in contemporary child-rearing books and seminars sponsored by local governments and community organizations for mothers. In child-rearing seminars and workshops I attended (some sponsored by prefectural governments), the importance of bonding and "skinship" (sukinshippu, a term initially coined by Ashley Montague) was repeatedly emphasized; and it was this close, loving bond with "mother" that was thought to form the foundation for social participation and "humanity" itself (ningenrashisa). (I describe this material further in chapter 5.) In one child-rearing seminar I attended at a local church, a professor of education described the importance of breast-feeding this way:

> The cultivation of *sukinshippu* and a mother-child rhythm is most important. A baby listens to the love, the heart in a mother's breast when drinking. Breast-feeding is not just about food, it nourishes [cultivates] the heart. It is the reciprocal expression of love. A child smells his mother while he drinks her delicious milk. They look into each other's eyes. "I love you Mommy," he's thinking. This is how relationships of "basic trust" are formed. A [psychological] wound or sense of deprivation at this stage will remain forever. Fundamental relations of trust are built little by little every day. This bond must be *tight [shikkari musubu]!* (Saitō, October 15, 1992)

It is important to note that the notion of motherhood as the most important of women's roles and of motherly nature as inherently nurturing is a relatively recent ideological construction. The notion of *ryōsai kenbo,* or "good wife and wise mother," which had been promoted by Meiji statesmen and intellectuals in the late nineteenth century, was an important move toward entrenching gendered divisions of labor and establishing child-rearing as an essential task of womanhood. Yet *ryōsai kenbo* ideology stopped far short of postwar conceptions of the nurturing mother, full of loving kindness *(yasashii okāsan).*[14] In Meiji writings, the home had been described almost in political terms, as "an essential building block of the national structure," a "public place . . . where private feelings would be forgotten" (Ekken [Meiji Greater Learning for Women], cited in Nolte and Hastings 1991: 156). As Kanō has noted, the Meiji *ryōsai kenbo* ideal described a role ideal imposed from without. In contrast, postwar ideals, in the context of the postwar rise of the middle class and the privatized mother, described nurturance and child-rearing as inhering in women's nature (Kanō 1995: 59).

The view of the mother-child relationship (characterized by mutualism and shared understanding) as a template for all Japanese social relationships has powerful implications for power relationships in Japanese society. It also has consequences for women's issues. As Tomiko Yoda has pointed out, a central conceit of the notion of maternalism was that while it upheld the maternal role as central to human relations in Japan, it also emphasized the "passive role of the child": "According to the theory of maternal society, in other words, Japan is a society occupied not so much by mothers but by children who depend on and yearn for maternal love and nurturance" (2000: 868). Yet an entire culture of people who presume upon the unconditional indulgence of society could hardly be viable. The subjectivity of the mother (the provider of nurturance and indulgence) is absent from Doi's analysis, while the psychology of the recipient becomes a proxy for all Japanese people.

The metaphor of mother-child relationships obscures the dynamics of power entailed both in family relationships and more broadly in Japanese society. The image of love between mother and child obscures the possibility of an abuse of power on either side. The care of a mother (or protector) is imagined as benevolent and nurturing, and thus the mother's intentions cannot be questioned or challenged. Conversely, a child's innocent need for its mother makes it difficult to articulate when the child has crossed the line from innocence to selfishness and exploitation. To construct all relationships as *amae* relationships is to undermine the possibility of approaching social conflict and conflicting interests through the language of rights and entitlement—or at least to make these claims difficult to articulate.

THE REORGANIZATION
OF AUTHORITY IN DAILY LIFE

Beyond the reconfiguration of family life, the immediate postwar decade witnessed dramatic shifts in the organization of social order and authority. The war did enormous damage to prewar notions of male authority. Government officials and military leaders who had dominated the wartime regime of military authoritarianism were eclipsed, at least temporarily, following Japan's defeat, and the pervasive influence of the army, which had been "the central socializing agent" for male citizens during the wartime and prewar periods, grew more removed from public life (Tsurumi 1970: 89). The Ministry of Education dismissed all military officers teaching in schools and attempted to eliminate the influence of the military on pedagogy.[15] Early education, including preschool and kindergarten, became more popular, and hence the number of female teachers increased (Beauchamp and Vardaman 1994); public announcements and television news increasingly used women's voices.

Broadly speaking, studies of social order and social control in postwar Japanese classrooms and elsewhere point to the attenuation of centralized authority and the presence of more informal forms of suasion produced through social participation, peer relations, negotiation with moderate factions, and separation of authority from power to preserve legitimacy (Rohlen 1989; Upham 1987; Haley 1991; and Hamilton and Sanders 1992). Studies of law enforcement in postwar Japan reveal an emphasis on rehabilitation in addition to punitive measures, and an importance accorded to contrition, suggesting the criminal's readiness to rejoin society. Juvenile crime, for instance, has been managed by nonuniformed female employees *(fujin hōdōin)* and youth assistants *(shōnen kyōjoin)* who provide counseling and "guidance" to youth on matters ranging from sexuality to future plans (Ames 1981: 82). Ethnographies of Japanese classrooms in the 1980s reveal, at least in the early years of education, comparatively large degrees of "chaos" and decentralized forms of imposing order through learned routines, often set to music, and small-group work that encourages children to monitor and discipline one another. When two students begin to squabble, a third student may be appointed as mediator. Authoritarian intervention by the teacher is rare (see Rohlen 1989; Peak 1991; and Lewis 1989).

Central to the ideology of a tightly woven middle-class society "protected" by a motherlike presence was the emergence of the company as a large-scale employer. The firm granted workers a considerable degree of stability and security and offered more meritocratic systems of promotion and education than had small enterprises and family-owned shops. In the growing middle class, the corporation was seen as being decisively more democratic than the traditional shop floor of a small craftsman or family business, dispensing with what were disparagingly regarded as "feudalistic" forms of obedience and loyalty to a single master rooted in heredity, and instead producing loyalty to the firm through the opportunity to cultivate one's own competence (Ezra Vogel 1963: 161).[16]

These shifts toward greater job stability and security and toward more democratic social forms of promotion created an environment in which institutions such as companies could claim to fulfill a familylike function with respect to employees, despite tremendous extraction of labor (Andrew Gordon 1993). Large organizations described themselves as "total providers," offering a family wage and a range of welfare benefits, including health care, pensions, company-owned facilities for family vacations, and monies for recreation. It was in this context that the voluminous literature on "Japanese-style management" *(Nihon shugi keiei)* emerged in the 1970s, proclaiming the "humanity" of Japanese managers and the Japanese company as a tightly woven community (see Andrew Gordon 1998). Businessmen such as Matsushita Konosuke (founder of Matsushita Electronics) published volumes of essays describing their managerial philosophy: concern with the "human quality" of business relations, care for employees, and a view of the company as a lynchpin of society. A collection of Matsushita's writings entitled *Not for Bread Alone* (reflecting an imperative to work for spiritual as well as material sustenance) includes such essays as "Everyone Is an Asset," "Bottom-up Communication," "Employees Need Dreams," and "Participatory Management." In one essay, "A Priceless Opportunity," Matsushita proudly tells the story of a junior executive who made an inexcusable error. Matsushita called the young man into his office and asked how he would feel if Matsushita presented him with a letter detailing his misconduct. "If you don't think you deserve it," he said, "then there is no point in giving it to you. But if you acknowledge your wrongdoing and are sorry for it, then it is worth the trouble, as it might help you improve your performance in the future." Just as Matsushita was about to hand over the letter to the young man, his immediate supervisor walked into the room. Matsushita pounced on the opportunity to share the letter with the young man's boss. He proudly recounts that, upon reading the letter, he told them how lucky both were to have someone to admonish them. "If I made such a mistake," he says, "there would be no one who would say anything right to me . . . [and] I would go on making the same error. It is good that you have me and others to point out your mistakes and tell you to shape up. After you are promoted to top positions, no one is going to protest, no matter what you do. That is why you should consider this a priceless opportunity" (1984: 33). This anecdote demonstrates the ethos that characterized "Japanese management": genuine concern for the employee and the company combined with the paternalistic sense that a boss knows what is good for his underling, and that the underling must naturally abide by this, since it is "what is best for him."

Of course a system that draws workers in by offering "total care" has the potential to simultaneously subject them to demanding regimes of production in the interest of the larger good. Such exploitative practices have included prolonged and grueling competition for promotions, heavy demands for overtime work, lack of control over job definition and labor conditions, and frequent transfers (Andrew Gordon 1993; Kumazawa 1996).[17] Although the scholarship on labor relations in Japan often seems to suggest that such exploitative practices give the lie to notions of corporate beneficence and paternalism, in fact it is possible to see the two sides of the story as compatible. The promotional systems that were put in place were in part the result of demands by workers' unions for employment stability in the immediate postwar years. And yet these same practices came with heavy trade-offs, diminishing worker autonomy and avenues of protest for workers' unions.[18] Large-scale companies provide for workers by guaranteeing job stability, access to promotion, a family wage, benefits, on-the-job training and mentorship, and after-hours collegiality, in return for employees' loyalty. At the same time, notions of loyalty and commitment make workers vulnerable to exploitative demands for unpaid overtime labor, frequent job changes, and transfers that take them away from their families. The paternalistic protection offered by companies facilitates the exploitation of employees, and yet it is important to note that the protection offered is real. The fact that employees did benefit at least in certain respects from the labor policies hammered out after the war, and that these regimes were in fact constructed partly in response to their own demands, makes us appreciate the very compelling nature of these postwar regimes, and the difficulty in protesting them.

The deeply rooted ideologies of the postwar family, company, and classroom are, as ideologies, compelling. Simultaneously, we know that these ideals have concealed (in fact sustained) specific forms of exploitation and injustice, making these appear natural, inevitable, or beyond contest. How to protest the boss who positions himself as the gentle mentor and guide and yet makes untenable demands on his underlings? Protest itself may be construed as a selfish violation of shared understanding. The ideology of commitment to the firm in return for "total care" deprives workers of the recourse to a language of rights and contractuality. "Benevolent paternalism" makes exploitation of the system more difficult to name (what is the line between paternalism and exploitation?)—and to resist.

Yoda writes that the generalization of "matricentric domesticity" to the nation more broadly helped to displace "a growing sense of loss—the irreversible costs of capitalist modernization," and helped to "absorb and displace" the growing criticism of capitalist society (2000: 880). Indeed, the language of dependency and nurturance in some sense preempted a language of exploitation, making exploitation impossible to articulate in the context of presumed good will. These tensions are at times thinly masked, as revealed in Dorinne Kondo's ethnography of a family-owned Japanese confectionary company that did not have the resources to treat employees as well as larger companies do. Kondo reveals the importance of the "company as family" myth to the small company and the many ways the ideology was reinforced in employee and managerial discourse. Yet the workers wryly note the many discrepancies between ideology and reality—including, for example, the indiscreet use of the loudspeaker and video camera on the shop floor (Kondo 1990: 204–12).

For the women at the Center, struggling to come to terms with a family member's substance abuse, these kinds of questions were central. Women have been the most literal providers of the care that the postwar system demands and glorifies. Similarly, as middle-class women whose husbands were involved in Japanese industry in the heyday of Japan's rapid economic growth, they largely shared the ideologies of families acting in the national good and the possibility of the company as quasi-family. Yet in caring for their families in the context of this crisis, women also began to ask rather pointed questions about the kind of social contract defined by the maternal society. It must be remembered that for many of these women, *amae* was their chief mechanism of social control over their families in a context in which authoritarian control was neither sanctioned nor possible. Yet was such a form of control really healthy? In a sense, in return for their care of husbands and children, women expected compliant behavior from their families (hardworking husbands and filial children). Yet these contracts were being broken, and meanwhile women were paying a high price for such services. Similarly, wasn't it time that husbands and children learned to assert themselves and to care for themselves in certain respects, rather than waiting to be cared for?

Above all, women questioned the beauty and virtue of waiting to be cared for that Doi so celebrates in his book. This was too much the story of their own lives, and where had it gotten them? They also questioned the virtue of giving through self-sacrifice and the entitlement that such sacrifice ideally should bring. Many of the women in the group spoke of being more assertive in public life, in addition to taking steps to change relationships within the family. In taking up the language of codependency, women became more attuned to the implicit social contract lying beneath these deeply held ideas: the virtue of waiting to be cared for and the entitlement born of self-sacrifice. In challenging key prescriptions for the wife and mother, women were challenging not merely a "role" but a national ideology that proclaimed the virtue of Japanese culture in addition to the virtue of women. What is remarkable are the many ways in which the women at the Center continued to see compelling aspects in the protective society, despite the hardships and irreconcilable impasses they faced in renegotiating family life. They chiefly sought to impose limits on the kinds of care they would provide, but in many respects, they did not challenge the fundamental premises of the mutualistic society that postwar national ideologies proclaim. Given the deep crisis these women faced and their centrality to the culture of caregiving, this, above all, is testimony to the compelling and ideologically persuasive nature of this postwar discourse.

Chapter 3 | GOOD WIVES
Negotiating Marital Relationships

Al-Anon promotes "firm sympathy" in dealing with a drinker: a delicate balance between coping and setting limits and between support for one's husband and what is called "loving detachment" (Al-Anon 1977). Ideally, a wife will find a way to carry on her life in the face of her husband's alcoholism, while at the same time continuing to welcome his recovery.[1] Although Al-Anon praises the virtue of endurance to a point, a woman who can no longer stand the trial of a husband's alcoholism is encouraged to draw the line by making explicit what she will tolerate. Because it is ineffectual to persistently threaten to take action (for example to leave) and not carry through, each woman must decide for herself where this line will be drawn and then stand by her commitment. Yet the nature of this delicate balance and the question of where lines are drawn is of course heavily inflected by culture.

According to Al-Anon teachings, drawing the line begins with a confrontation in which a woman states the terms she requests and the consequences if the terms are not fulfilled. This "intervention" usually begins with the statement "I love you" and then follows with "but I can't continue to stay in the relationship on these terms. If things don't change in the following ways (specify the terms) I plan to leave."

The Japanese women at the Center were taught these ideas in a series of educational seminars that all women were required to attend before they could join the group meeting. The language of the intervention was translated word for word into Japanese *(Anata o ai shite iru . . .)* to tell women how to approach their husbands. To my knowledge, though, few if any women ever delivered such an ultimatum to their husbands. In fact, the fundamental premise of such an intervention did not fit with the way the women imagined their marriages. Most women continued on in their marriages, coping with their husbands' drinking, seeking neither total reconciliation with their husbands nor divorce.

In the first place, most of the women did not have the economic resources to get divorced, and prospects for finding work and supporting a family outside of marriage were scarce. Nor was divorce regarded as a successful outcome at the Center. Only one of the women who attended meetings during my year at the Center left her husband to live separately in her own apartment, and she was able to do so because her husband continued to support her. But economic concerns were only one aspect of their decision, and few mentioned it directly. In fact, most women did not see their relationships with their husbands as the central aspect of family life— as a relationship which, if soured, would be sufficient reason to leave the marriage. Instead, women viewed their marriages as one part of the broader project of managing a family. Although most were financially dependent on their husbands, they led their lives relatively independently, with separate friends, separate hobbies, and separate vacations. A husband's alcoholism caused a breakdown in family ties when he became abusive or excessively disruptive (bringing home drunken friends in the early hours of the morning or having frequent accidents due to drinking) or when he lost his capacity to support the family economically. But an attenuated relationship between husband and wife was not in itself a deal-breaker for most women, or even their central concern. In fact, in some cases it allowed women leeway in coping with their husband's drinking and carving out some space for themselves.

WHAT IS LOVE?

The notion of the marital relationship as foundational to the family, and the notion of romance and sexual intimacy as essential to marital relationships, are attitudes we take for granted. In fact, they are relatively recent historical constructions that crystallized in Western Europe in the context of industrialization in the late nineteenth century. The "conjugal family," defined as a married couple and their children, has always described marriage as the centerpiece of the family. In the conjugal family model, marriage means the establishment of a new family; when children are born, the family is extended, but when those children marry they start their own families, and their children are not part of the conjugal family but of the extended family. In Europe and the United States, the notion of love that emerged among the Victorian bourgeoisie emphasized sexual passion and the perfect match of two individuals who were destined for one another, a sharing of souls.[2] Courtship increasingly came to emphasize a woman's beauty and sexuality, since she was seen as having little to offer as a "productive" (i.e., wage-earning) laborer (D'Emilio and Freedman 1997; Watt 1983).

In contrast, the Japanese "stem-family" system has historically emphasized vertical ties between the generations; marriage did not establish a new family, but rather served to perpetuate the ongoing family line, traced through the eldest son. In practice, the Japanese stem family is imagined above all as an economic enterprise, prioritizing continuity, economic cooperation, and self-sufficiency, so that the perpetuation of the family line and vertical ties (between parents and children) were prioritized over horizontal bonds between husband and wife (Befu 1966; Nakane 1967).[3] Little emphasis was placed on the cultivation of romantic intimacy between spouses, and by and large, family members and especially women were expected to sacrifice "selfish" desires for the good of the whole. Obedience or filial piety of children toward their parents and devotion of a mother to her children were the central emotional components of family life (Yoshizumi 1995: 187). Romance between husband and wife was deemphasized in favor of a partnership based on a division of labor.[4]

The American-imposed constitution, written during the occupation, legally encoded equality between the sexes; later, the Civil Code, revised in 1947, attempted to redefine the nature of family, describing marriage as a private relationship based on the mutual decision of the two parties and placing the spousal relationship at the center of family life (Yoshizumi 1995: 189). In the postwar urban context, the word *kekkon* (marriage) became widely used, replacing the prewar concept of *yomeiri* (literally, "inserting the bride [into the household]"); the mass media also celebrated notions of love and happiness as associated with marriage, and public opinion polls showed that increasing numbers believed that young people should chose their own marriage partners rather than having their marriages arranged by their families (Hendry 1981: 29). Yet the reality of Japanese marital ideology has certainly changed more slowly than the rhetoric. Takie Lebra's ethnography of women and gender in a small city outside of Tokyo in the mid-1970s describes how women giggle in response to questions concerning love between a husband and wife and distance themselves from the very idea. Love was thought to grow out of marriage rather than to be the impetus for it. Some of her informants insisted that the traditional practice of arranging marriages was more successful in producing love than the "love marriages" that were slowly becoming fashionable (1984: 122–23).

The notion of love—defined as shared interests, friendship, communication, and enduring romantic passion—did not permeate middle-class life in Japan in the same way that it did in Europe or the United States. Nor did the notion of the marital relationship as the pillar of family life. The women at the Center, largely in their forties, fifties, and sixties, continued to view marriage in a largely old-fashioned way. Although many called their marriages "love marriages" (ren'ai kekkon), meaning that they had not been formally arranged (they had met their husbands themselves while working or through social organizations), few knew their husbands very well before marrying them and most felt that "endurance" was the single most important quality for a successful marriage. At the first meeting I attended, Koike-san said: "A woman I work with told me that when she got married thirty-nine years ago, she was told by her father, 'Any time things get bad you know you can come home.' I thought that this was a big-hearted father. My father wasn't like that—to stay and endure was something taken for granted [gaman suru no ga atari mae]." At least for this generation of women and, to a surprising degree, for younger generations as well, marriage is based on the notion of separate yet compatible spheres of labor, with women managing matters within the home and men supporting the family through the family wage.

In fact, one could argue that the gendered division of labor has become increasingly polarized in the postwar period, with middle-class women cultivating their chief intimacies with their children and social relations with other mothers, and men cultivating key relationships in the work context, returning home late after drinking with colleagues, and spending weekends socializing with friends (Allison 1994; Vogel 1978, 1988; Brinton 1993). Contemporary surveys of Japanese couples have found that men perform an average of five to seven minutes of housework a day and that many men do not even perform basic tasks to take care of themselves (Brinton 1993: 92–95). In Suzanne Vogel's early ethnography, one woman complained that her husband could not open the refrigerator and would wait at the table, helplessly, until she returned home to make his snack (Vogel 1978: 14). The view of the husband/father whose only role is that of wage-earner is reflected in a cartoon published in the *Mainichi Shinbun* in the early 1990s. It shows a family seeing their father off to work in the morning as he glumly puts on his shoes in the entryway. "Papa— fight for that spring promotion!" they cheer. Lining the walls are three banners, which read "A Hawaii vacation!—Mama," "A personal computer, please!—Tsutomu," and "A 50% allowance raise!—Yumi." The model of the husband as the resident wage-earner with little other role in the family has created a dilemma for families, particularly after the husband retires and is at home, now only a burden to other family members. Women I knew often half-jokingly repeated the postwar saying *Teishu wa genki de rusu ga ii* (A good husband is healthy and not home).[5]

Nor do men see the home as a haven from working life. In Anne Allison's ethnography of a Tokyo after-hours club, she explores the family relationships that lie behind men's after-hours drinking. She finds that both husbands and wives have come to accept the routine of men returning late from work, men's absence from the home, and even men seeking sexual and erotic pleasure outside the home (1994: 136). In turn, men confided to Allison that they did not feel particularly relaxed or welcome at home; home was not "their castle," a comfortable place where they were pampered and respected. Rather, when one salaryman was asked what he would like to change about his life, he said that he wished for more time away from home *and* work (103).

The upshot of this pattern has been that marriage does not revolve primarily around sexual compatibility or spousal romance. Sex for pleasure or fun is constructed as something to be pursued outside the home (Allison 1994). Nor is a woman's sexual attractiveness to her husband seen as the key to marital success. Indeed, women's role in the family has been notoriously desexualized. The image of the "young wife" *(wakai okusan),* dressed modestly and adorned with an apron, is seen as a compelling, even attractive one in Japanese popular views; rather than a woman's ability to fulfill her husband's sexual needs, it is a woman's capacity to meet the needs of her family, as well as her status as a mother, that makes her beautiful and attractive in the eyes of others. Indeed, a Japanese saying describes the first year after a child is born as the height of a woman's beauty—a bewildering idea to anyone who has ever had a child.

DIVORCE WITHIN THE HOME

In an account of a 1990 symposium on alcoholism and the family sponsored by the Psychiatric Research Institute of Tokyo, one audience member makes the following comment:

> You learn to cope with your husband coming home late and drunk. First with anger, and then with resignation. It's the way the *society* is. . . . We're not talking about a company; it is *life* here in Japan.
>
> So you develop a routine as a wife with kids, and learn to get your kids' schooling done and bath and bed. You may hope he comes home after 10:00 P.M. so you can get two hours to yourself. And if he does come home earlier, you don't want him! . . .
>
> So, a drunk husband after a long commute and a fourteen-hour day is easy to handle! No sexual demands. You get him in the bath, you put him to bed, he passes out; it's great! He brings his paycheck home, it's fine! (Reported in Saitō, Steinglass, and Schuckit 1992: 225)

The story illustrates how men's heavy drinking can be accommodated in "normal" family life, in which women and men occupy separate spheres within the home. It also suggests that such a separation of spheres may even allow women leeway to cope with their husbands' drinking, making their absence from the home tolerable, even desirable.

For these reasons, certain Al-Anon interventions were more easily incorporated into Japanese cultural practice than they perhaps are in the United States. Al-Anon tenets of recovery involve constructing boundaries and learning how to disengage, maintain distance *(kyōri o oku)*, and recognize that "I am I, and my husband is my husband." In some respects, for Japanese women, these concepts proved to be manageable in the context of everyday life and did not necessarily provoke great self-reflection.

The distance women felt from their husbands was clear. They felt little shame in poking fun at their husbands in meetings, and in fact it was not uncommon for women to baldly express dislike or even violent impulses regarding their husbands. Women often said very matter-of-factly that they "didn't have anything in common" with their husbands and spoke of how hard it was to cultivate "couples talk" *(fūfu kaiwa)*. In one meeting, Koike-san said coolly: "On Thursday evening I was surprised to learn that my husband had called an ambulance and gone to the hospital and I hadn't even noticed. I heard a sound in the entryway and it was him returning home. He said his hiccups wouldn't stop and it was painful so he'd phoned the hospital. I was sound asleep and didn't hear a thing. Maybe I was just too tired, or maybe I've just become callous. Anyway, I went right back to sleep." At a later meeting, she matter-of-factly commented: "The other day when my husband was taken off to the hospital I felt entirely cool and composed. I'm not sure if that was on account of my studies here at the Center or else that I just dislike my husband."

Women took holidays with their friends, not their husbands. Women also seemed to face little opposition from their husbands in coming to meetings at the Center. Most women did not seem to keep it a secret from their husbands; men simply had very little idea what went on and were largely indifferent to how their wives spent their days. A few of the women in the group even established separate living spaces within the home, which they described as their "separate residences" *(bekkyo)*. The term "divorce within the home" *(kateinai rikon)* is used to describe situations in which estranged couples continue to live together and function as a family, despite little contact between the spouses. Although it is difficult to know how many couples use such an arrangement, it is easy to see how such a solution is in many ways compatible with both dominant constructions of marriage and the demands of Japanese society.

The original Al-Anon texts pay a great deal of attention to the importance of rebuilding the lost intimacy between husband and wife, suggesting that the growing distance between husband and wife and the isolation of the husband are key problems that can perpetuate the disease itself (Al-Anon 1977). Marital intimacy and communication are seen as foundational to the family, and an intimacy that cannot be rebuilt is viewed as a situation that must be resolved one way or another. In one testimonial, "I Learned to Love," published in *Al-Anon Faces Alcoholism,* a woman tells the story of how she was able to find some distance from the situation and learned to love her husband again.

> After five years of marriage, I now love my husband in spite of the fact that he is still drinking and our life is still very difficult at times. I began to see many beautiful and admirable things about him. I care for him as a person. I feel warmth and compassion for him that I have never known.
>
> In my earlier meetings at Al-Anon, my friends there must have thought me very good at the "detachment" that is recommended in dealing with an alcoholic problem. I was, indeed, detached, not from his alcoholism but from *him*. I just didn't care what happened to him. Now I do care, very much, although I am trying to maintain detachment from the illness itself. (95)

The treatment discourses embraced by the Center described the hazards of overly intimate parent-child relationships from which the second parent (the husband) is increasingly marginalized. One aspect of the Japanese family system that repeatedly came up for criticism in Dr. Saitō's books and Center seminars was the tendency for husbands and wives to refer to one another as "Mom" and "Dad," even when the children were not present or after they had grown up and left the house, a holdover from a household system in which marital relationships were deprioritized in favor of parent-child bonds. Dr. Saitō advised women to abandon this practice as a step toward privileging the bonds between husband and wife.

The women dabbled with these ideas, often playing at the idea of cultivating romance with their husbands. But they did not seem to take these ideas terribly seriously. In one meeting, Fukuda-san recounted, to much applause, that she had experimented with a new way of addressing her husband.

> Last week when we all went out for tea after the meeting, we were talking about the idea of couples calling each other by their first names, and I decided to put it into practice. My husband's name is Yoshichiku, but since we've had kids we've been calling each other "Mother" and "Father." I just couldn't bring myself to say Yoshichiku, but during dinner I took the plunge and said, "Yo-chan, how do you like dinner?"[6] [Laughter.] I'm a bit embarrassed, but since this actually happened I'll continue. . . . He answered

(because my name is Sachiko), "Sa-chan, it's delicious." [Laughter.] I thought he'd get angry, but he took it with good heart. It was only possible because it's just the two of us at home these days. "Sa-chan, you really outdid yourself tonight!" he said. From now on, I want us to call each other by these names. [Applause.]

In many ways, the Japanese ideal of marriage allowed women to dismiss this pressure to reunite or fall in love again with their husbands. Many of the women seemed to regard the ideal of love and romance as superficial and even insincere. They viewed the idea of spouses saying "I love you" as a fatuous form of flattery. Once, when Hata-san recounted that she and her husband had been learning to communicate, they were unconvinced:

Koike *desu*. Twenty years ago my husband told me that he loved me. I wasn't the least bit pleased [*Jitsu wa zen zen ureshikunakatta*]. It was so obviously just flattery [*kuchi saki*] that I actually got mad. I just didn't want to hear it.

Ehara *desu*. I'm subjected to such flattery all the time. I come down in the morning, and I have no makeup on. I'm wearing crummy old clothes— nothing special at all, and he'll say, "Gee you look so nice today" [*Kyō wa kirei desu ne*]. Then the next minute he'll say something like, "Who needs you anyway, why don't you just return to your parents' home where you came from!" [*Omei nanka wa iranei kara jikka ni kaere!*] And then he'll actually ask me to do him a favor! [*Are kore shite kure to iu!*] Really I think he's an imbecile [*baka*] sometimes. Just this morning he said I looked nice in what I was wearing, and then the very next thing he said was, "Are you going out in public looking like that?" I felt very manipulated [*Zuibun furimawasarete iru to omotta*]. . . .

Koike *desu*. I wish I could be more like Hata-san and try to cultivate a kind of relationship with my husband and make conversation. But it's just too much of a nuisance.

In the end, the notion of marriage as separate but compatible spheres offered women a window for establishing distance from their husbands without creating great upheaval. This model of marriage allowed women to struggle on in their marriages, sometimes creating a space for instituting small but important changes in marital dynamics, as we will see. However, it may also have perpetuated the status quo of women remaining in their marriages, without overturning dominant gender definitions.

WOMEN'S INVISIBLE LABOR

Although the women did not emphasize romance in their marriages, it was not the case that marital intimacy simply did not exist. Rather than revolving around sexual attraction or romantic passion, marital intimacy has historically been described as a seamless partnership in which husband and wife independently go about their labor, while sharing a quiet understanding and empathy. As Lebra (1976: 40) and others have noted, the ability to meet the needs of another without being asked constituted a source of pride for women of an older generation.[7] An acquaintance in her mid-thirties told me the following story:

> My father had only his job in his life. My mother's job was to look after my father. He couldn't turn on the gas in the house; he couldn't even use his own bank card. She handed him his clothes and those items he needed before he left the home each morning. He was so absentminded and engrossed in his work that she had to literally put things into his pockets, because if they were in his hands, he'd leave them. If he looked like he wanted to smoke, she would hand him his tobacco and lighter. She used to brag, "I know every single thing about your father" *(Otōsan no koto wa nan demo wakaru).* It was a source of pride for her.

Women were expected to provide total care for their husbands, meeting their every need without a moment's delay—much the way a mother is expected to attend to a child. Sumiko Iwao has said that the traditional ideal of a husband and wife's relationship was to be like "air" to each other. This meant that the couple could understand one another without verbal expression and that their mutual affection and understanding need not be explicitly expressed. "When we become conscious of the air we breathe, it is a sign of physical crisis; when the marital relationship had to be consciously dealt with, it was thought, the bond was in danger" (Iwao 1991: 6). Ideally, family members are thought to simply understand one another without explicit communication; the notion of *ishin denshin,* or separate hearts communicating as one, is often held up as testimony to Japanese homogeneity and cultural uniqueness in popular *Nihonjinron* discourses (texts on Japaneseness).

In *The Anatomy of Dependence,* Doi writes that family members simply understand one another, that to explicitly thank someone with whom one is intimate would be "too coldly formal": "It is precisely because the two are part of one whole that it is impossible that one of them should bow his head in thanks to the other. Any Japanese, I suspect, could understand this reasoning. . . . The more intimate the relationship the fewer the expressions of gratitude; between husband and wife or parent and child words of thanks are normally almost unknown" (1973: 91).

In Takeshi Ebisaka's wry analysis of why young Japanese women are postponing marriage, he comments that Japanese men's perceptions of a happy marriage "rest on a deplorably low plane of consciousness": "The majority see a wife as someone who takes care of their personal needs and does the housework; the comfort and order of the home depend on how well the wife performs these duties" (1988: 46). He quotes one happy husband who boasts, "When I see my wife doing the housework for me even though she'd rather not, I can't help feeling love for her" (46). These are the notions of marital love and intimacy that women had to combat in redefining their roles with respect to their husbands.

The idea of "air" obscures the labor entailed and renders impossible or even unnecessary any communication between husband and wife regarding marital problems. It became increasingly clear for women in the course of their participation in the group meetings that there is an extremely fine line between "unspoken sensitivity" and being taken for granted. What fills the interstices of family needs and demands is not "air" but rather women's continual efforts to manage resources efficiently and to smoothly meet all demands. This becomes particularly clear when one looks at the dynamics of a typical Japanese household of this generation, in which men consider all aspects of household maintenance a woman's job.

A "good" human relationship is often defined as "smooth" *(sumūzu)* and free of "emotional tangles" (*ningen teki shigarami,* literally a weir that obstructs objects in a water stream, preventing them from moving freely). A "mature" woman is expected to smooth over and mollify the situation, disregarding her own desires. In one example, I was visiting a usually harmonious couple's home when they began quarrelling heatedly. I felt that the husband was behaving rudely and irrationally, and there was clearly no hope of reaching any kind of resolution. Finally, he stormed out of the room and went to bed, while the wife and I sat at the table wondering what had angered him. Later, the wife confided to me that the next morning was awkward and her husband left without eating breakfast—perhaps because he was ashamed. So rather than saying anything to make the situation more awkward, she tucked a note in his briefcase saying simply, "Sorry for making you upset." I was surprised to learn that she had apologized, since the matter didn't seem like her fault, but she said, "Well, I generally make it a practice to apologize after an argument. It makes things go more smoothly" *(sono hō wa umaku iku)*. When I told the story to a Japanese friend in her mid-thirties, she said, "What a good wife—she knows how to manage her husband so that things go smoothly later."

Women often talked about the work they did for their husbands as "service" *(sābisu)*—the same language is used for service that is provided in commercial venues and in the home. The concept of service entails a great deal of attention to detail. Attentiveness is seen as a virtue and obliviousness as rude or selfish, particularly in women. Women hosting guests often monitor exactly what each guest eats, making sure the dishes they prefer are within reach, refilling glasses of alcohol after each sip, and timing the presentation of each course, all the while declining to feed themselves. Since rice is served after the alcohol has been largely consumed, they judge when everyone has had the right amount to drink before serving this last course. Although the custom of women sitting in the kitchen while guests enjoy themselves at the table has become less common, I was often surprised by the extent to which women took care of guests and attended to them, even in fairly informal contexts. When guests arrive at a house, they leave their shoes at the door; when they leave, the shoes have magically been turned around to face the opposite way. When I stayed with my Japanese family, my things were often moved around ever so slightly, and used towels hanging in my room were replaced with clean ones. My toothbrush, left on the ledge above the sink, was placed in a small glass cup. Almost anything I left lying out was put into some kind of case or container. If I went in the kitchen to wash my hands, a towel magically appeared to dry them.[8]

I have many examples of this tendency from field notes on Japanese "total" service as a distinctive element of everyday life. Japanese workers in the service sector are trained not only to respond to customers' needs but also to anticipate them. Many Japanese people associate this level of service with being cared for and looked after—despite the often intrusive nature of these ministrations. I remember well the cafeteria of a hospital where I used to work, where the woman behind the cash register often gave me advice on the items I had selected for lunch: "Will that salad be all right without dressing? *[Ano sarada wa doresshingu o kakenakute ii desu ka?]*" she would ask; or, "I think soy sauce on that chilled tofu would be tasty *[O tōfu no ho ni wa shōyū kaketara oishii to omoimasu]*." I found the suggestions invasive, but my colleagues were touched by her "finely tuned sensitivity" *(kime ga komakai)*. "I think it's very kind," one remarked. "Service like that is hard to come by these days—even in Japan."

Indeed, there is a rich lexicon in Japanese to describe this quality of attentiveness. The idea is captured in a number of Japanese expressions that describe alertness (literally, the way one holds one's *ki,* or "animating spirit") as a social virtue: *kizuku* (*ki* is ignited, connoting "noticing" and awareness), *ki o tsukau* (to use one's *ki*), *kimawashi* (to circulate one's *ki*), and *kikubari* (to hand out one's *ki*) all describe the importance of being attentive to the needs of others in a preemptive way. A person who is inattentive to others, whose *ki* does not ignite *(ki ga kikanai),* is seen as oblivious, lazy, or unreliable. For a woman, this is unforgivable.[9]

Within a home, too, a housewife's work means anticipating family members' needs before they are articulated *(sakidōri, sakimawari).* In what Takie Lebra has described as "around-the-body care," women often scurry around managing their husbands' needs when they are at home together: picking up their laundry, setting out their clothes, putting out their futons, drawing their bath, and so forth. I have even seen Japanese women function as a kind of human address book or calendar for their husbands, who call home when they want to know a friend or colleague's telephone number. Lebra describes one household in the 1970s in which the husband, while relaxing and watching television in the evening, would call out, "Channel 8!" whereupon the wife would rush in from the other room to turn the dial. Another woman packed her husband's suitcase (independent of any help from him) before he went away on business (1984: 132).

The codependency conversation called women's attention to these dynamics. They often talked about themselves as "service wives" *(sewa nyōbō),* or the "go-all-out wife" *(tsukushizuma).* Some engaged in what might be called forms of "everyday resistance": refusing to wait up for their husbands to return from work, becoming "loose" *(rūzu)* with household chores, putting the same food out for dinner as they had for lunch, or buying food of inferior quality that was more convenient. They joked about being the "wicked wife" *(akusai)* and began to talk about the thankless way in which they were expected to minister to their husbands. The language of code-pendency seemed to sensitize women to the ways in which their work was often unspoken, unseen, and unremunerated. They began to see this in-visibility as one aspect of the behavior that had led to complicity in their husbands' drinking and destructiveness. At one of the first meetings I at-tended, Fukuda-san, whose husband had stopped drinking relatively re-cently, told this story: "Fukuda *desu.* I'm here because of my husband's al-coholism. At the moment there is a plate of sweet bean cakes sitting on top of our table at home. Since my husband has stopped drinking, he enjoys sweets. But I'm always the one who brings home the sweets. I remember when he was still drinking, it was always I who devotedly bought his sake. These days I'm starting to think that I'm just repeating the same old pat-tern." Hata-san talked about how her husband had finally grown to treat her as a "fellow human being." He thanked her after being given a cup of tea, and another time offered her some of the peanuts and bean bread that he had bought on the way home from work. She said, "Until that moment he never gave anyone anything." When Nakamura-san told the story of how she had hung up the phone before her husband could ask her for a ride home from the station in the rain, the social workers later remarked on her progress. They told me she had once been the super-service wife, who would check the weather report before her husband left each day to determine whether she needed to hand him his umbrella.

In a more humorous moment, which occurred toward the end of my year attending the meetings, Fukuda-san recounted a story that reflected her husband's infantility and the minuteness of the care that women are expected to provide for their husbands:

On Sunday, my husband and I went to a Buddhist memorial service for a friend. Lunch was served and the couple sitting opposite us was related to the deceased. The wife cut and prepared all the food that appeared and fed it to her husband—even peeling the skin off the shrimp. "What the heck is she doing?" I thought to myself. "How odd!" But of course I realized I used to do the same kinds of things. Now I can appreciate how strange it is. Well,

I don't do it for my husband anymore, but now I'm doing it for the dog. We've had a dog for seven years, and I lovingly tear up his food in tiny pieces for him to eat. I suppose there is still a part of me that just needs to dote on someone. Occasionally I wonder if I'm putting a burden on the dog. [Laughter.]

The notion of *enryo,* meaning to show reserve in the presence of people with whom one is not intimate, was a recurring topic of conversation. People *enryo* when, as a guest, they are offered something to eat but decline for fear of imposing. In urging his or her guests to partake, a host will often say, *dōzo, enryo shinai de* (please, don't hesitate). Men *enryo* when they resist leaving the job early (despite having finished their work) for fear of appearing irresponsible to their superiors. At home, children and men are not expected to *enryo;* women, however, are expected to *enryo* even in the context of their own families—declining, for example, to take the best piece of food at the family table or being the last to bathe.

In *The Anatomy of Dependence,* Doi romanticizes the intimate relationship between parent and child that (for the child) requires no *enryo.* As relationships grow more distant, *enryo* increases proportionately. According to Doi, "Everybody believes that if possible an absence of *enryo* is ideal, which is itself a reflection of the fact that, basically, the Japanese idealize the kind of relationship of oneness typically embodied in the parent-child relationship" (39). Needless to say, his statement reflects the perspective of the child and not that of the caregiving parent.

One conversation provoked by the topic of codependency focused on the different expectations placed on men and women with respect to attentiveness and restraint. During a humorous conversation that took place over tea after the meeting, Fukuda-san announced that she and her husband had just recently decided that it was acceptable to pass gas in front of each other. Fukuda-san asked if I knew the Japanese *senryū,* or satirical poem:

A bride's gas
circulates about the five viscera
and the six internal organs [the bowels]

[O yome no he wa
gozōroppu o
kakemeguri]

Hoshi-san explained, "That's because young brides have the least status in an extended family, so they have to restrain themselves in front of everyone." They all laughed and talked about how their husbands expected them to be more restrained because they were women. Takahashi-san said, "My husband expects *me* to *enryo*, but he himself lets loose whenever he feels like it! Men have no self-restraint! If I so much as make a peep, he says, 'And for a woman, too!' *[Onna no kuse ni!]*" Takahashi-san said that she had heard on the radio that if you hold them in, they enter your bloodstream. "So it's really true that too much self-restraint can actually hurt your body," she said. "It is *gas* after all," Hata-san agreed.

Yet in the end, for women the work of caregiving was their central source of validation, and few seemed inclined to give it up. As Lebra has pointed out, the dependency relationship is often the only point of intimacy between husband and wife; it also provides women with a sense that her services are valuable. Women who described their husbands as "bullies" or "macho" were often referring to the husband's desire to be independent rather than the husband's tendency to rely on his wife (Lebra 1984: 133–34).

In a perfect world, the women wanted to continue to be the ultimate caregivers but to be appropriately appreciated for it. They saw its exploitative dimensions, but they did not dismiss the possibility of achieving satisfaction from it. For example, they still seemed eager to indulge one another. When a woman in the room where we held the meetings once complained that it was stuffy, three women leaped up to open a window. When we went out for tea after the meetings, they often exchanged small gifts and passed around little homemade cakes for the other women to take home. A story of Fukuda-san's that was widely appreciated illustrates this point:

This week I experienced something for the first time since I was born. At two in the morning my eyes popped open when I heard a BANG BANG sound like a pistol. I listened closely as I wondered what to do. It began to come closer. My son came down the stairs and yelled out "Fire!" and there turned out to be a fire just about thirty meters from our house. Two houses were completely burned to the ground. We went all out to take care of the three people whose houses had burned; I exhausted myself attending to them like I haven't in a long time.

Afterward I thought that perhaps I'd inadvertently returned to my former self. But then I decided that there is after all a place and time for taking care of people. I want to save that little part of me for times like this.

It's funny, though, when I heard "It's a fire!" I remember waking my husband up, but after that I really don't know what happened to him. I just remember that I was standing outside cradling the dog. "What should I do with the dog? Where can I put the dog?" I kept thinking to myself. [Laughter.]

Although the act of helping a family whose house has burned down hardly seems an extraordinary (let alone codependent) act, I took the point of Fukuda-san's story to be that the best scenario was to be able to choose when to go into service mode: to do it when it was rewarding (and it still was rewarding for some women sometimes) and to let go of the role when it was undermining.

EFFECTING CHANGE

Although a few women remained paralyzed by the demands of their husbands' alcoholism and never seemed able to implement the ideas they were given, most of the women used the idea of codependency to begin to effect at least small changes in the world they inhabited. For example, a number of women told stories about learning to assert themselves in public, closing the door on unwanted salesmen or speaking up when they felt a retail merchant had made a mistake in calculating change. In one meeting, Hata-san told the story of how a young boy's tennis racket was poking into the back of an elderly man on the train. She said the person on the other side of the boy was glaring at him, but she felt that if it had been her sitting there, she would have asked the boy to move the racket. She commented, "I thought about how much I've changed since coming to this center."

In a few cases, women were able to accomplish momentous things. A key challenge that women faced was being able to persuade friends, family, and neighbors that they were doing the right thing in letting their husbands suffer the consequences of their drinking. For women to truly implement the lessons of codependency, they had to confront neighbors, bosses, and extended family; and for these people, the notions of both alcoholism (an addictive disease that takes its own course) and codependency (the notion that caregiving can be harmful) were counterintuitive. How could they reconcile these views with the belief that a woman should take care of her husband in all respects and that a good wife facilitates family relations so that family conflicts do not become public disruptions?

As women attempted to educate their extended families about the problem, few found that their families (even their natal families) understood. Koike-san told me: "I talk to my mother and brothers and sisters, but they don't understand. They can't shed the idea that my husband is just weak-willed [ishi ga yowai] and that's why he can't stop drinking. No one in our family has ever had an alcohol problem, so they have no familiarity with it. Still, they don't criticize my husband or tell me to leave him. They feel sorry for him!" Hoshi-san's mother-in-law enjoyed drinking and often enjoined her son to join her. She didn't understand the concept of addiction. If her son refused a drink, she would say, "But surely a little is okay!" Hoshi-san once told me, "My mother-in-law must have thought I was very cold. For example, if he was drunk and urinated in his pants, I just left him. Then Grandma would come and change his underwear. She must have thought I was very cruel. At night he would leave and not come back, and she would wake me up to worry. I'd say, 'If anything happens we'll hear from the police.' She'd think I was very callous, refusing to look after her dear son. She doesn't understand the situation at all." Hoshi-san told me that although she had bought the Al-Anon book for her mother-in-law at the hospital bookstore, it simply didn't sink in.

The idea that a skillful wife can manage her husband's outbursts allowed women to endure years of their husbands' drinking and, in some cases, verbal or physical abuse. A husband's abuse is often perceived as a source of shame for the wife—a failure on her part to meet his needs or to diffuse his anger. As an acquaintance of mine once put it, a neighbor hearing a husband yelling across the street would most likely ask, "Why did that wife make her husband yell?" (Nan de ano okusan wa goshujin o donaraseta?) The process of men exploding and women concealing evidence of their outbursts from neighbors and extended family perpetuates the dynamic whereby men do not have to take responsibility for their own loss of control (Lebra 1984: 130). This dynamic has been remarked upon in the American recovery movement literature, but it is particularly true in Japan, where women feel the pressure to keep family disruptions quiet, and there is little understanding of the idea of codependency and no pervasive critique of domestic violence. Exposing domestic violence or asking neighbors for help is perceived as evidence of a wife's weakness.[10]

For this reason, Saitō's books encouraged women to break this dynamic by calling on neighbors for help and exposing their husbands' outbursts to public scrutiny. Of course, women took a risk that such tactics might backfire, but for some women the idea seemed to produce an important psychological shift toward allowing them to believe that their husbands' behavior was not their fault and that they were not responsible for hiding it. In one meeting, the following conversation transpired:

> Kurita *desu.* Today before I came here the two of us [she and her husband] were going at it. In Saitō *sensei's* book, he recommends letting the whole neighborhood know, so I deliberately opened the front door as we were yelling. When was it that I said he was driving me to distraction? I don't really let it get to me anymore. . . .

> Fukuda *desu.* About Kurita-san's story of opening the door. I used to hate the thought of letting the neighbors know [about what went on in the house], and I used to shut the windows and curtains [when things got rough]. I kept myself pent up inside the house because I didn't even like to see the neighbors. After he began treatment at the hospital, I decided to openly explain to everyone that my husband suffered from alcoholism. Immediately I had the physical sensation that an enormous load that I had been carrying on my back had slid right off and left, and I felt a sense of relief. I understood the enormous burden created simply by not telling anyone and carrying something like that around inside.

Koike-san once took a considerable risk when she left her drunken husband sleeping on the curbside around the corner from her house. She received little understanding from the neighbors, despite her attempts to explain the nature of alcoholism and codependency. Eventually, a neighbor brought her husband home.

> Koike *desu.* I'm here because my husband has alcoholism. . . . The other day he began a drinking bout in the neighborhood and ended up crouched on the sidewalk unable to stand up. Two neighbors came by to inform me that he was there, but I told them, "Please just leave him until he realizes

and picks himself up. He is an alcoholic, so that's the best thing to do."
They looked at me very strangely. Later that day, one man brought him
to the doorstep. When I asked my husband later how he thought he got
home, he said he had no idea.

THE HOME AS SOURCE OF STRENGTH

In making sense of the stories women told about their triumphs, one might
ask why no explicit critique emerged of the gender system in Japan,
specifically the limited opportunities afforded to women in the commercial or public sector. Answering this question requires a more careful exploration of Japanese marriage and domesticity and the great resources
they have afforded women. For this generation of Japanese women, marriage has been not simply an entrapping sphere of exploitation but also,
in some cases, their sole source of empowerment.

In addition to the many ways women were beholden to their husbands
and the fact that few women would have been able to sustain themselves
economically had they decided to leave their husbands, there were more
deeply rooted reasons for staying in the marriage. The historical notion
of housework and child-rearing as fostering the broader public good contributed to a worldview, available to middle-class Japanese housewives of
the postwar period, that allowed nonworking (nonwage-earning) women
to consider themselves productive citizens. In contrast with American
housewives of the 1950s, who performed the work of housekeeping and
child-rearing but deferred to their husbands in matters of finances, children's education, and the family's social networks, the Japanese housewife
role has always been more encompassing. As others have documented,
women manage family purchases, make decisions about children's education, perform home repairs, organize the family's financial investments,
purchase insurance, and so forth. Often they receive the husband's pay-
check, depositing it in the bank themselves, while men may not even know
the ATM number required to access their account.

In addition, the entirely different spheres in which men and women
operate and the fact that a woman's primary emotional sustenance comes
from her children rather than her husband give women a sense of independence, despite their financial dependence on their husbands. The image of the childlike, fragile, or frivolous housewife that populated Victo-

rian drama and literature (for instance, the image of Nora in Henrik Ibsen's *A Doll's House*) was not as popular an image in Japanese renderings of the postwar housewife (see Borovoy 2001a; Sievers 1983).

The reality for most women who found themselves in unhappy marriages (in this case, to men who were alcoholics) was that marriage was both a source of discontent and their salvation. It was through their role as household managers, and particularly as mothers, that they found their key avenues to economic stability as well as social respect, authority, and self-sufficiency. This is illustrated in the story of Koike-san, a housewife in her early sixties who was a regular participant in the group. Her husband had been diagnosed with schizophrenia in addition to his alcoholism and had not worked for several years. Before that, he had switched jobs so frequently that he was never able to secure a stable upwardly mobile position that would provide the kind of pension benefits to which many middle-class families are entitled. Despite the fact that she had been single-handedly supporting the family for several years and no longer felt an intimate attachment to her husband, she decided to stay with him. Although she testily broached the possibility of divorce at meetings, she never took steps in that direction.

In speaking with her, it became increasingly clear that the affordable, city-subsidized apartment block *(tōei jūtaku)* in which she lived and the community she had constructed there were as important to her in making the decision to stay in the marriage as was her relationship with her husband. When her children were young, Koike-san had found work through the apartment block, where companies often came to recruit women laborers looking for piecework before day care was readily available. (Jobs included drawing up menus for employees living in company housing, sewing and tailoring, coloring animation films, and collecting insurance fees in the immediate neighborhood.)

In response to the question of whether she had ever considered seeking a divorce from her husband, Koike-san once told me,

> Well, the apartment is registered in my husband's name, and I don't want to move. Our rent in the city-subsidized apartment building is 30,000 yen a month [about three hundred dollars according to current exchange rates], and I have lots of friends there. We've lived in the same place for twenty-five years. We have a small garden there that we planted together, and in the

spring the flowers bloom. And after twenty-five years it's just difficult to think of moving. Despite my husband's situation, people don't look at me harshly. For me, it's the place where I feel at home. I'm open to my friends about everything—my husband's alcoholism, my son's school-refusal syndrome. Together with my friends, I knit, paint pictures, travel. The place where I work now is ten minutes away, so very convenient. I'm thinking I'll stay there until I die.

Koike-san's explanation shows that the broader community was just as important as her feelings for her husband. Marriage and family are women's "passport" to community participation and social activism; through marriage and family, women derive social credentials and resources that are independent of their relationship to their husbands (see Borovoy 2001a; Imamura 1987; LeBlanc 1999; Suzanne Vogel 1988). The same constraints that kept Koike-san in her marriage also created opportunities to cultivate independence. From this perspective, it made little sense to seek a divorce.

The privileges of the middle-class housewife were brought home to me once again in a conversation I had with a social worker. I expressed bewilderment that the women did not focus more on the broader social inequalities they faced as they tried to cope with their family problems. She said she felt the reason women did not talk more about gender inequality was that they had not in fact experienced it. Because they were housewives, she argued, they were sheltered from the inequalities of the workplace and from wage discrimination and sexual discrimination. In her view, the support and respectability that the housewife received eclipsed the encompassing inequalities that confined women to the home to begin with. I came away feeling that the Western emphasis on romance in marriage, equality (defined as sameness), and autonomy (defined as receiving a wage) inclines us to see Japanese marriage as oppressive, while making it difficult to see the privileges of the middle- or upper-middle-class Japanese housewife: her time with her family, her independence, and the social and economic stability she enjoys throughout her life.

However constrained a Japanese housewife's life may appear from the standpoint of American middle-class feminism of the 1960s and 1970s (which urged middle- and upper-middle-class women toward financial independence), Japanese housewives were accorded many privileges in

Japan's postwar era: economic stability and social standing in the community are among the two most important. Indeed, Japanese women regard the life of the full-time housewife as enviable because of its stability and privilege. Fukuda-san was considered the ultimate success story at the Center, in many ways because she preserved these values. As I explore in the next chapter, she took full advantage of her status as housewife, capitalizing on what already were her strengths so as to be more strategic in managing her husband. She took pride in the years of hardship she had endured, and used these as a means of dominating her husband after he had become sober; she sought to rebuild civility in the relationship after it had ruptured; and she spoke fondly of the values of attentiveness and care that were supposed to be the underpinnings of codependent behavior. Each of these statements drew great admiration and praise from both the clinicians and the other clients at the Center meetings.

Two other stories that deviate from this path—and the reactions they elicited—illustrate the way in which "success" was defined in terms of the middle-class housewife, or, put another way, how the promoted path to recovery took advantage of the strengths common to woman of this generation. Perhaps the most notable case of a woman who rethought conventional definitions of a wife and mother and took steps to move away from them was Hoshi-san, who ultimately separated from her husband, leaving him behind, along with her mother-in-law and three children (ages nineteen, twenty-one, and twenty-three), to live in her own apartment. She was forty-eight, a bit younger than the other women, and she came from a somewhat more elite family. She and her husband lived in a fashionable district of Western Tokyo.

She began to think about leaving her husband when she realized that as long as she was living at home with her family it would be impossible to live by the Al-Anon ideas and refuse to cover for her husband. She told me:

> I was doing everything: managing the house and all the economic matters. He didn't know anything. I used to give him his money but he spent it all on sake. I got sick of him drunk, lying around sick. I told my husband I had to think of myself and that I wanted to live separately. He said no. His mother was there, the kids were there, and so I *had* to take care of him, I couldn't just leave him, it wouldn't have been appropriate. Eventually, someone I consulted at the community health-care center told me that some drinkers stop when

their wife is there and others stop when she leaves. I decided that my husband was the type who would not stop so long as I was there.

Eventually Hoshi-san decided that since her children were all grown and working, they could look after themselves. She moved into her own apartment and took a job as a night janitor at a company. Her oldest daughter bought her a phone, television, washing machine, refrigerator, table, vacuum, and gas heater with $3,000 of her own savings, and her husband continued to send her a weekly allowance. What made Hoshi-san different from the rest of the women was that she seemed to have different expectations of what marriage should be. She had romantic ideals and once described a time in the happier years of her marriage when she and her husband would cuddle together listening to classical music before bed.

When I first began attending meetings at the Center in October, Hoshi-san had been living separately from her husband for ten months. They met on the weekends, and she described being torn between believing that her husband "missed her" and valued her and feeling that her husband wanted her home merely because he missed her services. She began writing letters and poems to him every day, and they went to movies together. "When we went out for tea, we'd reminisce about things, and my husband remembered everything," she said. Eventually she decided to return to her husband. She told the other women at the meeting,

> I realized that over the year I've inflicted terrible pain on my husband, and that I'm a foolish, arrogant woman, and I'm embarrassed about my egoism. I felt so terrible about this part of myself, I called my husband to ask him to forgive me. I apologized. He said that it was his fault. I had the feeling that maybe we could try again and that made me very happy. The following week I went to see them and visited the room of Grandmother. I'd made things rough for her for one year, but she welcomed me back and thanked me. I've lived with her ten years and I've never seen her with such a happy face! I prize her. I'm happy that I will be able to return home next month.

After this story, a number of women spoke up and said how touched they were, and that Hoshi-san was truly seeing herself and looking fairly at her husband. One of the social workers said that she cried (although not all the social workers agreed that going back was the right thing to do).

Yet, the following week, Hoshi-san reversed her decision. She had returned to the house to make preparations and found that her husband had not gotten around to doing the cleaning he had promised. She explained:

> It's been a week of feeling heavy in the chest. Since January I'd been looking back fondly on my old feelings for my husband. In February we met on a regular basis. I thought we could work things out. But after cleaning the house and returning to my apartment, I wondered why I was thinking of returning. . . . For me, the reason to live together is if we share feelings for each other. I think my husband's reasons are, first, because his mother is getting old, and second, because he wants me to teach my daughter how to cook.
>
> My husband told me that he'd like to me to return home by his mother's eighty-eighth birthday. At that moment I felt that he wanted me home not for me but for Grandmother's sake. For that alone I won't return home. I've lost confidence in myself. I wonder if I'm becoming selfish again. My own feelings have changed totally from last week, and that makes my chest heavy.

One month later, Hoshi-san did decide to return home. She described her life as significantly improved. Her husband was more considerate: he did the dishes, and one night he walked home in the rain, saying it "wasn't much," rather than phoning her from the station. Her children were also more appreciative. Everyone in the family did their own laundry, and instead of preparing meals for everyone before she left the house, she simply left a note on the board about where things were.

Yet her husband was ultimately unable to stop drinking, and before long, things began to slip back to their old ways. In the fall of 1993, she once again decided to move out. At the meeting she announced, "My husband underestimated me; he assumed once I returned home I was there to stay."

Hoshi-san stood out among the women in her decision to leave. Her financial situation was such that she could consider moving out on her own. But, more importantly, she had different ideals than the other women did regarding marriage. The fact that so many of the women found her decision to move back in compelling suggests the conservative nature of prevailing views toward marriage. Although divorce or separation perhaps inevitably invites self-scrutiny or self-blame, Hoshi-san continued to live with the feeling that she had done something unforgivable to her husband and family. By my visit in the summer of 2000, her husband had passed away, and when all the women gathered, Hoshi-san reflected back on her decisions with a mixture of guilt and liberation:

> I came to the Center in Heisei year 2 [1991][11] because of my husband's alcohol problem. I attended the educational program and participated in meetings weekly. After a long period of time when my husband kept drinking, I began to feel resentment and hate. I myself started to feel mentally unbalanced. I felt I would become a cold, callous person if I stayed on. But I felt that I couldn't single-handedly decide to leave with the children there and Grandmother. But I finally decided to leave and not worry about the others. I left by myself and slowly a path opened up. I was lucky. I felt comfortable by myself. My husband would pursue his recovery, and I would pursue mine. I left and then went back, but again I became miserable; I couldn't live with my husband when he was drinking, and so again I separated. That took a lot of courage. I also feel grateful toward my husband. Every month he sent me living expenses.
>
> Last year, on New Year's, his drinking level increased and he died. When I looked at his face after his death, it seemed a peaceful face. I still think it may have been unforgivable to leave my husband and Grandmother. I rented my own one-bedroom apartment. But now I'd like to return home and set my feelings straight.

Even after her husband's death, Hoshi-san continued to ask herself whether she had really been entitled to leave him. In a context in which sacrifice and patience are the ultimate virtues, it is not surprising that these questions were not easily resolved for her. Her steps were not entirely against the grain of the Center's ideas and the other's women's decisions. After she announced the first time that she felt selfish and ashamed for having left her husband and that she would be returning home, a considerable outpouring of support occurred—though the members of the staff were divided in how they felt. Her steps were transgressive in this context and yet certainly not a total break from what the other women did. She moved away from her husband to allow herself her own space, but she never sought a divorce. Nor did she seek new partnership or complain about the scanty economic opportunities offered to women who seek to subsist independently. She accepted all this with a sense of resignation and gratitude, which onlookers like me found surprising, given her steps to move out. Further, she remained close to the other women in the group and attended all of the reunions upon my visits to Japan. Her pleasures continue to revolve around family ties, particularly the pleasures of spending time with her grandchildren, and the freedom to pursue her own hobbies.

The only woman who formulated a critique of the Center, Koike-san, did so from the position of a different political standpoint from the rest of the women. In addition to living in public housing, she was also a long-standing member of a Marxist-influenced women's group, the New Japan Housewives Association *(Shin Nihon Fujin no Kai)*, a group primarily concerned with women's labor issues. (She had also been politically active as the head of the Residents Association at the public housing community, which lobbied the city for better services.) When her husband died, she received a meager pension from his company (because her husband had not been working in his later years) and little aid from the state. (The Japanese government often matches pension benefits to those earned through company pension plans, thus accentuating existing inequalities.) She described herself as "poor" and went on to explain, "I've worked this hard only to find that the women who are ultimately rewarded are the women who don't work and just marry rich men."

When I returned to Japan in 1998, I arranged to meet Koike-san for a cup of coffee. I had remembered her as a somewhat severe-looking woman, with dark black hair and dark gray jacket. As I waited at the station exit, I was surprised to see a sprightly woman with white hair arrive in a brightly colored flowered blouse. She had stopped dying her hair and appeared a good deal happier and more energetic. After we sat down, she told me that her husband had passed away. I tacitly understood that her husband's death had meant both grief and yet also liberation. Because she could not consider divorce, this was the only form of liberation she could obtain. In some ways, Koike-san's story makes clear a further dimension of the Japanese postwar gender system. Because the work of the housewife has historically been upheld as important by the state and by Japanese enterprise, and wives of white-collar workers have been in a sense subsidized to stay at home, many Japanese women have been able to find economic stability, social validity, and personal fulfillment as housewives. Women who are unlucky in their marriages, for example women who marry men who are alcoholics, must cope with a bad situation, but they are able to make use of the resources of a wife and mother to distance themselves from their husband, take over management of the household (which they had largely been doing anyway), and find community outside the home. Yet women who are not able to count on their husbands for financial support in many ways face the worst of all worlds: they must support themselves and their families through their own wits and labor, they enjoy little emotional support or camaraderie from their husbands, and they must both manage the home and work outside the home, often working overtime. This same situation holds true for many working-class women who share financial responsibilities with their husbands (Kondo 1990). It is perhaps not surprising that the majority of the women at the Center were not working women—that is, they did not work full-time, instead relying chiefly on their husbands for financial support. Just as men were unlikely to identify as codependents, since they did little of the caretaking work around the house, working-class women were also less likely to identify with either the problem of codependency or its solution (developing better caregiving strategies, seeking community outside the home, and so forth).

Koike-san's politicization and the distance she placed between herself and others in the group were other signs of the depoliticized nature of the group and the women in it. Yet one can see how the major movements of North American and European feminism, rooted in their particular historical contexts, have not exactly met the needs of mainstream middle-class Japanese women. Both liberal and Marxist feminism, which see paid work outside the home as the key to women's liberation, have been less immediately compelling in a society in which women have historically been empowered through their role as homemakers. Liberal feminism's emphasis on equality—defined implicitly as sameness—cannot explain how separate but independent spheres might empower women, and its emphasis on autonomy cannot explain why domesticity might be attractive. In the liberal view of human nature, which sees maximization of individual gain as the centerpiece of individual autonomy, the unpaid labor that women perform at home can only be viewed as "irrational" (Collier 1991: 6; Jaggar 1988: 45).[12] Radical feminism, too, in its Anglo-American version, has had little to offer. Radical feminists have seen the home and marriage itself—particularly motherhood and women's sexuality—as the foundation of women's subordination (Jaggar 1988: 271; Firestone 1971; Rich 1976). The radical feminist focus on the internal contradictions of marital sexual relations (that sex between a husband and wife is supposed to be driven by emotional passion but is conducted in the context of economic subordination of the wife to the husband and patriarchal power disguised as love) pose fewer problems for Japanese women, who view romance as peripheral to the marital bond and do not construct themselves as economic dependents. Similarly, the facts that Japanese women inhabit worlds largely independent of their husbands, that they manage home life, and that they do not see being sexually attractive to their husbands as a central role make these claims less immediately important.[13]

I have tried to portray a more complicated view of Japanese marriage and the trade-offs it entails. The privileges of the housewife are not meant to suggest that women lead rosy lives. On the contrary, the miseries of the women are apparent. Yet dominant constructions of marriage, gender roles, and women's nurturance, precisely because of what they offer women, make it difficult for women to find the language to criticize their situation.

Chapter 4 | A SUCCESS STORY

In this chapter I narrate the story of one woman, Fukuda-san, as she told it to me, from her childhood during the American occupation to the years following her husband's sobriety. In looking at the way her life changed as she managed her husband's alcoholism and attended meetings at the Center, I explore the meaning of being a good wife for this generation of women and the kinds of "resistance" that were possible from within this ethic. Fukuda-san learned to stand up to her husband and refuse to buy liquor for him; she learned when to engage him and when not to; she learned how to say no to household tasks; she learned to walk away when his temper flared up; and she learned to see herself as someone who could do these things, rather than as someone who was obliged to continue to endure him. The key element of her success was her ability to distinguish what she came to call codependency from the ideal of nurturance, care, and service that she admired.

Fukuda-san was widely regarded as a success story by staff and other women at the Center, and this reveals a great deal about the strengths that were perceived to adhere to the role of wife and mother. Fukuda-san was seen as successful because she responded to her husband's alcoholism by engaging in careful strategizing, displaying unlimited endurance and a good deal of self-reflection, all without giving up on the marriage. She spoke a great deal about her attempts, after her husband became sober, to restore civility to the marriage, in the form of everyday greetings and shared conversation. As her story reveals, she emerged from her husband's alcoholism (he was one of the few husbands who eventually became sober) a stronger and more thoughtful person. This path of self-cultivation, self-strengthening, and self-reflection was praised by the staff and other members of the group. And Fukuda-san herself spoke of her accomplishments with pride, noting that the experience changed her life: "I think I owe my change in character to my husband's alcoholism. If he hadn't become an alcoholic, I would have lived out my entire life as a 'service wife' and later as a 'service grandmother,' interfering in my son's life and quashing my own selfhood. And with that my life would have been over." In another story she captured a small moment that revealed how she herself had learned to accept favors and to be taken care of.

> Fukuda *desu*. I was telling my husband that the day of the weekly meetings has been changed from Wednesday to Friday, and he said that he would be able to drive me here. "Okay," I was able to say, sincerely. I think formerly I wouldn't have been able to accept and would have said, "No, no, really, that's okay, it's too much of a nuisance etc." As we were riding in the car together I was able to think to myself, I feel really happy now. Watching the junior high–schoolers and the kindergartners going to school with their new school bags I thought to myself, I'm a first-grader too. I feel a sense of "newness" as I approach this process of recovery.

Though Fukuda-san told her story as a success that could even be appreciated by American popular psychologists (she reintroduced humor into the marriage, she learned to say "no," etc.), many of her accomplishments were brought about by virtue of her sheer endurance. Yet this endurance conferred on her a sense of entitlement, which she took advantage of in the years following his sobriety. She withdrew after that from certain household chores (such as preparing the family taxes), claiming her eyes were failing her, and she more frequently walked away from her husband's demands. In a sense, she had learned to protect herself and protect her dignity in the context of a vastly exploitative relationship.

Some would see Fukuda-san's accomplishments as merely a concession to Japan's enduring regime of gender inequality. Strength by virtue of endurance is not a value that we feminists have an easy time embracing; it comes too close to diminishing or romanticizing women's hardships. And yet, as I believe the narrative below reveals, Fukuda-san's accomplishments were real. One should read her story as evidence of the very complex mix of oppression and empowerment that characterized postwar marriages rather than as a failure to abandon or transform the marriage altogether. The story reveals the exacting standards the family historically placed on the wife, mother, and bride. It also reveals the strength and pride that women derived from meeting these standards. In coping with husbands' alcoholism, women are able to overturn some ideas about what makes the "good wife" or "good mother," but they also build on the strengths already provided by the traditional construction of the role. Fukuda-san's story reveals both these strategies.

The story also displays the major historical transformation that women of this generation traversed in their coming of age. Born before the war and socialized into prewar notions of family, household, and marriage, they grew up in the context of the postwar period of "democratization." In the case of most women, historically rooted notions of family as a "vertical" entity built on cooperative ties between parents and children persisted, although they commingled with imported ideas about romantic spousal love. Notions of duty (to family, community, and nation) commingled with notions of rights. In Fukuda-san's recounting of the occupation era and her own family's response to it, we see excitement about radically new postwar ethics of democracy and equality mixed with a sense of bewilderment and contradiction: how would these new ideas be integrated into a historically rooted system that prioritized family loyalty, self-sacrifice, and marriage as a social contribution rather than a means of self-fulfillment? The story belies any notion that the occupation automatically ushered in a new value system that was easily understood and embraceable by the Japanese population—and the notion that postwar Japanese social change has been a story of "Americanization."

Fukuda-san was fifty-eight years old in June 1993, when I first asked her to talk to me about her life history and the significance of the treatment program at the Center. She had been coming to the Center for almost two years. Her husband had been a heavy drinker for over ten years, growing increasingly violent and unruly, before finally quitting. The alcohol had left his legs temporarily paralyzed, and he rarely left the house. "I'd like to kill him with my own two hands," a staff member quoted her as saying when she first came to the meetings. Later she said that she came to think of that period as the time when she was most caught up in the "pathology" *(byōki)* of her husband's alcoholism.

When I asked if she would sit down with me for two afternoons and talk about her life history, she seemed surprised: "Could it really contribute to your research?" she asked several times. Fukuda-san narrated her story to me in two seamless stretches with few interruptions. This is her story, largely unedited.

FUKUDA-SAN'S STORY

I was born in Tokyo in 1935, six years before the beginning of World War II. My mother died when I was only eight years old, at the age of thirty-three from a kidney disease. She had weak kidneys and checked into the hospital a lot. Her mother took care of her there. There were no medicines available because of the war, and she was finally sent home from the hospital to die. I recognize her in photos by her swollen face—a result of the kidney problems. I was very well behaved through it all, never running around being a menace *[choro choro shinakatta]*. I remember the nurse brought me some sweets, I was sitting so quietly. "For the little girl," she said, putting them in my hand. I was an only child, because my two younger sisters had both died when they were babies. My father remarried when I was twelve.

I have lonely memories of my childhood, but the house where my birth-mother *[umi no haha]* grew up, where my grandmother, grandfather, aunt, and uncle lived, was very close by, and they owned a barbershop. My father was a veterinarian. I used to go with him on his rounds; I was very close to my father—his pet *[otōsan ko]*, maybe because my mother was so sickly. He was completely taken with me *[chichi wa watashi no koto ga kawaikute shō ga nai]*. I always bathed with my father, never with my mother.

My father used to say, "When you get big, you'll be a nurse," and I told all my friends that when I grew up I'd be a nurse. We lived in Tachikawa near the naval hospital, and my uncle would take me to the hospital when he went to cut the patients' hair. I always admired the style of those nurses—tall hats and long skirts—I still remember! At school when they asked us what we wanted to be when we grew up, I always said "a nurse." Other girls said "a bride *[oyome san].*" For girls, to become a bride was thought to be the happiest life path *[O yome-san wa onna no ko ga ichiban shiawase na michi to sarete ita].* Of course, I also admired the nice kimonos that women got to wear when they got married. "I want to wear one of those too!" I thought to myself.

I was seven when the war began. We managed to stay in Tokyo through it all. We had enough food, and Tachikawa was spared, fortunately, but the neighboring town of Hachiōji was burned down. There were some terrifying moments. A few times we had to escape into the mountains in middle of the night. (That's why it's so strange to be talking with you about all this now!) I remember seeing the B-52s flying overhead majestically— they were so big! They lit up the sky.

But frankly, I think it's a good thing we lost that war. Japan was so poor (and the United States was so rich) and [Japanese] men were so dictatorial *[otoko no hito ga ibatte ita]*—especially the military. Women couldn't walk in front of men back then, you know. If Japan had won, things would have really become insufferable. We'd be slaves now in my opinion. I *know,* because I've now experienced both kinds of lives.

My stepmother brought me up from when I was in the sixth grade until I got married. She married for the first time when she was thirty-three years old. She was an active woman who had been to America, Argentina, and China by boat. In those days, she was considered a real oddity *[tonde iru onna].*[1] Her relatives were in the trade business, wool and threads, and she had worked as their maid, traveling with them overseas. They finally encouraged her to get married, but she continued to work well beyond marriageable age.

And here I was, a quiet, sheltered little kid, and this was the woman who was to be my mother. She was incredibly strict, and she had me do everything for myself. I washed my own underwear. She said she would wash the clothes, but things that went directly on the body were my own responsibility. She made me do all kinds of housework and wake up early in the morning to help make breakfast. None of the other kids had to do this. "These are the things that women do; when you get married you'll have to know how to do this," she told me. And I did everything I was told.

I learned later that all my relatives felt sorry for me. Apparently there was once a big fight between my stepmother and my birth-mother's family. They told her she was too strict. "She's my child and I'll thank you for not interfering [*Watashi no ko dakara kuchidashi shinai de kudasai*]," she told them. I think she was admirable to say that.

She knew how to sew Japanese clothing and had gotten a license to teach this skill to other people. And she could also make Western clothing, so she would take apart things that were the wrong size that came from the United States and resew them, so I could wear things that no one else had. Everyone was very jealous of me. When I got married, she said to me, "Once you've stepped out the door, please try not to come back."[2] She was strict, but I didn't dislike her, because she had a nice side too.

After the war, my father sometimes worked as a vet at the Tachikawa base. Lots of Americans would bring their pets to him and he would talk to them in English. Boy, did he seem impressive at those times! One soldier brought in a sick dog and said that he hoped to take it back to America with him. So my father stayed up all night doing everything he could, so that he could bring the dog back with him to America. Now that I think about it, I've actually had quite a bit of contact with America [*Kangaete mireba, kekkō America to en ga arimashita*].

My younger sister was born when I was twelve, and my father died of a stroke when I was fourteen years old, in 1949. When he died, the family of my stepmother asked her repeatedly to come home, along with me and my sister. She ignored them [*Sore o zenbu furikitta n desu*]. My birthmother's family—my uncle the barber—wanted to take me into their family, to keep the family together. But my stepmother insisted that the three of us should stay together. And things were tough, because my father died suddenly and didn't leave a lot of money. But we had our own house and our own land, so at least we didn't have to pay rent. My mother made a living by sewing. I used to sit by her and learn. She was such a tough [*tsuyoi*] woman, and her teaching methods were severe. I'd listen to her with my heart pounding, and if I asked her a question she'd say, "You *still* don't get it?" or "Think it out for yourself." She herself once admitted that it wasn't in her character to be a teacher. And she's still that way to this day.

I have good memories of the period just after the war. In front of my house was the path to the naval base. There were rumors that if a young girl stepped outside wearing red or other colors that were not discreet—or if she showed her legs—she would be snatched away. We always wore black or brown. The American soldiers were so different from the Japanese soldiers. They were cheerful *[akarui]* and chatted loudly with each other *[becha becha shabettari shita]*, laughing and chewing gum. We used to play in front of the house, and once when we stepped out onto the road they waved! And they also threw us chocolate and gum, but we were told by our parents that it was poisoned, so at first they wouldn't let us eat it. But after a while they stopped telling us that. And that chocolate was so delicious!

Entering Marriage

I've only been to school up through junior high. I wanted to keep going, but my family situation was such that I couldn't. I wanted to be able to help out at home as soon as I could. My mother absolutely never slept—even while we slept at night, she worked. And we rented out the second floor of the house and used the two rooms below for ourselves. We used to rent the upstairs to couples—really nice people who were fond of me *[kawaigarareta]*, though I have no idea why, since I wasn't really a very cute child. I was quite serious.

Half of my class from junior high went on to high school; the other half went to work. I had a hard time finding a job. The economy was bad and I didn't have a high school education, so basically the two choices were to work either in a factory or else as a waitress in a beer hall. I ended up working in a small factory that was subcontracted to make watch parts. I worked there for two years, but the dirt floor made my leg start to hurt, and I had to stop because I developed rheumatism. I lost my job, but we decided that it wasn't worth ruining my body any more than it already was.

And, well, there was another reason why I left that job too. . . . There was a man working there, he was twenty-three and I was seventeen, and the boss of the factory tried to marry us *[kekkon saseyō to shita]*. If it had been the prewar days, I suppose I might have gone ahead and done it, because that was how we did things in Japan in those days. When I told the boss I was thinking about quitting, he said he wanted us to get married. I was shocked! I never even noticed this was happening. He wasn't a *bad* person, but I just didn't feel like getting married at that point. I told him, "I'm not ready to get married yet." But he pushed me. "You're going to get married sometime, aren't you? He's a smart boy, and he likes you, and you don't have to get married right away, anyway." But I still refused. My stepmother simply said, "It's a little early yet, isn't it?" And then it became even harder to stay at the factory, so I quit.

Looking back on it, that was the first time in my life that I exercised my own will *[hajimete watashi no ishi ga dete kita to omou]*. Until then, I'd really done what I was told—I acted "feminine" *[onna rashii]* or docile *[sunao]*.

My next job was an office job at a seafood wholesaler. I got to be really good with the abacus—I had a knack for it, and the time would just slip by. That's where I met my husband. He worked in the office doing tax calculations. He had been to a vocational high school, so he was doing skilled work.

[How did you meet?]

How did we meet? . . . I'm not exactly sure what to call it . . . I suppose it was a kind of love marriage. My husband initiated everything, though, not me.

[But you weren't attracted to him at all?]

Well, in a way. He looked a bit like my father. And I was my father's pet *[otōsan ko]*. In fact, people used to say that *I* looked like my father, which is something people usually only say about sons. Anyway, he became a kind of surrogate for my father *[Chi chi oya to dabutte ita]*. He was tall and sturdy. But I wasn't thinking about marrying him! I was young and naïve *[ubu]* and very cautious *[hikkomijian]*—not at all precocious *[masete inakatta]*. He wanted to get married, but of course he couldn't say that to me directly, so he got a close friend of his to help him.

His way of communicating was strange from the start. There was a group of about ten workers who all used to do things together—go to the mountains, go to the beach. One of the older members of the group set us up. He invited me to the mountains for the day, and I thought everyone was going together, but when I got there it was just the three of us! When I asked where everyone else was, he said, "They couldn't make it." I made the mistake of later showing the pictures we took to my mother. "There's something funny about these!" she said. "Why are there only two people in each picture?" [Laughing.] Of course, in the old days it was unacceptable to be out alone with men.

He finally brought his uncle and came to my house to "get" me *[morai ni kita]*. He told my mother, "I'd like to have her as a bride" [here Fukuda-san emphasized the words *get* and *bride* to indicate these as customs of the time]. I put out tea but then left. I was waiting in another room. I had a good feeling *[kōkan]* about him. Afterward, my mother asked me how I felt, since I was eighteen years old. I said I didn't mind marrying him *[Ii yo, kekkon shite mo]*. Of course, I was an only child, so theoretically I should have stayed to carry on the family business. The barbershop was still there, and my mother's family asked me to stay. But my fiancé was the oldest son, so he couldn't marry into *my* family, and it was also after the war, and those kinds of customs were falling by the wayside anyway. And I still had a younger sister, and that sister was the *real* daughter of my mother. If I stayed on, then my sister would have to leave. I didn't dislike my mother, but I thought somehow she and my sister (her daughter) should stay together. So I decided to get married.

The Self-Sacrificing Bride

After we were married, we lived an ideal life for a while. I quit work immediately and gave birth to a daughter when I was twenty, in 1955. We stayed in my house for a while because my husband's siblings were still living at home and they didn't need our help immediately. The children were really the center of my life, and I had the feeling that I pleased my husband *[otto ni ki ni irareru]*, that I was loved *[ai sareta]*. I quit my job and was determined to be a good wife. I was totally engrossed in raising the kids, my husband wasn't making trouble, and everything was fine.

[Did your husband help out with the kids then?]

No, not really. Well, he did on weekends. One day he took our daughter to a friend's house. He didn't come back, and it was time for her to have milk and her diaper changed. It turned out that he had taken her to a bar, and the *mama-san* was looking after her. Finally he forgot and left her there, and I had to go back to get her. Once he was looking after her and fell asleep, and she ate his cigarette butts so I had to make her vomit. I suppose he was really a typical father of his generation. My daughter's husband is really wonderful—a whole different story. No matter how tired he is when he gets home, he plays a game with the children before bed. They wait up for him. My daughter wants to give her own children the things she never had.

My daughter told me that, when her husband told her he was a second son, she had an overwhelming sense of relief. Not that I had bad relations with my mother-in-law, but I know how arduous it is to marry an oldest son. When I was pregnant with my son, my second child, my husband's father got throat cancer and I had to look after him. So we went to live with his family. He [her husband] was the oldest son, after all, and I didn't really object to the idea. But, well, that was in the end much, much harder than I had imagined. Altogether there were nine people in the family—Ojiisan [Father-in-law], Obāsan [Mother-in-law], four brothers, my husband, me, and our daughter. My son was born just a few days before Ojiisan died. And my new life began [*Umarekawari no seikatsu ga hajimatta*]. I'd strap my new son on my back and cook, do the laundry, and do the shopping. I was being a *yome* [a young bride] [laughing].

I really think, looking back on it, that I was able to do it because of my children. The reward of bringing them up spurred me on to do everything else. My hands were cracked and all that, but I just thought, this is a *yome's* job. It was hard, but I never once cried.

Each year on New Year's, I would return to my own home and family, and I used to look forward to that—because I could sleep! I'd hand my kids over to my stepmother. I'd breathe a deep sigh of relief and just pass out for the duration. She watched the kids because, after all, she was my mother. I literally slept day and night while she looked after the kids, and they were at their most difficult age, too. Of course, she got mad at me a few times, because I used to just hand over the kids as soon as we arrived. "Aren't you coming home to sleep! [*Omae wa neru tame ni kaette iru no kai!*]," she would say.

My mother-in-law took advantage of her old age and didn't help out at all. She was a real Meiji era person. She liked traveling, and also worked at part-time jobs. When she would leave on a trip, I'd wake up early—no matter how early she was leaving—to make rice balls for her, and sometimes she would ask for some for her friends to take with them. I'd see her to the front door, saying, "Take care, come back safely!" I just assumed that was all part of my job. But after talking to other *yome-san* in the neighborhood, I found out they didn't even get up! The mothers-in-law in the neighborhood used to tell me that their *yome* didn't do such things for them, and they told me that I was praiseworthy for treating her so well [*anata wa yoku shite ageru kara erai*].

[Why do you think you felt compelled to be so diligent?]

Well, I suppose I just thought that was the job of a *yome*. Also, my mother-in-law used to tell me that when the kids were older and she was too old to travel, she would stay home so *I* could go. But of course she died before she could fulfill her promise! [Laughing.] And she always brought me back little presents, things to wear. I saved them away like little treasures. We really didn't have the typical kinds of battles between daughter and mother-in-law. Of course, it was a short period that we lived together—only eight years.

I got married very young, so I really didn't know how to do much around the house. I didn't know how to make pickles, *ohagi* [rice balls with red bean paste eaten the week of the equinox], or *sekihan* [red rice eaten on festive occasions]. Obāsan taught me all that. My husband used to hand over his monthly salary check to his mother, and she managed the family budget. She gave me a little money for household expenses, but nothing at all for myself. So Obāsan bought me everything, all my clothes. (When I went back to visit my stepmother, she would give me just a little money to buy my own things.) Obāsan would also give me money for haircuts and things, and I kept all the change, hiding it away. She knew, of course. I saved it all up until after she died, and then I bought myself a very, very thin gold necklace.

In 1963, she got cancer of the ovaries and uterus, seven years after Ojii-san had died. She was in the hospital for ten months. When she entered the hospital, she handed over the family purse to me. At that time, my daughter was eight years old, and there was a tradition of handing the purse to the *yome* when the first child was eight. Those two events just happened to coincide. Her younger sister and I took turns taking care of her while she was sick.

Managing the Problem of Alcohol

[When did you begin to think that your husband's drinking was a problem?]

After my daughter was born, my husband changed companies and went to work for his father's company because the salary was better. His father had changed jobs after the war and was working at a coal company. We used lots of coal after the war, so it was a big business. That was where he learned to drink alcohol. He was in charge of delivering coal by truck to hospitals and schools. I think because it was heavy labor [*chikara shigoto*], they all used to go out drinking at the end of the day.

In 1970, when Japan stopped using so much coal, he quit and went to work for a painting business. They used a lot of paint thinner, which weakens the effect of the alcohol, so you have to drink more and more to get the same effect. His dependency kept getting worse and worse, and by 1980 he was completely addicted, but at that time I didn't know anything about the disease of alcoholism. I just thought that, more than anything else, he really liked his alcohol [*Nani yori mo osake*]. He was still working at that point.

One time he had to drive down to Kyoto, leaving in the evening. When he arrived, he passed out in the car—unconscious. He was taken to a hospital in Kyoto, and they diagnosed it as a liver problem. It was the first time he had ever been to a doctor. They told him he was healthy, and he stayed there for ten days while they treated his liver. I stayed with him, sleeping next to his bed. Then we came back to Tokyo. Not one single person told him to stop drinking! The doctor said, "If it's just a little, it shouldn't be a problem." I myself thought the cause was that he worked too hard. Anyway, he was drinking beer on the way home.

He started drinking heavily again. In 1983, I went to the local public health center [*hokenjo*], and they told me it was an alcohol problem [*arukōru no mondai*]. They gave me a referral to a hospital and I went for a consultation in secret. (The trip to the local health-care center had also been in secret.) If I had suggested to him directly that he had an alcohol problem, it would have been a terrible scene. But I knew something was wrong; he was a different person. If I said one thing he didn't like, he'd turn over the plates, throw things, say crazy things—I thought he'd gone insane [*kichigai*]. I really thought his brain had gone funny [*Nō miso ga okashikunatta*].

I cried while telling the doctor about what had been going on [*naki naki hanashita*]. I had gone a little sick myself, a little funny [*Watashi mo sukoshi byōki ni natte ita. Okashikunatta*]. "Please admit him to the hospital no matter what," I begged. But they said that to be admitted he had to consent. "See if you can persuade him as his wife," they told me. But I didn't know how! I had no experience with such a thing, and in the end I couldn't get him to do it. He stayed shut up in the house all day drinking, not working, not eating, just being a burden to me and the children.

I brought him home a pamphlet and tried to talk to him about it calmly. If I said, "Now, Dad, your drinking habits are not normal anymore," he would start throwing things. Once he threw a fruit knife that stuck in the wall behind me. "What is this hospital? Some kind of hospital for lunatics? Are you trying to call me a lunatic?" he'd yell. "I'm no drunkard!" [*Nani kono byōin? Kichigai no byōin janai ka? Ore o kichigai ni suru ka? Ore aruchū janai!*].

One month after my visit to the hospital (in 1982), he himself suggested going. I instantly called the hospital, but they told me to wait until afternoon to bring him. I said, "Please let us take him now! He might change his mind in the afternoon!" So they agreed to see him. My son took the day off work to take him himself.

They diagnosed it as cirrhosis of the liver and told him he needed to check in. But my husband resisted being admitted because he had delivered coal to mental hospitals before, so he had seen people behind bars. And the doctor said he *would* be put behind bars while he went through withdrawal. He argued with the doctor for an hour but refused to be admitted. I sat next to him, saying over and over, "Doctor, please admit him, please make him check in," until finally the doctor got mad and threw me out of the room. My husband decided to commute as an outpatient. They prescribed some antabuse and he brought it home, and that's how he stopped drinking.

At that point I was a sick person myself. I tried going to Danshukai meetings for alcoholics and their families, but my husband never went and I myself really couldn't talk. I would just kind of weep. They told me to keep coming. "If you keep coming, your husband will definitely start to come," they encouraged me. But I stopped going.

In 1988, six years after my initial visit to the hospital, he started drinking again. I went to the local hospital [a different one] to consult an internist. The internist said, "There's really nothing you can do at this point. If he died, wouldn't it be for the best?" [*Shindara ii janai ka?*] This internist was a woman. "Don't worry, I'll write the cause-of-death certificate for you," she promised. Because, you know, in Japan if you die when you're not under the care of a doctor, the detectives and police come to investigate. After she said that, I breathed a big sigh of relief. That doctor became my ally [*Sensei wa mikata ni natte kureta*].

One morning, he began convulsing and I had to call the ambulance to take him to Tachikawa General Hospital. A specialist in alcohol-related problems came to the hospital once a week. It was December 22, Friday— I still remember. And it just so happened that that was the day the specialist was in. "You need to go to a hospital that has an alcohol treatment facility," he told him. We *all* told him—the nurse, the internist, me, my son—but he refused to go! And they wouldn't admit him to the general hospital, because he was an alcoholic and he would be a danger to the other patients if he caused some incident. Instead he decided to commute to the hospital as an outpatient. So once again I brought him home.

At home, he went into withdrawal. At least he wasn't violent. He just behaved very, very strangely. He cut up the tatami mats with scissors and dumped out the contents of the drawers. He backed into the [gas] stove and set himself on fire. He drove nails into the doghouse. My son and I took turns guarding him day and night. This went on for three or four days. There was no time to even cook meals, so my son went out to pick up *bentōs* and things. But we hardly had time to eat or even bathe.

After the withdrawal period was over, he was suddenly unable to walk. His legs were paralyzed. "It hurts, it hurts," he'd complain. He couldn't go to the toilet, so we had to put diapers on him. "I don't want these! *[Konna iya da!],*" he'd yell, and take them off again. We would heat his legs with a blanket, and he would say, "It's cold! Change it!" being tyrannical and throwing his weight around.

Since then, he's pretty much been clean. There was one episode over New Year's when he drank steadily for four days. But by then I was participating in meetings at the Center, and I told him, "This is your problem, not mine." And I refused to buy sake for him. So he bought it himself and heated it up on the stove. But on the fourth day, he announced that he was stopping and said, "I'm going to the hospital."

That night we talked until two or three in the morning on our futons. It was the very first time that we'd talked about any of this. I told him about those three days when he was going through withdrawal. "I don't remember a thing," he said.

Mine has really been a life of upheaval. But I really have a lot of things to be thankful for too. When I look back, especially on the time I was slaving away as a *yome-san* in my husband's house, I sacrificed my own self. But there was a particular kind of reward in that. I was the last to go to sleep and the first to wake up. But when they praised me, when people said I was a good bride, I couldn't have been happier. To suffer is a bride's fate, I thought *[kurō suru no ga yome-san no shimei].* I thought I was fulfilling my destiny.

I did absolutely everything. But when I was washing the *bentō* boxes and I saw that they had eaten everything up *[kirei ni tabete kureta],* I was very happy. I thought to myself that the meal I made must have been good. Looking back on it, I don't know where that good bride came from or who she was. I was actually enjoying sacrificing myself *[Jibun o gisei ni suru no ga tanoshinde ita].* I thought there was a certain beauty in it. When

Obāsan got cancer, I looked after her until she died. And one week before Ojiisan died, I gave birth to a son. I knew how happy it made him that I'd produced an heir. And I felt that I had fulfilled my mission as a *yome-san*. Looking back on it, it all seems crazy. . . .

Sometimes I wonder if my husband was lonely during that time. I was so busy with the family. We had no married life. All he had to look forward to was drinking. He basically just came home to sleep.

Revenge, Strategy, and Entitlement

[Tell me how you think you've changed since coming to the Center.]

The first time I went to the Center for an educational seminar was in 1991. A specialist in psychosomatic medicine *[shinryō naika]* from Tachikawa General Hospital recommended it to me. At first I said I had no interest in going. Kadoyama seemed very far, and I'd never been on the Keio [train] line—I'd never even been to Shinjuku before! But the doctor said, "Now don't be making objections; it will really be for your own benefit to go," so I just mustered up the courage and made up my mind to go *[Sono toki yūki o dashite, "yoshi" to omotta]*. I decided I needed to start taking on more challenges in my life. That was always a flaw of mine—I never took enough initiative *[sekkyoku sei ga nai]*.

So that's where it all started. I became very serious about going, never missing a meeting. At first I couldn't stand it, talking in front of everyone. My heart was pounding—boom boom boom. I wouldn't hear a word that the person next to me said. It really took a year. After one year of listening to other people, I developed my own confidence.

I've done quite a lot of experimenting—taken lots of chances since then—with regard to my husband's sickness. When I pull something off, I praise myself inwardly, which I never did before. For example, when things between us were really bad, we stopped saying "thank you" to each other, ever. We used to say it after we got married, but after he started drinking and we'd been through all that, a kind of hatred developed between us and we stopped saying things like "good morning" or "thanks." I was the one to try again *[Watashi no hō kara chōsen shita]*. At first he didn't respond at all *[mutto shita]*. I'm sure he was wondering what in the world I was saying.

He'd been drinking for so long (1969 was the first time he collapsed). After he quit, he developed tuberculosis. His character changed and he became silent, depressed. We never had any conversation. He also lost the use of one of his legs. He used to just sit in front of the television in silence. He'd wake up, eat, take a nap, eat, watch television, and sleep again. He really wasn't a human being. So I didn't really have the desire to greet him.

But after he'd stopped drinking for one year, I took up the challenge of saying "Good morning." And gradually he started to help out around the house. He'd pull out the futons, wash the dishes. And I'd say "thank you" when he did those things. At first I couldn't say it, I was so embarrassed *[Saisho wa terekusakute ienai]*. But finally I said, "Thanks, Dad—that was a big help!" After that first time, it just popped right out. Human beings are like that—the first time is the hardest.

We drink tea, so I would say, "Okay, the tea is ready!" And he would say, "Right, thanks" *[arigatou]*. And I would say, "Not at all." Although recently we've taken to saying *"Sankyū"* [in English].

So then, after that I started experimenting with a lot of things. For example, once when I was coming home from the Center, I saw him coming home from work. I waved at him. For a second I was completely ashamed, but then he waved back! Now we do it every morning when he leaves.

[He's working again?]

He's working at a small business. For his age, he gets paid relatively little, but he also has to go to the hospital each week and so forth. We have enough to live on if we're not too indulgent *[zeitaku shinakereba]*. Once people start to indulge themselves, there's no limit. For me, it's enough that he's not drinking.

You see, since we got married I've always been the intervening type. I would check how much sake he'd had, continually tell him not to drink so much, and so forth. My whole attitude toward him used to be "don't do this, don't do that." Now I don't make those perpetual comments *[ichi ichi iwanai]*. I don't complain. Even now, when he has to go to a company New Year's party or something, I don't even say, "Don't drink" or "Be careful" before he leaves. He probably does drink something, but I figure that's his own problem *[sore wa honnin no mondai da kara]*. I don't ask him when he gets back either. When he slipped and started drinking again over New Year's, I didn't get involved one tiny bit. I refused to cooperate with his drinking behavior.

Of course, it was an enormous inner battle; I was terrified of his anger. "Buying sake is a wife's job!" he'd say. "You don't listen to what I say! *[Ore no iu koto kikanai no ka!]*" he'd yell. Once I told him we had no money, and he told me to go work as a prostitute! It was cruel. I told him about all these episodes later, but he has absolutely no memory of it. I think he may be feigning ignorance. Not that I don't forgive him. I wouldn't still be here if I hadn't forgiven him. But I can't forget. "That was really a blow" or "That was really awful," I say to him. If I tell him too much, he asks me to stop. In that case, I politely stop. "I'll resume at the next opportunity," I think to myself. Looking back on it, I really held my own.

I used to think, "Thanks to you, my entire life has been ruined!" I really had some horrible thoughts, you know, though I'm embarrassed about it now. I'd look at his sleeping face and feel infuriated; "I'd like to kill him," I thought. I considered strangling him. But that was when I was caught up in the pathology of the illness. After I'd been coming to the Center for a while, my daughter told me, "Mom, you've gotten so tough!" I used to be a teary-eyed woman who complained a lot and couldn't talk in front of people.

My daughter once told me that since he'd made me so miserable, she wished he would just hurry up and die *[konna ni haha o kurashimete shinda hō ga ii]*. I felt terrible that seeing my misery drove her to say such a thing. She said that if he died she wouldn't shed a tear. I've felt a lot of regret about spurring her to say something like that.

But now I've got much better strategies for dealing with him. Number one is to allow myself time. When he starts getting angry *[ka tto naru]*, instead of responding in kind right away, I go to the sink and slowly, slowly drink a glass of water. Then I come back and calmly say, "Now what you are saying is that, but what I am thinking is this."

For example, the other day he was separating the seeds from their pods one at a time when he was working in the garden. He said, "Help me with this, would you?" Now, before I would have said, "Yes, yes of course *[Hai hai!]*," but instead I said, "Oh me? That job's not for me. And I've got dinner to make. . . ." Then he said, "But it takes so long!" So I said, "Well if it's that much of a nuisance, why don't you just forget it?" "Because I'm doing it because I like it, that's why." So then I suggested that he do it more efficiently by letting the pods dry and then pounding on them. He said stubbornly, "I'm doing it because I like doing it this way." A couple of days later, I noticed he was pounding them. But I just stood and watched. I didn't say a word.

[Did you ever think of getting divorced?]

I thought I'd like some separation *[hanaretai to omotta]*, but I really couldn't just leave him behind. When I used to leave the house for even just a bit, I would forget everything. Then coming home again would be so awful. As I was turning the corner on my bike, my chest would tighten up painfully. But if I weren't around, he'd just be a burden to the neighbors and the relatives, and I didn't like that idea at all.

My daughter is *very diligent.* Just like me—I have that quality. I can't stand quitting in the middle of something. It just goes to show that there can be virtuous aspects of a fault. For example, with the housework, if I decide that I'm going to do something today, then I just cannot forgive myself for putting it off until tomorrow. "Diligence" would be a positive way of putting it.

TWO LIVES

In the context of Japan's unconditional surrender and the American-governed occupation, America came to represent individual liberty, self-expression, and egalitarianism to many Japanese. A mnemonic device taught to Japanese children to help them remember the word *democracy* was the phrase *"Dare demo kurashi ii,"* literally, "Anyone can live well." Images of American ebullience during the years of postwar prosperity (the land that "fed" the Japanese after the war) and the Kennedy years were piped into Japanese homes through television in the 1950s, as were glorified images of eccentricity and domestic cheerfulness on American sitcoms such as *The Brady Bunch* and *Bewitched.* In the 1980s, many Japanese still imagined a historical trajectory in which the 1950s were the heyday of American culture, a moment which was eventually soured by the country's defeat in the Vietnam War. There was a stark contrast between American postwar prosperity and national pride and Japanese defeat followed by the postwar years of poverty. Fukuda-san's observations about American soldiers who "were cheerful *[akarui]* and chatted loudly with each other *[becha becha shabettari shita],* laughing and chewing gum" are indicative of continuing Japanese perceptions of Americans as bold, loud, and uninhibited.

The grandiose agenda of the occupation was no less than to "democratize and demilitarize" Japan, an agenda that encompassed institutional reform from the ground up (Dower 1999: 69–72). Others have noted the irony entailed in the project of fomenting revolution by decree (a "revolution from above"), and in their stories of the occupation years, women often remarked on the many disjunctures between newfound ideologies of liberalism and democracy and continuing realities.

Occupation reforms dictated equality between men and women and sought to redefine marriage as a mutual agreement between partners, but change does not come so quickly. The projects women pursued in their recovery—self-expression *(jiko hyōgen)*, true self *(jibun rashisa)*, spontaneity, and self-care *(jibun o daiji ni suru)*—which were inscribed in the language of American popular psychology, reflected the values of American individualism, though, as I shall show, women rarely achieved them or even sincerely aspired to do so. This was particularly true in the way that women approached the question of marriage and family.

The household system was initially formulated by the Tokugawa feudal government (1603–1868) to establish the village as the basic social and economic unit in rural Japan and the household as the production unit responsible for revenue. Peasants cultivated land under their own management, and every household became a separate unit, in theory with no differentiation among households of a village community. The household became the central organizing structure of economic cooperation, property, and political relations. Solidarity of the household was based on performance of duties and obligations between the members. And households often banded together to form *kumi*—local neighborhood organizations of households—to cooperate in labor exchange, credit associations, marriage ceremonies, and so forth. Thus, it has been argued that the household, the local corporate group, and the village formed the basis of Japanese social organization. Later, these became an efficient basis for social control and state administration (Nakane 1967; Robert Smith 1961).

The Japanese kinship system, promoted as a universal standard during the Meiji era, constructed the family as a corporate entity, in which family property and the management of the family business or farm were passed down through the "main line" *(honkei)* of the eldest son. In what is known as a stem-family pattern, the eldest son married and brought his wife into his household. Younger sons were required to marry and form their own branch lineage *(bunkei)*. Daughters married out of the family and moved into another family, their names crossed off the family register and added to their husband's. (This is still the practice today, although the kinship system has been formally reconfigured.) In a family with only daughters, the eldest daughter would bring her husband into the family line as the next male heir in a practice known as adoption (*yōshi*). Thus, in contrast to the Chinese descent system and other unilineal descent systems, which privilege biological descent, the Japanese stem-family system prioritized economic productivity and continuity of family property over biological heredity (Befu 1966; Nakane 1967).

The stem-family system emphasized above all economic productivity and self-sufficiency. Working-class women and farming women were chiefly counted as workers, valued for their productive labor and their capacity to contribute to the family enterprise, particularly through producing heirs (Befu 1966; Nakane 1967; Lebra 1984: 78). Women were situated at the bottom of the family hierarchy, particularly when they first joined their husbands' families as young brides (*yome*). The role of the *yome*, particularly the wife of a first-born son (the heir to the household, property, or business, and head of the main family line), was an exacting one, and in many households women had few rights, privileges, or privacy, and no disposable income.[3] In the contemporary context of the meetings at the Center, the *yome* embodied the very ethic of self-sacrifice and the privileging of role over self that Fukuda-san disavowed; a daughter-in-law was considered the "wife of the house," not just the wife of the first-born son. Ueno Chizuko cites Yanagita Kunio's description of the wedding ceremony: "The bride exchanged cups of *sake* with the bridegroom three times; but before exchanging cups with her future husband—not afterward—she exchanged cups with his parents, her future parents-in-law. The wedding ceremony was thus an adoption ritual rather than a marriage contract between two individuals; the family first adopted a girl as a daughter-in-law and then married her to the successor of the house" (Ueno 1987: 132).

Many scholars have noted the extent to which the consciousness of *ie*, or extended household, continues to permeate Japanese family life. Although Fukuda-san described the *ie* system as customs that were "falling by the wayside" at that time, her decision to leave her adopted mother and to marry into her husband's family (since he was the eldest son) reflect these practices, as she notes. Fukuda-san's mother defied these practices to a greater extent. By insisting on staying and keeping her own home and by continually fending off advice from the extended family of her birth-mother and father, she essentially founded an independent female-dominated household, where authority was not derived and legitimated through the presence of a father.

The system Fukuda-san described and her work as a *yome-san* reflect a view of marriage as very much in service of the family rather than as an expression of love between the couple. The pride she took as a young bride ministering to the needs of her family suggests that women's satisfaction came from meeting these needs. For the women at the Center, marriage was first and foremost about being a good provider for husbands and children—creating a positive household atmosphere and meeting the needs of each family member. Providing a household in which children were successful in moving up was central to women's pride. Fukuda-san acknowledged that she derived satisfaction (when the family ate everything in their lunch boxes), credibility (when older women in the neighborhood praised her for looking after her mother-in-law so well), and ultimately authority (the family purse was ultimately handed down to her) through her work.

Fukuda-san often described herself as having lived two lives, one before her husband's alcoholism and the other after. Yet, although Fukuda described her life in these terms, it is possible to see continuities between the two. In the context of the household system, the young bride gradually gains authority and entitlement in the home as the mother-in-law's power fades. Women pay their dues when they are young and must learn the ways of the household. Later empowerment is sanctioned by earlier sacrifices. (Similarly, Fukuda-san's mother-in-law claimed entitlement to travel with her friends and relax while Fukuda-san managed the house.) Fukuda-san's early struggles were instrumental to the emergence of her present self, even while she wished to claim that her "new self" was the product of leaving these "old values" behind.

Although Fukuda-san described her "recovery" using an American vocabulary of "independence" and "self-realization," it was also embedded in traditional views of gender and entitlement. It was partially enabled by her husband's illness and subsequent recovery and the suffering she endured during that time. She never thought about separating from her husband, nor did she talk about the problems she faced in terms of social equality. The power she later attained came not from redefining marriage or gender roles but rather from acting more strategically within them: for instance, carefully choosing her words while going to the kitchen sink for a glass of water. Fukuda-san was still financially dependent on her husband, and she was still regarded by family and neighbors as responsible for his health and well-being. Her consciousness-raising at the Center did not change this. However, it did make her more savvy at managing her husband. Though Fukuda-san's encounter with the Center was dictated by her husband's illness, it was both her husband's recovery and her own history of sacrifice and adherence to prescribed wifely conduct that enabled her, ultimately, to take certain liberties in her relationship with him and to cultivate herself. That is, rather than ultimately breaking free of conventional social expectations, Fukuda-san capitalized on her years of enacting them. Fukuda-san's success was very much imagined in the context of traditional constructions of gender roles and women's empowerment.

Chapter 5 | THE INESCAPABLE DISCOURSE OF MOTHERHOOD

LEARNING TO BE A MOTHER

We at the City of Chigasaki Department of Social
Welfare aim to support all those mothers and fathers
who are engaged in the endeavor of childrearing—to
enjoy the production of a home with charm and taste.
We understand your extreme busyness, but we are offering
a "How to solve your childrearing difficulties" workshop
as delineated on the attached schedule and are [humbly]
awaiting your attendance.

When the city of Chigasaki announced a five-week seminar on "Solving
Your Child-Rearing Difficulties" *[Kosodate nayami o kaiketsu shiyō]*, several young mothers in my neighborhood began making plans to go. The
seminar was conducted and taught by the "child-rearing advisor" of one
of the city's day care centers, the chief counselor of the community child-
rearing counseling service, and several workers from local day care centers.
The schedule was as follows:

1. Playing with mother—creating a rhythm
2. Discovering the heart of childhood
3. Let's learn to play with cloth books
4. Children in groups—reports from the day care centers
5. Child-rearing question and answer

The motivation for the seminar was to combat the growing trend toward pressuring children from an early age to begin climbing the ladder to social success by preparing for entrance exams, attending cram schools, and undertaking numerous extracurricular activities at the expense of having time to play. "Nowadays children must make an appointment to play," the child-rearing advisor admonished. "But when they grow up, it won't matter if they can't play the piano, swim, or how good their grades are. The *only* thing that matters is the ability to interact with others *[hito to kakawaru chikara]*. Kids must master the art of human relations," the child-rearing advisor announced at the first gathering. To illustrate the point that children were growing up too quickly, the adviser told the (seemingly apocryphal) story of a family where both parents worked: "The mother came home and found her son had invited his elementary school friends over and served them brandy and cigarettes! They greeted her with high spirits and red faces."

A central theme of the seminar series was that a mother's presence is key to her child's social development and that social development is more important than educational accomplishment. In this context, the Chigasaki child-rearing seminars set out to teach mothers how to play with their children. At each session, we sang songs, danced dances, looked at handmade cloth books with pockets and pop-outs, all sewn by hand by workers at the local day care centers. We played the "name game," and after each child inserted his or her name into the song the day care advisor (who was sixty years old) would sing, for girls, "What a cute name . . . !" and for boys, "What a strong-sounding name . . . !" We played clapping games. "Pachi pachi, ton ton" (onomatopoetic words for clapping sounds), the daycare worker called. "All kids will smile when they play this!"

"See how big mommy's hands are?"

"Now look at your kids and feel *their* hands—do they have a fever?"

Some of the dances were rather complicated, but the mothers were determined, some of them carrying their children while proceeding through the steps: lie on the floor, kick, jump, squat, bend in all directions, clap, leapfrog. Many of the mothers seemed to know the steps already, as well as the lyrics to the songs. Finally the teachers made a tunnel and we passed under their arms and proceeded out the door to the tune of "Dinah Blow Your Horn." Outside, as the young mothers settled their children into the small back seats attached to their bicycles, they cooed, "Wasn't that fun?"

"Isn't that nice, you got a balloon!" "You don't need to go pee-pee before we go, do you?" and "You made so many friends, didn't you?"

In part, the child-rearing seminar was simply a performative space for mothers, a place to validate the importance of child-rearing. Nobody there needed to learn how to play—the entire room was pandemonium from the minute we walked in to the minute we left, with children running wildly about and jumping up on stage, mothers in hot pursuit, fathers frantically videotaping. Mio, a young woman who lived next door to me, usually disappeared as soon as we arrived, chasing her two-year-old son, Shion, up and down the stairs while he explored the building. As the principal of the day care center had once informed us, "Children like to be followed—not to follow." Usually, the day would began with little Shion reaching over to take my pen and then beginning to scribble on my notepad. Initially, I assumed his mother would demand that he return it to me, but instead she shrugged helplessly and casually offered the thick colored felt-tip she'd brought from home. After each meeting she would say—a touch self-righteously—that she had been too busy playing with her son to absorb the lessons of the child-rearing experts.

Many of the lectures and presentations emphasized the difficulty and importance of child-rearing. A public day care worker who made a presentation on "a day at the day care center" spoke minutely about the daily day care schedule, how they created a daily "rhythm," how they taught children to enjoy and appreciate food, how they carried children who didn't want to walk, and how they gently cajoled children into following the daily day care regimen. For example, for those children who only wanted to eat white things, they sprinkled a little seaweed on their rice until they gradually got used to eating other items. A school counselor came and spoke of rising rates of children's problems, including school-refusal syndrome and borderline personality disorder. The presentation proceeded in an alarmist, quasi-scientific vein, as the counselor handed out a list of "character liabilities" that can cause vulnerability to Borderline Personality Syndrome (*Kyōkai Jinkaku Keisei Shōgai*)—a highly vague and broad diagnostic category in the Japanese context. The lecture repeatedly emphasized that good mothering could prevent these problems. One child-rearing adviser began his comments by saying, "One must be so *smart* to be a good mother these days. Did you know that only one out of every four children is born smart? Sixty percent of children's intelligence comes from their mothers."

As we pedaled home, Shion fell asleep and Mio asked if Americans think that raising children is a very difficult task. "Because, in Japan, it's considered *very* difficult," she said emphatically. Kyōko (Mio's cousin-in-law, who lived in the area) added, "The family is the smallest unit of society. And women are the 'sun' of the family. The entire color of a home can change depending on her mood *[Okāsan no kimochi de ie no iro ga kawatte kuru]*. That's why we all need to study little by little."

A session entitled "Let's Learn to Play with Cloth Books" revealed how motherhood is associated with agrarian communalism, and through this, "traditional" values of community, cooperation, hard work, frugality, and the appreciation of material goods.[1] I began to notice that many of the games we played involved vegetables. Vegetables evoke not only Japan's agrarian past but also the image of home-style cooking *(katei ryōri)*, domesticity, and, of course, mother. A typical home-style dish, boiled vegetables *(onimono),* is associated with loving and painstaking home cooking, since vegetables are best flavored by simmering in a fish-based broth on low heat for a long time.

"The Vegetable Song," which was handed out on a photocopied song sheet so that we could all sing together, went like this:

> A cabbage goes *kya kya kya.*
> A cucumber goes *kyu kyu kyu.*
> A tomato goes *ton ton ton.*
> Lettuce is *pari pari pari.*
> And bean sprouts go *mosha mosha mosha.*
> [Tickle your child.]

Other songs focused on the making of agricultural materials into packaged products—a reminder that these items too originated in nature:

> The potato in the field (hey!), the potato,
> *Moko moko* woke up one day, woke up one day,
> *Goshi goshi* he washed his face, washed his face,
> He took off his pajamas and was too fat!
>
> *Ton ton ton*—to be more slender,
> He soaked in a hot oil bath,
> And became potato chips . . .
> They're done! They're done!

During the "How to Play with Cloth Books" session, the senior day care mother (she was in her fifties) proudly demonstrated the story of the salad. She began the lesson by praising the virtues of books. "Mother and child playing together, a book tucked in between them: this is an ideal way to be affectionate with each other." Then she put on a large felt apron and read, "Once upon a time, all the vegetables lived together happily in a big field." At this point she pulled a number of stuffed vegetables out of a large pocket and stuck them to her chest with velcro—radish-*san*, carrot-*san*, and pepper-*san*. (She appended the honorific suffix -*san* to the word *radish*, which adults do when engaging with children to convey a sense of appreciation.) The vegetables invited each other over for a big gathering. Parsley-*san* and lemon-*san* came too. "Thanks for inviting us," they said graciously. Then mayonnaise-*san* arrived. (Mayonnaise is a popular salad condiment.) "'Let me into your group too, please!' he said. And they all became playmates—full of vitamins A, B, and C!" Then suddenly, as she squeezed the mayonnaise, a yellow ribbon flew from its top, and the vegetables escaped in all directions—each making its own distinct noise. "Then they all became a delicious salad," she happily concluded.

The child-rearing seminar was one glimpse into the way in which child-rearing is viewed as a project that is difficult, important, and fun—messages that permeate Japanese society and are sent by the state and the social services supported by the state. In this chapter, I explore the discourse of motherhood, which is both constraining and compelling, through the lens of the mothers at the Center, who attended meetings to learn how to cope with their troubled teenagers. The women at the Center who were attempting to cope with their children's drug addiction faced a particularly difficult dilemma. For women married to alcoholic men, there were avenues of recourse that would allow them some freedom, while they remained within the dominant construction of a good marriage. Although many women lived in tragic situations, the wives' meetings were characterized by witty stories (often poking fun at husbands' idiosyncrasies) and stories of days away from home with friends or pursuing other activities. For mothers, no such sphere existed. The tenor of the meetings was typically somber and fretful and rarely featured humor. The social demands placed upon Japanese mothers and the demands of "recovery" defined by American discourses seemed entirely at odds.

In contrast with their attitudes toward their husbands, women enjoyed indulging and caring for their children. They spoke of "not being able to resist" taking care of their children, indulging them in small pleasures, and bailing them out of difficult situations—even when this was linked to destructive behavior on the part of their children. In daily life (though not among the women at the Center, who were coping with serious problems), women often speak with pride about the way their children are *amaete iru* (overly indulged) or refer playfully to their children as "little troublemakers" *(itazura),* implying their indulgence. A forty-year-old housewife once told me that she hadn't been sleeping well because at 4 A.M. each night her sons came into the parents' bed, making up all sorts of excuses, such as they "saw a bug or their buttocks are itchy." She told me, "Really, our house is the epitome of *amae.* Of course, we're always saying to one another that we really must be more strict, but . . ." *(Uchi wa amae sono mono desu yo. Itsumo motto kibishiku shinakereba to iinagara).* Her complaint was somewhat disingenuous; having her five- and seven-year-old sons come into her bed at night was a source of pleasure and pride.

To successfully implement the notion of tough love put forward by the Center, women had to make distinctions between being a good mother and letting their children take advantage of them, distinctions that were difficult to make in the context of a discourse of motherhood that celebrates the "merging" of mother and child and imagines a woman's self-cultivation as taking place largely through the process of raising children.

In addition, despite continuing ideologies of motherhood and "total care," the life of teenagers has changed dramatically in the past fifteen years in Japan. In the 1950s, 1960s, and 1970s, the pressures of the exam system meant that the lives of most teenagers were largely confined to home and school (Rohlen 1983). Historically, most middle-class teenagers did not work, and participation in after-school club activities was a central aspect of social life. Yet the wealth of consumer opportunities, the new demand for part-time workers, and growing class disparities have created a new sphere between home and school, where increasing numbers of teenagers earn their own spending money and spend greater amounts of time relaxing, shopping, patronizing video arcades and karaoke bars, and enjoying time with members of the opposite sex (White 1994). At the same time, these profound changes have not been accompanied by a new ethic of individual responsibility, and a rising incidence of petty crime, drug abuse (most commonly paint thinner, amphetamines, or alcohol, as these are the only drugs that are readily available), alcohol poisoning, and teenage pregnancy has accompanied these new freedoms. Mothers at the Center had to cope with these changes and contradictions, and their children's drug abuse was commonly intertwined with other issues, including juvenile delinquency and debt.

MOTHERHOOD AS WOMANHOOD

Much has been written on the links between motherhood and the projects of nationalism and modernization in Japan, as well as on the centrality of motherhood to women's lives. I will a highlight a few historical points here in an effort to convey the broader social and historical roots of the pressure women felt to continue to support and indulge their children.

The endorsement of motherhood by the state has its roots in the Meiji era (1868–1912). The idea marked a departure from Edo period views of the "breeding mother," which emphasized the importance of reproduction, while paying little attention to child-rearing. Women's lowly status and mental incompetence were thought to make them unfit to raise children.[2] Meiji era discourse, in contrast, described child-rearing as "the essential task of women" and emphasized that the teaching and socializing of children required training and education, making women worthy of an education, at least according to some (Niwa 1993: 73). The important shift that occurred in the Meiji era was not the absolute rise in the status of women. In reality, women had few political rights (including the right to vote) and the education of women in practice lagged far behind the ideology (Niwa 1993: 75). Yet women were seen as useful servants of the state and were drawn into public discourse and public roles through their status as mothers.[3]

The image of the good wife and wise mother, discussed earlier, described women as quasi-civil servants, raising children and keeping house with diligence and frugality in order to better serve the state (Nolte and Hastings 1991). In the prewar and postwar periods, women continued to use their maternal credentials as a passport into broader social and political spheres. Most of women's many gains in the subsequent years were realized through the state's support of motherhood and women's support of the state. Middle-class postwar feminist organizations, such as the New Japan Women's League, explicitly sought to represent "the voice of housewives and mothers in politics" (Garon 1997). "Yours is the voice from the kitchen," Oku Mumeo told her audience in 1946, as she was campaigning to become one of the first women elected to the Diet (Obituary, *The Economist,* July 19, 1997). Even today, dominant strands of feminist activism (consumer movements, environmental movements, neighborhood improvement organizations, etc.) continue to be dominated by motherhood feminists who see their status as mothers as a key impetus to their activism (see for example, Lewis 1978; LeBlanc 1999).[4] In fact, some have even claimed that women's movements, such as the antinuclear movement, rely so heavily on participants' identity as mothers that they exclude those who do not have children.

In the postwar period, more than ever, the role of motherhood became central to most women's identity. The totalizing division of labor that occurred in the postwar years placed women fully in charge of the family domain, managing children's daily life, purchasing their clothing, school supplies, and equipment, and participating in the broader politics of education through the PTA. Moreover, as the standardized exam system created increased opportunities for upward mobility, children became central to a family's social status. The "pedigree society" *(gakureki shakai)* that emerged meant that a degree from a prestigious university could be key to determining one's future. In this context, child-rearing came to be viewed not as a "discrete task," but rather as the cultivation of resources or human capital (White 1987: 154). Children's (particularly a son's) success in the educational system bolsters a family's social status and economic stability (if the son returns to support the parents in their old age). The importance accorded to child-rearing also gained support from the view of children as moldable. The exam system that serves as the gateway to children's academic success emphasizes (and rewards) students' efforts in studying for exams; the importance of innate intelligence is minimized. A mother's work is central to this effort (White 1987).

As others have pointed out, a mother's work is seen as the foundation of family members' success outside the home. Mothers' work is actively solicited by schools in the form of frequent meetings with teachers, participation in the PTA, help with homework regimens, and preparation of school supplies and equipment. In her experience enrolling her own son at a local (private) kindergarten, Anne Allison describes the tireless work that is demanded of women as partners in their children's education, including implementing "summer discipline," making daily routines "fun" (by participating in morning exercise together or communicating over a "hearty breakfast"), and preparing the many items Japanese schools require students to bring with them, such as homemade bags, smocks, and hand-stitched labels. In each case, a mother's love is seen as the enabling factor in embedding the child into the disciplinary routines of the educational system (2000: 112–14).

In a range of works that explore the importance of motherhood in facilitating the demands of postwar economic growth, Allison demonstrates that Japanese mothers' work not only makes the reproduction of human labor possible, but actually makes regimes of discipline and productivity outside the home more palatable, changing the complexion of public life (1991, 2000). She writes, "It is women, as mothers, who not only oversee the educational regimens of their children but also, and more importantly perhaps, fuse these closely with practices of maternal nurturance, indulgence, and love" (2000: vii–viii). In her ethnography of the Japanese lunch box *(obentō)*, Allison shows how the demanding regimen of the school day is facilitated by the home-prepared lunch box. The lunch box, which children must bring with them to school each day, is a symbol of Japanese tradition and aesthetics. It is consumed by children in the context of a daily regimen (children must first wash their hands, eat together at the same time, and finish their meals) that is meant to instill good values: order, discipline, good hygiene, and the prevention of wastefulness. In Allison's analysis, the *obentō,* which signifies a mother's love and caring attention, when consumed in the context of the school, allows the child to associate the mother's love with the necessity of discipline and good manners, "suturing" home and motherhood to the regimes of productivity and discipline demanded of children at school. The *obentō* makes the "habitual desirable" (2000: xv), rendering the constraining practices of classroom order, self-discipline, and punctuality ideologically compelling to the child by linking these to the mother's love (1991).

The many arms of the welfare state that support and educate families continue to reaffirm motherhood as women's primary purpose. Although the state's presence in the management of family life has waned since the prewar years, to a surprising degree motherhood continues to be administered by the state and children continue to be viewed as national resources. In the context of the local welfare offices that administer vaccination forms, health-care guidance, and various social support services, women are taught that being a mother is cherished, difficult work. On government forms, it is the mother (not the father) who is typically listed as the child's "custodian" *(hogosha)* (though the father, as wage-earner, is considered the head of household). Community health-care centers sponsor childbirth classes and mother-child "play groups," which include instructions for making baby food. Once registered at the ward office as the mother of a young child, one is likely to receive invitations to monthly get-togethers sponsored by community social services, at which mothers chat while cooking seasonal snacks or making crafts. Schools and day care facilities require intimate involvement on the part of the mother, sometimes including the preparation of homemade goods, bags, and foods. Some local governments even sponsor courses on global issues, the environment, and self-development. The message is that being a good mother is more than simply giving birth and providing for a child materially; it involves education and self-cultivation (Sasagawa 2002). Included is an understanding that motherhood is a public project that betters society, not only the family itself.

Given these structures of motherhood, it is perhaps not surprising that for many women, their children continue to be both their chief claim to accomplishment in life and their most intimate human relationship. Because the state and all its constituent institutions (as well as ordinary people) view women chiefly as mothers, for most women, motherhood eclipses all other identities. A woman with a small child is apt to be addressed as "Mother" by a range of people, from her husband to the day care worker to shop clerks.

The culture of motherly nurturance is entwined with a culture celebrating childhood and childlike innocence—the often remarked "culture of the cute" *(kawaii bunka),* which permeates consumer goods and media entertainment. Childhood beguiles and commands resources, and childlike products appeal to all age groups. Depending on the place of residence, children may receive full health-care coverage until the age of six. Public day care centers are funded to provide the best care possible, including homemade, high-quality food for infants; pedagogy for children is taken quite seriously, starting at birth. And as is often remarked, children are treated quite permissively, forgiven for public disruptions or transgressions of etiquette in a way that others would not be.

The fascination with and love of young children was brought home to me when I returned to Japan several years later with my son. Although a foreign baby is always an object of exotic admiration, we were stopped not only by middle-aged women, but by construction workers, teenagers, and even elementary-school girls, who cupped the baby's face in their hands, petted his cheeks, and made a bit of conversation with him. One evening, when I joined a family with whom I was acquainted for dinner, it wasn't long before the father, a restrained middle-aged businessman, began pinching our son's cheeks, making every attempt to engage him, including calling the family phone on his cell phone so that my son could hear the ring and answer.

"TOUGH LOVE"

The notion of "tough love" has been central to American therapeutic movements that have sought to counsel parents on dealing with troubled teens. "Tough love" (*tafu rabu,* in its Japanese translation) describes a style of parenting that is meant to be effective in managing an adolescent who is "acting out." Like techniques for managing a substance-abusing adult, tough love involves setting clear rules and limits for teenagers and declining to rescue them from the consequences of their own bad behavior. On their web site and in their book, *Toughlove: A Self-Help Manual for Parents Troubled by Teen-Age Behavior,* the founders of Tough Love International, Phyllis and David York, advise parents to set limits regarding the major issues they face with their teenagers ("I will not pay my teenager's traffic fines," "I will not fight with school officials about my teenager's behavior," "I will not tolerate disrespect/violence in my home," etc.) and then enforce these limits while refraining from either rancor or guilt. They offer a "Parents' Bill of Rights," including the right to "a night's sleep without worrying about where your child is," and encourage parents to "stop 'helping' your child and start taking care of yourself." The web site quotes Erma Bombeck, the syndicated columnist, on the process of raising children:

> I see children as kites. You spend a lifetime trying to get them off the ground. You run with them until you're both breathless—they crash—they hit the rooftop—you pat and comfort, adjust and teach. You watch them lifted by the wind and assure them that someday they'll fly.

Finally they are airborne; they need more string and you keep letting it out. But with each twist of the ball of twine, there is a sadness that goes with joy. The kite becomes more distant, and you know it won't be long before that beautiful creature will snap the lifeline that binds you together and will soar as it is meant to soar, free and alone. Only then do you know that you did your job.[5]

The notion of tough love revolves around the assumption that the project of adolescence entails separating from one's parents by developing autonomy and an independent identity. The language of rights is an important aspect of this discourse, particularly the rights of the parents to set rules and to be respected. While the notion of tough love makes sense from the standpoint of managing juvenile behavior, the assumptions that underlie it were entirely foreign to the way the mothers at the Center were accustomed to view child-rearing and the social role of the mother.

For example, the kinship system that became universalized in the Meiji period constructed children as almost property of the household (particularly the eldest son). Parents invest in children and children in turn repay their parents, chiefly by taking care of them when they grow old. In earlier periods, women talked about the "three belongings": first to the father, then to the husband, and finally to the eldest son. Although these ideas have changed in principle in the postwar period, when the family was officially designated as two generations, in practice ideas did not change so quickly. The expenses of education, combined with the shortage of social assistance or government money for caring for the elderly, ensure that children continue to depend on their parents and that parents continue to depend on their children. The question of when this investment of resources should stop remains ambiguous.[6] Parents transfer money to children through a weekly allowance *(okozukai)*, New Year's gifts *(otoshidama)*, and so forth. Yet these small gifts often blur over into more substantial forms of support. Parents are expected to fund children's weddings and first homes, and even into adulthood family finances are often blurred.

As teenagers grow increasingly interested in big ticket items, such as computers and motorcycles, they often turn to black-market lending organizations, usually run by mobsters, which offer loans with phenomenally high interest rates *(sarakin)* in return for keeping the business secret and requiring little collateral. The potential for accruing debt is high, and debt is generally viewed as irresponsible and slovenly in a society that uses credit cards largely for convenience and encourages savings as a matter of national policy. The issue of whether to bail a teenager out of debt was a key tension that women confronted at the Center. While the dictates of tough love demanded that they shouldn't, the dictates of Japanese society demanded that they should. Often it was only when fathers became involved (and that was rarely) that women found legitimation to turn their children down.

In addition to being permitted continuing financial dependence, middle-class children are generally not expected to perform household duties and are often discouraged from taking on after-school employment. In what White has referred to as the "reproduction of immaturity," many middle- and upper-middle-class housewives expect little from either their sons or daughters in terms of domestic chores, because they feel they should protect them through the long ordeal of exam preparation necessary for academic advancement (2002: 142–43). In part for financial reasons, many young people continue to live with their parents through college and into the early years of working life. In one of the families White studied, Ichirō, a twenty-five-year-old worker at Chiba Motors, chose to commute two hours to work rather than rent an apartment near his office. His mother prepared his breakfast and dinner, ironed his suits, and nursed him through his hangovers (142–43).

For women in particular, continuing involvement in their children's lives is strategic: they offer help in child-rearing and added financial support (often materialized as small gifts, gifts for grandchildren, etc.). For mothers, particularly women who don't work, there are pleasures associated with continuing intimacy with their children and a continuing sense of purpose. As children require more financial help to get started in their lives and as a generation of middle-aged adults born just before or after the war increasingly has the money to give, children's prolonged ties to their families—both financial and emotional—have become a topic of broader social criticism.

Indeed, the Oedipal narratives that have been central to Anglo-American psychiatry—the imperative that the child renounce his love for his mother for fear of punishment (castration) by the father and the accompanying notion that a child must renounce the nurturance and femininity associated with the mother in order to join the world of political power and autonomy associated with the father (Chodorow 1991)—have not animated Japanese psychiatry or psychology, nor have they permeated popular culture. As Anne Allison has written, the Oedipal narrative is even less resonant for boys than for girls in Japan, since boys are under more pressure to succeed academically, and thus rely more heavily on the mother's continuing help (2000: 24). In Allison's essay "Transgresssions of the Everyday," she analyzes a number of sensationalized stories of "mother-son incest" that appeared in the popular press in the 1980s. The stories reveal what is perceived to be a fine line between socially sanctioned, indeed required, motherly behaviors (gently guiding and encouraging a son through the exam preparation process) and unhealthy, transgressive behavior such as incest (Allison 2000: 123–45).

It is noteworthy that the discourse on mothering that emerged in Japan in the 1950s and 1960s (which is still very much present) suggests that childhood dependency lays the foundation for future success and social engagement; the path from motherly nurturance to adult competence is imagined as one of continuities more than ruptures. Furthermore, the mother's nurturance is regarded not as something a child needs to overcome or "get past" in order to advance in the world but rather as essential to his or her success. In the limited number of child-rearing seminars that I attended, *sukinshippu* (skinship, a term initially coined by Ashley Montague, the anthropologist who promoted motherhood as women's chief role, emphasizing the virtue of "touching") was continually emphasized as the foundation for social participation and humanity itself *(ningen rashisa),* and women were told that "dependency leads to independence" *(izon kara jiritsu e).*

In the 1960s, Japanese developmental psychologists drew on conservative thinkers such as Montague and on John Bowlby's notion of "attachment theory," both of which emphasize the central importance of the formation of a bond between mother and child through continual physical proximity.[7] Comparative studies of child-rearing manuals have shown that a distinctive feature of Japanese texts is their strong support of co-sleeping, cobathing, and continual physical intimacy with the child, including the traditional practice of the mother carrying the baby on her back throughout the day rather than putting the baby down to sleep by itself (Boocock 1999: 10).[8] In contrast with American mothers, who expend much energy verbally engaging with the baby and trying to draw it out, the Japanese mother "views her baby much more as an extension of herself" (Caudill and Schooler 1973: 327).[9] Similarly, a child's success in school is credited to the skills of the mother, just as his failure speaks badly of her. The continual collaboration of the mother with the child in his studies, as Suzanne Vogel noted, historically has been seen not as over-protective but rather as a praiseworthy sign of devotion and self-sacrifice (1978: 19). The notions of "motherly nature" *(bosei)* and "motherly love" *(boseiai)*—the love a mother "instinctually" has for her child—are touted not only among psychologists and child-rearing specialists but in popu-lar discourse. Once, when I was purchasing a used bicycle from the local mom-and-pop store, the owner of the store told me that although the basket (where my son would sit) was a little beat up, with a bit of "mother's love" *(okāsan no aijō de)* I could make a cushion to make my son more comfortable.[10]

Indeed, the stories women told at the mothers' meetings revealed the intimate level at which the mothers were involved in their children's daily lives—the absence of boundaries between their own concerns and their children's. This involvement was almost taken for granted in their narra-tives, and even the social workers (the implementers of tough love) often seemed not to question it, but to me it was surprising. In one story, a young mother matter-of-factly remarked that she knew that her daughter was sexually active, but that she had been checking her daughter's underwear regularly and was relieved to know that her daughter was menstruating (and therefore not pregnant). In another example, a young mother recounted a story that she felt described her newfound ability to let her college-age son lead his own life. Her son had moved out of the house and was rent-ing his own apartment:

Mizuta *desu*. My son is living alone now and for the first time in a while I went to visit him at his apartment. He had lost some weight—like me, he has a tendency to eat a lot and be heavy—and looked pretty good. He had been to the dentist to take care of some teeth problems. And he was keeping active. But his room was a mess! He said that he had cleaned it two days ago, but everything was strewn around. He does his laundry but he doesn't fold it afterward, so it was all wadded up in balls. But I was very casual and paid no notice to all of this and said I'd be on my way *[ki ni naranai de "Ja ne" to iu kanji de]*.

Mizuta-san had taken in virtually every detail of her son's life and environs, but surveillance of her son's personal hygiene, the order of his space, and his schedule was not regarded as unusual for a mother. In fact, she told the story as evidence of her own "recovery." These intimacies, which struck me as breaches of privacy, were simply taken for granted; indeed, they were constructed as aspects of being a good, caring mother.

The notion of the nurturing mother as overly domineering or as a noxious influence on the child has emerged only recently in Japanese popular culture, as mothers' motivations are seen as having shifted from self-sacrifice to selfishness, based on the cultivation of the child as a "pet" and on a desire for middle-class upward mobility. (I discuss these emerging discourses in greater depth in the concluding chapter.)

WHO IS RESPONSIBLE FOR A YOUNG ADULT?

The notion of women's enduring responsibility for their children and the centrality of motherhood to women's identity form the backdrop of the dilemma of the mothers at the Center. Iwao (1993) has pointed out that mothers are often both praised and blamed in public for their children's accomplishments. Investigations of criminals and reporting on criminal cases often mention the perpetrator's mother and even drag her into the media limelight.[11]

Parents' responsibility for teenagers is deeply imbricated with systems of education, kinship, and social control. The parent's assumption of responsibility for a child (rather than the child's responsibility for him or herself) is so deeply assumed that one often sees parents quickly step forward and apologize when their children act out or misbehave in public, without saying so much as one thing to the child himself. In one case presented during the weekly case supervision conference at the Center, a high school student had borrowed large amounts of money from several of his classmates and failed to pay it back. To punish him, the principal contrived with the parents to have them come to school and to have the student watch as his creditors lined up and his parents humbly bowed, apologized, and then paid back each of them in turn. This tactic rests on the assumption that parents are nominally responsible for their children's behavior, and that seeing his parents suffer for his bad behavior would persuade the student to repent. When the social worker who supervised the case conferences heard this story, she virtually howled with laughter. "That's no punishment," she quipped. "That's incitement to do it again!"

Women at the Center were often called upon by teachers, dorm mothers, legal officials, neighbors, physicians, and relatives to intervene on behalf of their children or apologize for them. The women continually asked themselves if they had done something wrong to make their children into substance abusers, and these doubts were reinforced by welfare bureaucrats, legal officials, social workers, and others. One woman, on a visit to the juvenile delinquency office after her daughter got in a fight, was asked to fill out a questionnaire that included a question on whether or not she had breast-fed her children.

In one of the more poignant moments I witnessed at the meetings, Hanawa-san spoke of the early days of her marriage and her and her husband's struggle to build their small business. At the end of a story about her son's recent rebellion, she recounted, "I wanted to be able to give him breast milk but I didn't have that luxury. We built our small shop out of borrowed money . . . I didn't have time to feed him milk, so I strapped a bottle on the side of his basket so it wouldn't fall—I worry that his mother-child contact [sukinshippu] was insufficient. We put him in day care from an early age. He really didn't get a lot of physical attention until he was in about second grade." Her voice started to tremble and tears trickled from her eyes. "It was terrible for my child, and perhaps that's why he grew up this way," she ended.

At another meeting, Abe-san told this story: "Abe desu. The other week I met up with my siblings to go and visit our father. At dinner, my older sister said that I'd botched my child-rearing [kosodate ga shippai shita]." As she said this, Abe-san, who was ordinarily extremely stoic and chose her words with great precision, suddenly burst into tears. She continued, "I've had this thought myself before but never had it put to me so bluntly. It was a shock. At that moment, I felt so remote from my siblings. They all have successful, proper families [seikō shita, chanto shita katei o motte iru]. My sister feels that the fact that I was working is what ruined my children, since I didn't need to work for economic reasons."

In a similarly heartbreaking episode, Abe-san spoke of her daughter's abortion and how to manage her daughters' emerging sexuality. The women at the Center were all from generations that condemned premarital sex, and knowing that their daughters were sexually active troubled them. Early in the year that I attended the meetings, Abe-san described how her daughter had become pregnant and had an abortion. She emphasized that she herself felt responsible for the incident:

> Abe *desu*. I'm here because of my daughter's paint thinner. Now she's much better and the house is a more cheerful place, but I've had other things to worry about. She had been going over to a boy's house, and in June we thought she might be pregnant, but then she bled a little, so we figured everything was normal. Then it turned out that she was pregnant after all. A test at the hospital showed she was already five and a half months pregnant. I blamed myself, even though I know she's eighteen years old and should herself be responsible for her actions. The boy is twenty and wanted her to have the child. His parents also said they would welcome her into their family as his bride. We thought about the possible damage of the paint thinner and urged her to have the surgery [abortion], which she did without a problem. I think she's become an adult as a result of this experience. And watching her, I think she has recovered. I need to come to grips a bit better with that dependency-oriented *[izon teki]* part of myself.

Although this is a rather extreme example, in which a parent's involvement is certainly not unexpected, the story shows the wrenching position in which women find themselves—wedged between two worldviews, one that expects them to be there for their children and another that advises letting them be. What becomes clear in Abe-san's story is the extent to which she was intimately involved in her daughter's problem from the start, knowing there was a chance of pregnancy and carefully monitoring her daughter's menstrual cycles.

SETTING LIMITS, DEFINING BOUNDARIES

Women had difficulty setting limits for their children. After years of being socialized to believe that they should cater to their children's every whim, there was no discourse that legitimated drawing these boundaries, denying their children something that they wanted, or protecting their own needs or rights—the right to privacy, the right to say no, or the right to prioritize other things (work, friendships) over their children's needs, if only occasionally. The lack of a sense of entitlement to set limits, particularly in the face of a child's need for intimacy, was noticeable in conversations at the Center, as well as among other mothers I knew.

The issue of physical and verbal abuse particularly from children who were using drugs was central for the women at the Center. And yet because there is no language that delineates the rights of a mother or her entitlement to her own space, there is also no language that distinguishes a child's presumption of intimacy from his (or her) abuse of a mother's generosity or indulgence. The issue of children's physical violence *(katei nai bōryoku)* toward parents has gained attention in the past ten years, and I knew from the weekly case conference that some women were subjected to physical abuse from their children, particularly in instances where children were abusing drugs. Those who counsel families with this problem report that violence tends to come out in the open (the family seeks help from doctors or the police) only when it is directed at fathers. This suggests that mothers might be enduring the violence, perhaps regarding it as part of their role. Assumptions about relationships of nurturance can prevent recognition of abuse. Both parent abuse (particularly mother abuse) and child abuse have been unrecognized and underdiagnosed in Japan, because intimacy is thought to include both parents' invasiveness in children's lives and tolerance of children's aggression and misbehavior. Though no one spoke at the meetings about being hit or hurt by their children, women hinted that they were not always treated respectfully and sometimes were subject to at least verbal abuse.

> Kikumoto *desu*. Sunday was the election, and my son offered to drive me to the voting booth. He was rushing, so he was using language like, "I'll drive ya' but hurry up!" I said I didn't need a ride, but anyway I ended up going with him. He has a big microbus—the kind that celebrities ride in—and I asked him not to park in a place that would block others, but when we arrived he pulled right up to the entrance and slammed on the brakes. He just doesn't listen to what others have to say, I thought to myself.

Although women faced opposition from nearly all the social institutions they encountered, the meetings served as a source of support for them to stand up to their children. One of the women who took steps to change her situation, Yamamoto-san, told the story of her son, who was in debt and had recently sold his computer to a pawn shop: "Yamamoto *desu*. The latest incident is that my son wants to buy a VCR and wants his father to become the guarantor for the loan. My husband refused and told me that he needs to learn an important lesson—that debt is a frightening thing—and instructed me absolutely not to help out *[zettai ni te o dasanai]*. I think my husband is right; he knows these things because he's had experience in the world of money and business. So I'm following his advice."

Sharing stories offered women the possibility of rethinking the assumption that because mothers were responsible for their children, they were also to blame. In one meeting, Yamamoto-san said: "It is very hard to think that my son's addiction is the result of his upbringing. Maybe that is one part of it, but I find myself thinking that just *can't be the only thing*. [As a parent] I have tried very, very hard *[Watashi wa isshōkenmei ni shite kita]*." Other women took great comfort in this comment. In another meeting, Yamamoto-san told about a dorm mother's phone call and her effort to ignore it:

Yamamoto *desu*. I'm here because of my son's drug problem. I had already forgotten that last weekend was a long weekend. I went on an overnight trip and watched a movie at home. But a call from the dorm mother where my son is living made me forget about the holiday. There's a new dorm mother and I hadn't met her yet, but on the phone she began asking me, "Why can't your son live at home—is there some particular reason?" "Are you helping him out financially?" "Have you been to visit his dormitory?" and so forth. I haven't once considered helping him out financially *or* going to visit where he lives. I'm leaving his life up to him now. I told my husband that I wondered if she didn't find me an incredibly heartless parent. I asked him if he felt like going over to visit the dormitory. "Heck no," he said. "Funny, he doesn't seem to be bothered by not going," I thought to myself. I have to say that I myself wasn't inspired to go have a look, even after being scolded. I'm afraid of the same old scenario [lending him money, etc.]. I'm very afraid of returning to our former modus operandi. I called Takemura-san [a staff member] for advice and she said to let the dorm mother's words roll right off my back. Being in that position of deliberating was agonizing, but I guess that's to be expected.

I didn't like myself for letting that phone call make me forget all about the nice time I had had on vacation. I see that I still get depressed when I'm taken to task like this. I'd like to be a bit more resilient in these instances.

One woman above all managed to rethink the social dictates of motherhood, and her toughness set her apart from the other women in a way that ultimately created a rift in the group. Katō-san was a thirty-nine-year-old divorced woman with a teenage son who had been in and out of a rehabilitation center. Struggling with her son for a year, she continually tried to help him but without success. In one incident she described, she went to visit him at a rehabilitation facility and found his hands and feet tied to the bed because he had stolen another patient's cigarettes. Eventually, she let her son go on national welfare, an almost unthinkable step in Japan, where parents support children and social assistance is rare and requires much bureaucratic intervention. At a meeting, she said,

I used to think that with a "mother's power" I could somehow fix this situation. But I finally reached the point where I can't attempt it. I need to move forward. I'm sick of repeating the same patterns. I'm determined to move in a better direction. If you keep rethinking each little incident from the past you don't move forward. I feel I've put one step forward in that direction. I told that to my kids. When I first came to the Center, I was clinging to the idea that I needed to do something to make things better. Now I feel I've been reborn.

Later in the spring, Katō-san talked of her daughter and the difficulties she was having. Again the question of limits was at issue. She spoke of having to find a balance between meeting her daughter's demands for a nurturing home and carving out her own life independent of her daughter. She described a conversation illustrating these tensions, which took place after they had been to a museum together: "After we'd left, I told my daughter that I was heading to a friend's house to spend the night. My daughter began to cry. She said that since we've been divorced, she feels she has no home [ie ga nai]. I did feel sorry for her. I felt I'd done the unforgivable to her. I feel she's twenty-five and so it's time for her to make it on her own. But in her eyes a parent's home is a place where you're welcomed and fed."

Several years later, when I reconnected with Katō-san and several other women in Tokyo, I found that they continued to wrestle with these same issues as their children grew older. Katō-san, whose story was by far the most tragic, witnessed her son descend further into the depths of stimulant abuse. He was arrested a number of times and at the time of our encounter was serving a two-and-a-half-year prison sentence. Katō-san had decided that there was nothing further she could do. She gave him her phone number and told him that she would no longer take care of him or provide money. She said, "I worry about him, but it's not something that I can do anything about. No matter what I offer him, he won't get better."

But even Katō-san, who had broken ties with her son in a way that would be unthinkable to many mothers (not only Japanese), felt nostalgia for the pleasures of motherhood and providing for her children. She had moved in with her daughter and son-in-law but lamented that her daughter prohibited her from cooking for them, claiming that it wasted too much gas. Her daughter made simple meals for herself and her husband, and Katō-san made her own meals. Katō-san, who, until her daughter chided her, had gone to great lengths to have a delicious dinner on the table to feed the family when they returned home, said that she felt "shrunken down" (*chiisaku naru*) and miserable (*mijime*). She longed for the old days, when everyone enjoyed her home-cooked meals (*tabete morate oishii to iwareru no ga hoshii*).

In later years when I encountered the women, many continued to be quite involved in their children's lives, living out their later years in the traditional role of the grandparent; though most did not live with their children, they often lived close enough to be of service to the family. Abe-san's eldest daughter moved closer after she had children, so that Abe-san could help take care of them while she was working. Abe-san kept herself busy going to her daughter's house to do the laundry, clean, and prepare meals. "There's still a part of me that is not comfortable unless I'm being useful to someone," Abe-san mused. At the same time, she felt uncomfortable that her daughter had a tendency to "take things for granted" (*atari mae ni suru*) after they had been done for her. She and her daughter were working out an explicit arrangement to share the costs of food, since Abe-san did much of the shopping.

Watanabe-san told a story of learning to put some distance between herself and her son. She said that her son had recently been complaining that he needed a job. So, "as a parent, I began looking around for a job for him." Someone eventually offered to hire him, but when she shared the news with her son, his response was that he would look for his own job. "Then I realized," she said, "it's true that he never asked me. After that, I stopped searching or saying anything. I stopped paying his expenses, too. Then his gas and water stopped. He was surprised to learn that it's really true that if you don't pay they stop your utilities! After that, he started being a bit more careful."

REJECTING TOUGH LOVE

Although several of the women resisted cultural pressures in important ways, the mothers, more than the wives, had difficulty engaging with the ideas the Center offered, because they were unable to get past their feelings that motherly love should be all-encompassing. Eventually, some of the women began to reassert the importance of *amae* and "a mother's love" for their children. Though they did not disavow the Center or the support they had received there, they began to suggest that they would have to find their "own way"—something in between the Center's dictums and what seemed intuitively right to them. Yoda-san talked about trying to find some balance between indulging her son and encouraging him to be independent:

> I've been blaming myself for being too child-centered, and wondering if something was wrong with *me*. I've given him everything I can and cradled him, but maybe I didn't raise him to grow up. Now I'm trying to be more of a parent in that way—to not quash my kid's own thoughts, to let my kid go first, and then I would follow, providing whatever was needed or missing. I cradled him, but did I love him? At the time when he should have "taken off" from the nest, he couldn't. But I really think that if a parent communicates her deep love for her child, the child will change. I'm looking for my own road to follow now.

Abe-san also asserted that she was moving away from the tough love stance:

> I feel I'm moving along the same path as Yoshida-san. I was told by Dr. Saitō that my bond to my children was "too strong" *[kizuna ga tsuyosugiru]*. But as time passes and I can look at the situation more calmly, I see that just following the textbook advice doesn't turn out very well. I mix what I've learned here with my own way. That's made me feel more comfortable.

Lately, on Saturday mornings I wake up early and experiment with all kinds of dishes for breakfast; then I wake everyone up at 10 A.M. I was told that waking them up in the morning wasn't good and making them do everything along with the family wasn't good, but if it's fun for the family, isn't that a good thing? Before, I was forcing myself to obey the rules. But it's more natural to do things one's own way. To feel that one has to do things the way everyone else does is painful.

I've been thinking that the time may be coming to graduate from here. It's fun to come here, but I want to be able to remove myself and resolve things by my own thinking. I've become too dependent on this place. When I can't follow the advice of the group, in a strange way I feel even worse. When I came here and tried to disclaim all that I had been doing before and do things the group's way, it made me depressed.

This conversation shows the women wrestling with the tough love ideal and continuing to cling to the importance (and pleasure) of motherly love and intimacy. Even women whose children were engaging in delinquency and substance abuse or who were being abused or harassed by their children were prone to see motherhood in this light. They still wanted to wake up early and make their children breakfast. Although the idea of tough love is compelling and persuasive, the women quickly saw through the more extreme aspects of the idea and questioned the foregone conclusion that independence is better than intimacy. In some respects they were responding to the dogmatic aspects of the codependency discourse and its tendency to pathologize dependency relationships. Yet, in other respects, their stories reveal the difficulty of thinking one's way out of motherhood in Japan— the compelling nature of the discourse as well as its burdens. The difficulty in embracing the tough love discourse reflects the difficulty of distinguishing love and nurturance from self-sacrifice, spoiling, and declining to hold children responsible for their own actions. The distinction between nurturance and self-sacrifice (or nurturance and overindulgence) is obscured by dominant discourses of childhood as a celebrated state of dependency and motherhood as the paramount accomplishment of womanhood.

CONCLUSION

The Home as a Feminist Dilemma

FEMINIST TRADE-OFFS

The constraints Japanese women often live under—loveless marriages, "divorce within the home," the management of virtually all the household labor—seem unthinkable from the perspective of dominant American ideologies of marriage, which emphasize equality, romantic love and passion between the spouses, and the notion of the spouse as a companion and partner (D'Emilio and Freedman 1997). Although Japanese women appear oppressed in these respects, the women's stories described here suggest that many Japanese women, particularly of this generation, have a sense of security in marriage that many American women do not share. Because marriage is organized around rigidly gendered, separate worlds, and because motherhood, rather than wifehood, is viewed as the central aspect of women's work, women do not fear that their husbands will "fall out of love" and leave them due to personality conflicts, changes in their appearance, or a husband's sexual wandering. Although the prevailing Japanese idea of marriage as a compatible division of labor that does not hinge on sexual attraction or shared interests seems "contractual" or "cold," as the students who take my courses on postwar Japan often comment, it also highlights the naïveté that underlies thoroughly American (Hollywood) ideals of marriage as comprising enduring passion and romance, even as life moves along and other priorities take hold. In this context, the Japanese ideal of cooperative labor and a shared sensitivity, though not always realized in the Japanese context (as we have seen), has its own appeal.

The anthropologist Lila Abu-Lughod once reflected that if our own cultural categories shape our knowledge of our informants in the field, they are also inevitably shaped *by* our encounters with these informants (1995: 347). In this section, I take the opportunity to reflect on the particularities of our own system through the Japanese lens. While Japan may not be the most logical basis of comparison for the United States, owing in part to the extreme differences, I use the materials collected in the book as at least an occasion to reflect on the things we've traded off in the United States in the interests of absolute gender equality and the pursuit of individual autonomy.

Of course, to hold up the Japanese system as an example to emulate would be misguided. The limitations of this system are more than evident in the book: women remain largely financially dependent on men; they often linger in unhappy marriages with little sense of choice; and it is difficult to draw the line where "caring" and "good service" blur into servitude, belittlement, and exploitation. The Japanese state does less for its parents in providing for child care expenses (cash benefits, subsidies, tax allowances, etc.) than many other industrialized nations—particularly relative to costs (Bradshaw and Finch 2002). To raise a child outside of marriage is also extraordinarily difficult in Japan, and thus the rate of marriage is high and the rate of out-of-wedlock births relatively low (Bradshaw and Finch 2002).

Yet within the context of marriage, Japanese nonworking women have been eligible for a remarkable degree of financial support and social validation. At the moment, as the Japanese economy faces a turning point in which housewives may no longer be "affordable" (I discuss this further later in the chapter), it is worth pausing to consider what the system of the subsidized housewife has offered Japanese women and how this can shed light on the often unspoken trade-offs of other systems.

While American women generally have better access to well-paid jobs, job training, and financial self-sufficiency than Japanese women, this may mean that they spend far less time with their children than they would like. A recent *New York Times* survey on the "juggling" that working men and women perform showed that working women, who on average work slightly fewer hours and do more around the house than their husbands, spend 1.5 hours per day on "helping" family members. (Working men spend on average 0.83 hours.) When one considers that some portion of this must include physical care (feeding, bathing, changing, etc.), the amount of time spent playing or in conversation is remarkably small.[1]

Furthermore, American women who choose to stay at home as full-time mothers face less stable situations than Japanese women. Not only do they confront the social stigma of not having an independent identity, but they cannot assume that their husbands are committed to staying in the family. Inadequate support for family and child care means that American women continually choose between being self-sufficient and spending time with their children.

The trade-offs of the two systems are revealed in interesting ways through the politics of divorce. A counselor at the Tokyo Women's Plaza (a city-subsidized hub for women's counseling, networking, and research) told me that she tells her clients who are debating whether to end their marriages that divorce is "better for the soul" but "harder for the body" *(kokoro ni wa ii kedo karada ni wa tsurai)*. In other words, women may experience psychological relief upon divorce, but they will most likely have to work very hard in order to survive. There is little question that divorced women face extreme hardship in Japan; family courts, which typically mediate divorce settlements, are notoriously conservative and tend to take the stance that marriage requires endurance on the part of women. Japanese alimony laws, while existent, are notoriously difficult to enforce, owing both to small numbers of lawyers and the fact that the laws still do not have teeth: courts do not have the right to take child care support from a man's salary in the case of a noncompliant husband, nor can men be fined or imprisoned for refusing to pay.

In my early period of exploratory research on women's support networks, I attended a lecture, sponsored by a local Tokyo women's counseling bureau, called "Divorce with a Smile" *(Niko-Niko Rikon-Sho)*. The bureau, organized by Madoka Yoriko, a psychologist turned women's advocate and entrepreneur, advised women on how to go about preparing for and negotiating a divorce in a society that is notoriously unforgiving to divorcees. The advice was remarkable: women should not think of divorce as a radical break from their married lives, but rather as a process that involves careful preparation and the utilization of institutions and resources already available through marriage. Because financial concerns are paramount, she urged women to plan ahead by withdrawing small portions of money over a period of time from their husbands' bank accounts. ("You earned that money too!" she insists.) She also emphasized the importance of motherhood. She exhorted women to prepare their children ("Children follow their mother in the way they cope with this" [haha oya shidai]) and to be careful not to hurt their husbands' pride. Even in the face of crisis, she said, it is above all important to remain "motherly" (haha oya rashii). The advice neatly revealed the entitlement women experience as wives—particularly the notion that women are entitled to their husbands' money and that saving small portions of it does not constitute stealing—and the absence of entitlement they face as divorcees (see Borovoy 2001a).

The increasing divorce rate among younger generations in Japan is one of the more dramatic changes to occur in the postwar history of gender and family. According to some demographers' estimates, a third of all marriages end in divorce within thirty years (Raymo, Iwasawa, and Bumpass 2004). (The "crude" divorce rate is, of course, much lower—2.27 divorces per thousand of population [Ministry of Health, Labor and Welfare 2002]). This puts Japan on a par with the highest levels in Europe (Germany and Austria) and well above France, Spain, and Italy (Raymo, Iwasawa, and Bumpass 2004: 404–405). Only the United States has a higher rate. Although one possible interpretation of this phenomenon might be that women are growing financially more independent from their husbands and thus more likely to strike out on their own, such an interpretation may be leaping to conclusions. Although increasing divorce rates are a common story among industrialized nations in recent decades, they have typically accompanied increased maternal employment and economic opportunities for women (McLanahan 2004, cited in Raymo, Iwasawa, and Bumpass 2004). Yet Japan is noteworthy in that the increase in the divorce rate has not been accompanied by an equally dramatic increase in the rate of women's labor force participation. Furthermore, in a comprehensive study that draws on census data relating educational level to average age of first marriage, Raymo, Iwasawa, and Bumpass show a correlation in the past two decades between higher divorce rates and lower levels of education. Divorces are increasing at a far more rapid rate among junior high and high school graduates than they are among college graduates (418–19); these less educated women are less likely to be financially independent and more likely to be married to someone who faces employment instability. Though it remains to be seen what will become of these young female divorcees, who seemingly possess few resources to support themselves and their children, the results could be interpreted as evidence that in many ways, although the divorce rate has increased among all educational strata (405), marriages among couples with higher levels of education, which are more likely to be premised on the postwar model of economic stability and different but complementary forms of labor, are, relatively speaking, continuing to hold together.

In contrast, American women seemingly have greater freedom and rights. The institutionalization of "no-fault divorce" and common property laws were meant to confer financial entitlements that would allow them to leave unhappy marriages, and they seem to have solidified the notion that individual freedoms should transcend the bonds of marriage. Yet the Japanese situation highlights in interesting ways the trade-offs of this arrangement. Although it is possible to tout women's right to leave a marriage as a feminist victory, the financial hardship that many women endure after divorce has been considerably underplayed. Older divorced women in the United States (whose numbers are growing) are at far greater risk of poverty than married women.[2] Rights in the abstract are important, but because in practice large numbers of American women still rely on their marriages for financial support, one must ask whether this legal and ideological victory is in fact sufficient.

While clearly neither Japanese women nor American women are in optimal situations, the Japanese case speaks to the drawbacks of privileging equality in the workplace while devaluing human interdependence and the work of caring for others.[3] The devaluation of domesticity in the United States continues to present obstacles to women's equality in the public sphere, due to insufficient commitment to day care, family leave, and so forth. For example, witness the growing number of highly educated professional women who choose to stay at home or scale back their workload and ambitions when they can afford to. A recent article in the *New York Times* entitled "The Opt-Out Revolution" spelled out these trends: U.S. Census surveys show that the number of children being cared for by full-time mothers has increased 13 percent in less than a decade. In addition, the percentage of new mothers who go back to work fell from 59 percent in 1998 to 55 percent in 2000 (Belkin 2003: 2). While the article is problematic in its suggestion that opting out is somehow "revolutionary" or progressive (since most of the women seem to have been edged out of their professions because these institutions failed to accommodate the demands of family life), it does indeed suggest the lack of resources available to support women who work full-time while raising families.

In contrast, recognizing the trade-offs involved in sending women off to work, many prominent Japanese feminists of the 1980s and 1990s resisted the view of remunerated work as the sine qua non of women's liberation. Though Japanese feminist groups and movements have been many and historically quite divided (like most feminist movements), it is fair to say that at each historical juncture prominent strands have defended the importance of the home and its links to social betterment (Mackie 2003: see, for example, 150–51; Nolte 1987: 97–103). In the 1970s and 1980s, as "professional housewives" began returning to work as part-time and temporary workers to meet the demands of the growing economy, Marxist feminist Ueno Chizuko (1988) warned that for Japanese women, seeking to replicate men's roles in the workplace would only serve to doubly exploit them, since they would still be expected to fulfill all responsibilities at home. Ueno insists that feminism will never be attained until women begin arguing for men's participation in the home—"the feminization of men," in her words. Japanese women's groups, such as the *Kateika no Danjo Kyōshū o Susumeru Kai,* who support equal education of boys and girls in home economics, may have foreseen the lesson that took second-wave North American feminists a generation to learn: that women's work in the public/commercial sector will not constitute liberation unless it is accompanied by a simultaneous revaluing of the home.

LOOKING FOR A DISCOURSE TO VALIDATE THE HOME

Several years after completing the research on alcoholism and codependency, I returned to Japan for another year of research, this time with my husband and one-year-old son. As a mother, I was afforded glimpses into dimensions of social life that had previously been less visible, and I could not help returning to some of the themes that had been so important to understanding the women at the Center. As working parents, we were eligible for state-subsidized day care in our Tokyo ward. In addition, because we were registered under the national health-care system, our son received free medical care and medicine (with some minimal copayments) until the age of six. The ward also sent regular reminders of vaccination needs and notices concerning health education.

Japan's public day care is of outstanding quality, though insufficient in quantity. Each day we received a detailed report of our son's activities, the number of ounces of milk he drank, his body temperature at various times during the day, the time and texture of each bowel movement, and a brief anecdote describing something he had done or said during the day. In return, each morning we were required to provide equally detailed information to the teachers on his home activities. Illustrated newsletters were sent home each month with anecdotes about what each child was doing or saying, describing any new members, noting the change of seasons, and in winter, documenting the latest viruses and educating us on how germs were carried and how we could avoid contracting them.

It is important to note that state-subsidized day care was never intended to support women who "choose" to work for their own fulfillment but was, on the contrary, meant to socialize working-class children into being good Japanese citizens in cases where the parents did not have the time and resources to do so (Uno 1999). In order to register our son, we needed to complete a litany of forms verifying our employment and need for day care, including documenting how we spent each hour of the day at our respective jobs. Hence there was a good deal of paternalism on the part of the day care workers, which a number of Japanese mothers I knew noted and resented. The Japanese mothers sometimes complained of being "disciplined" or "guided" in a heavy-handed way *(shidō sareru)* by the day care teachers, who saw their role as extending well beyond that of mere temporary caregivers. Yet my husband and I could not help but be struck by the seriousness with which child-rearing itself was regarded. Upon our departure from Japan, we were presented with a beautiful folding scrapbook on Japanese paper, with photographs of our son playing at day care, his hand- and footprint in paint, and farewell messages from all the teachers written on small balloons cut out of construction paper. On the back was calligraphed the song the teachers used to sing to him each day as he went to sleep for his nap. "Leon is a good boy. He is very precious. He's his parents' treasure" *(Reion-kun wa ii ko. Totemo daiji na ko. Otōsan, Okāsan no takaramono desu).* Throughout the year, I felt myself tolerating a considerable degree of fetishization of motherhood as natural and as a woman's most important mission. And yet, at the same time, I appreciated the message I felt I was continually being sent, by day care workers, physicians, the bureaucrats in the ward office, shopkeepers, and strangers on the street: that a mother's job is difficult and important. It was not a message I was used to hearing.

Of course, one can hardly hold up the situation of Japanese women as ideal; throughout the postwar period, women have been far too confined to the home, with little opportunity to achieve financial independence or personal gratification from work in the commercial sector. (I avoid using the term "public sector" here, since much of the work women do at home, such as neighborhood improvement, volunteerism, or environmental activism has historically been considered "public" work in Japan.) More than women in any other industrialized, capitalist nation (with the possible exception of South Korea), Japanese women have had a difficult time breaking into the commercial sphere and obtaining equal employment opportunities, despite recent bouts of legislation discussed earlier. For many women, with the exception of a small but growing number of elite, highly educated women, motherhood continues to be the only role that offers them support, stability, and some measure of social recognition.

Yet, in many ways, Japan—with its state-subsidized single wage-earner system and history of constructing the housewife as a crucial social role—offers an important lens for reflection. The second wave of American feminism in the 1960s, which called upon women to rejoin the workforce, created inroads for women to achieve equality in the workplace and economic self-sufficiency. And yet it left unanswered the central question of how to valorize the work entailed in caring for others (Gordon 1992). The classical liberal emphasis on autonomy as a central marker of personhood and the historical linkage between "paid work" and "productive work" have created an environment in which it is difficult to distinguish unpaid activities from unnecessary activities (Collier 1991: 6; Fraser and Gordon 1994). In addition, the Victorian, bourgeois notion of the home as a sanctioned safe haven from the values of industrialism and the marketplace (competition, modernization), a sphere of personal self-cultivation through hobbies, love, and leisure rather than a sphere of productivity, has made it difficult for feminists to reclaim the home as a sphere of public importance (Zaretsky 1976; Folbre 1991; Fraser and Gordon 1994; Borovoy 2001a).

As contemporary American feminists struggle to come to terms with this problem, what emerges is the dearth of vocabulary available to claim the importance of this work, aside from essentializing notions of "woman's nature," spirituality ("the Goddess within"), and motherhood.[4] Indeed, it is interesting to note that an emphasis on the role of the mother/caregiver over the role of the wife/partner—an emphasis that has given Japanese women a measure of autonomy and credibility—has also taken root among contemporary American women who decide to stay at home. One rarely hears these women refer to themselves as "housewives," with all the term's connotations of confinement, provinciality, and absorption in trivialities. Instead, "stay-at-home-mom" has become the term of choice.

Some have argued that currently in the United States, nurturance itself has become little more than a purchasable commodity, which some families outsource to nannies, babysitters, cooks, cleaners, therapists, and helpers of all kinds (see Hochschild 2003: 30–44). Arlie Hochschild has noted that the speeding up and rationalization of the workplace has been accompanied by the rationalization of the home space (the implementation of "quality time") (199, 203). She argues that for many, ironically, the virtues long associated with domesticity in the United States (nurturance and mutual support) are more likely to be found at the office, near the water cooler, than they are at home (1997). Indeed, as some American professionals and feminists have attempted to reflect on where we went wrong in prescribing the dual career track as an ideal trajectory, the logic of the commodity is explicitly present. In *The Price of Motherhood: Why the Most Important Job in the World Is Still the Least Valued,* financial journalist Ann Crittendon asks, if we were to actually account for the hours of labor and services that women provide through social reproduction and the cultivation of human capital (feeding, laundering, facilitating children's education, and so forth), not to mention the opportunity costs to their own careers, what dollar amount would we have to pay them? (Crittenden 2002).

State sponsorship and endorsement of motherhood in Japan makes it difficult for Japanese women to "say no" to motherhood—or even to be less than perfect mothers. As the narratives of the mothers in this book reveal, women are always ultimately held accountable for their children's behavior, and there is little agreement on where (if at all) women should draw the line in what they are willing to do for their children. Last year,

Japan's former prime minister, Yoshiro Mori, went so far as to suggest that, given Japan's declining birthrate, women who do not bear children should not be entitled to pension or welfare benefits. "It is truly strange," he said in a speech, "to say that we have to use tax money to take care of women who don't even give birth once, who grow old living their lives selfishly and singing the praises of freedom" (Faiola 2004). The "child-centric" model of the family continues to predominate, even as women give birth to fewer and fewer children on average (White 2002).

And yet, having experienced the superlative quality of state-subsidized day care in Tokyo, the well-paid day care workers who regard themselves as professionals, the free, government-subsidized health care for children under four, and the proud mothers chauffeuring their children around on bicycles at all hours of the day in our suburban neighborhood, it is difficult not to feel a twinge of envy. In contrast, in the United States, the government has all but withdrawn from support of children and child care except in particularly desperate situations. Overwhelmingly, the efforts of the state have been directed toward prodding women into the workforce (through "workfare" programs and the rollback of traditional welfare)— and encouraging them to pay other women to care for their children— rather than supporting them as mothers.

BEYOND MOTHERHOOD FOR JAPANESE WOMEN

While Western feminism has struggled with how to value "dependency work"—the work of caring for children and families, and of building communities—without compromising the liberal values of self-determination and autonomy (see Linda Gordon 1992), Japanese women and feminists have wrestled with a different but equally difficult dilemma: their history of intimate connections and complicity with the state, the protection and benefits women have received *as mothers,* and as some have argued, the infantilization of Japanese citizens, which has prevented them from taking political responsibility for their acts (see Inoue, Ueno, and Ehara 1995; Kanō 1995: 58–61). The question of whether women should receive support from the state *as* mothers (for example, whether they should be eligible for paid leave during pregnancy or menstruation) or whether they should seek progress through equal treatment with men has been a hotly debated question among Japanese feminists (see, for example, Mackie 2003: 55–57).[5]

In the important collection *Feminizumu Ronsō: 70 Nendai kara 90*

Nendai e (Feminist Debates from the 1970s through the 1990s), edited by Ehara Yumiko (1990), feminist scholar Asai Michiko argues that the illusion of the benevolent mother in postwar Japan is both the single best protector of women and the single worst enemy of women's liberation. While Western radical and Marxist feminisms have pointed to heterosexual patriarchy as the foundation of gender inequality, Japanese women, she argues, are oppressed by the powers and virtues associated with motherhood and femininity—what she calls the fantasy of "motherly nature" *(bosei gensō)*. In "Toward a Liberation from the Myth of the Modern Family," Asai argues that the image of the pure *(muku)*, nurturing wife and mother at the center of the family obscures the real-life exploitation of women, since motherhood eclipses womanhood. Motherhood, a double-edged sword, allows women empowerment through self-sacrifice and innocence *(junsui muku)*. At the same time, it protects women from the sphere of gender discrimination by desexualizing them—painting them as pure or desireless *(muyoku)* figures outside the purview of gender discrimination or violation, "able to turn the other way in the face of sexual oppression" *(sei ni yoru yokuatsu ni me o memuru koto go dekite)* (Asai 1990: 100). According to Asai, the discourse of motherhood loathes "maturity" *(seijuku kirau)* and applauds innocence. The fantasy of motherhood simultaneously empowers mothers and devalues maturity, equal rights, and self-assertion in women.

Asai's analysis of the maternal fantasy implies the very limited possibilities of empowerment for Japanese women and the important role of motherhood within these. Motherhood offers women respect and stability, as well as access to a social voice (i.e., enfranchisement through groups that hinge on their status as mothers, such as consumer advocacy groups or the PTA). It protects women from the dominant images of sexual objectification promenaded in mass media, popular culture, and the vast genre of male pornography, which invades mainstream magazines and occupies a prominent place at convenience stores and train station kiosks. Yet, at the same time, the place of motherhood prevents women from the realization of "womanhood," the cultivation of sexuality independent of motherhood, and the pursuit of equal opportunity outside the home. In Asai's view, a woman has two choices: she can play mother to her husband (who behaves like a child) *or* she can be subjected to sexual discrimination when she moves outside the context of the home (1990: 109).

Ueno Chizuko, who has acknowledged the power of the domicile for women (1987), has also argued that the path to empowerment through motherhood is ultimately illusory. Taking issue with the notion that maternalism in Japan constitutes "matriarchy," Ueno has argued that Japanese motherhood is better described not as matriarchy but as "transvestite patriarchy": patriarchy hidden "behind the skirts" of mothers. Mothers often act as agents of the patriarchy, socializing their sons to reproduce patriarchy in the next generation (Ueno 1996: 15). Furthermore, women may reproduce the patriarchy by absorbing and deflecting its negative effects (as seen in the narratives of the women at the clinic), making the consequences of male privilege appear invisible, at least at home and in the community. The valorization of home, while limiting Japanese women's entry into the commercial sector, has perhaps saved middle-class women and feminists from the unforeseen consequences of middle-class women's entry into the workforce in the 1960s in the United States.

In a context where self-sufficiency (defined as obtaining a living wage) is the key marker of maturity and personhood itself, American feminists have had to argue for the importance of caregiving and community in the face of the demands of the marketplace. For Japanese women and feminists, who have understood women's empowerment to emerge from the priorities of the home, the struggle has been to show how these priorities, while gratifying, can also be exploitative. The struggle to find a language to talk about the particular forms of exploitation—the fine line between nurturance and tolerance of abuse, for example—has been difficult. Borrowing Western feminism and American popular psychology has been insufficient.[6]

THE DECLINING VIABILITY OF THE HOUSEWIFE

As the new century unfolds with Japan increasingly faced with the pressures of neoliberalism, the Japanese housewife, who provided so much of the invisible labor that undergirded Japan's economy and society, is less and less affordable. The gendered division of labor that was explicitly supported by the government beginning in the 1950s has grown expensive and difficult to defend ideologically. The paring down of corporate salary and benefit structures and the gradual decline of "lifetime employment" and the family wage *(kazoku teate)* (where these had existed before) has meant that more women need to work to sustain economic stability. Women are staying in the labor force slightly longer before leaving to raise children, and more are returning to work afterward (White 2002). An impending labor shortage and the declining fertility rate are putting pressure on companies and the state to create an environment that supports women in the workplace—though women are still largely marginalized in the upper echelons of business and politics.[7]

In addition, a growing chorus of voices argues that the government can no longer justify its support for upper- and middle-class women to stay at home. Some scholars and social critics have pointed to the inequality of a system that supports full-time housewives through their husband's pension plans, rather than requiring them to buy into the national health insurance *(kokumin kenkō hoken)* and pension plan *(kokumin nenkin)* that support middle-income families (see Sechiyama 2000: 136, 138). In a powerful critique of the "housewife welfare system" *(sengyō shufu hogo seidō)* published in the political magazine *Ronza*, Sechiyama Kaku argues that while such a system made sense in a context in which full-time housewives provided services for the government such as care for the elderly, in a context in which the government is now taking steps to support these services itself, it can no longer afford to subsidize women to stay at home. In order for the government to respond to the aging society and declining birth rate, the state should make better use of women's productive (rather than reproductive) labor, and in return provide better services to families—including increased financial allowances for families who have children *(jidō teate)* and day care subsidies—rather than offering incentives for women to stay at home (139, 140–41, 142). The focus of national debate is now on how to sustain working women, and the government is now moving toward raising the wage level that would entitle a woman to obtain the spousal tax deduction.[8]

There are also signs that the respect once accorded to the housewife's role, and women's own sense of entitlement, is eroding. Time pressures and consumer convenience have gradually permeated the home (although a surprising number of women continue to hang their laundry to dry rather than use an electric dryer, and the vast majority of even working women continue to do their own housework), and comments that the housewife's job offers "three meals and a nap" *(sanshoku hirune tsuki)* have grown more pervasive in the context of an increasingly consumer-oriented society.

More important, perhaps, is the simple fact that the typical "housewife trajectory" that so many middle- and upper-middle-class women followed in the postwar years of rapid economic growth—from college (or junior college) to secretarial work to motherhood—is becoming less viable economically. In the context of slowed economic growth since the early 1990s and the deflation that has haunted the Japanese economy in recent years, mid-size companies and smaller entrepreneurial companies are increasingly rethinking the paradigm of the family wage in an effort to cut costs and treat all workers equally. The housewife track hinged on an assumption that women would be supported by their husbands, who would steadily make their way up the company ranks. Furthermore, the low-skill positions (such as serving tea or making copies) that women once filled in their postcollege years (positions that drew respectable salaries and benefits) are increasingly being filled with temporary or part-time workers. These changes are dramatically affecting the landscape of gender identity and the political economy of family and marriage in Japan in ways that are just beginning to be appreciated.

Japan's total fertility rate is now just over 1.3, the second-lowest in the industrialized world after Italy, and the average age of marriage for women is 27.3, a number that has been steadily rising since 1950, making its largest leaps in the 1990s (Statistical Research and Training Institute 2003). The growing population of single people in their late twenties and early thirties has come to be known as "parasite singles": women (and men) who live comfortably at their parents' home, often contributing little to rent or household chores. In the American mass media (and in the minds of many Japanese social commentators), the parasite singles are identified as women who refuse traditional Japanese gender roles. They prefer instead to "live for themselves" and "enjoy life" (Orrenstein 2001: 34), spending their income on hobbies, shopping and dining, and overseas travel. These women fill the fashionable districts of Omotesando and Shibuya (and designer boutiques in major American and European cities). They point to the way the employment and family systems prevent women from pursuing both family and professional fulfillment. Karen Kelsky (1994) first called attention to this phenomenon among young "office ladies" in the early 1990s, who, she pointed out, were more cosmopolitan than their male counterparts and questioned dominant constructions of work and family. These young women aspire to more emotionally intimate relationships with their spouses and a partnership with respect to family and household work, rather than simply being supported by their husbands in return for raising children and taking care of the home (Ueno 1998: 117; Yamada 2001).

And yet, the phenomenon of the parasite singles is far more complex than is usually acknowledged and may suggest that women have rather ambivalent attitudes toward family and the housewife role—that the longing for different constructions of marriage and greater professional opportunities is accompanied by a continuing sense of the importance of the work at home. In other words, the parasite single phenomenon may not be the indictment of domesticity, family, and child-rearing that conservative Japanese critics fear and American journalists delight in. Studies have shown that the delayed marriage age does not necessarily correlate with women's educational attainment or career advancement (Ueno 1998), though it does suggest that women are less inclined to give up their freedom.[9] Data collected on young women's consumption habits by the Japanese Family Economics Bureau shows that the late twenties (the early years of marriage) are the most difficult financially, particularly for young couples coming of age in the deflationary period of the late 1990s. Women often experience a decline in disposable income when they move from being single wage-earners with low overhead to being young mothers. However, women who wait to get married experience less decrease in disposable income than do women who marry earlier, since the income of their natal family may already be in decline by then, and they are more likely to find a husband who is higher in the corporate hierarchy (Higuchi and Ota 2004: 157). Furthermore, although interview evidence suggests that many women still wish to be supported by their husbands and to devote time to family, they may be unable to find a young man capable of supporting them until later in life (Yamada 2001: 82–84).

While much work remains to be done on the subject, the domestic ideal, particularly the role of the mother, apparently continues to be compelling to many young Japanese women, despite the many differences between their generation and previous ones. The discourse of motherhood is hard to resist. In conversations I've had with young elite college women who are being groomed for upward mobility and a professional career, they reveal ambivalence about the trade-offs put before them: they often tell me they want to keep working while they raise their children—but not if this means "sacrificing" their families. A television documentary from the late

1990s, which looked at young consumer-oriented *ganguro* ("black-face") girls, who congregate in the shopping districts of Tokyo sporting high platform shoes and raccoon-like makeup, traced them as they became young mothers. Perhaps not surprisingly, most were living quite traditional lives, though often in somewhat meager circumstances. They showed their husbands out the door each morning, took their children to the park (though they were hurt by being shunned by the other mothers), and generally aspired to a successful middle-class life. One scene featured two young women going out for their weekly shopping trip together, each holding a menu for the week carefully based on the items the store had highlighted as bargain items.

Japan is sure to undergo important changes as it faces pressure to shape its economy and society in order to meet the demands of increased global competition. And yet the question remains: if Japanese women are integrated into the professional sector, who will take over the work that has been so highly valued by the government and the citizens themselves—the work of facilitating family relations, making the home a hospitable place, creating safe and clean neighborhoods, overseeing children's education, and so forth? This is a question all industrialized nations face, and perhaps the United States is on one extreme in the extent to which it has ceded these spheres (particularly the home) to the realm of the market. But will Japan take this course? The women's narratives in this book suggest that forsaking the idealization of motherhood and state support for the family, even though it may be accompanied by an opening of broader opportunities for women, will be experienced as a great loss.

NOTES

PREFACE

1. To protect the confidentiality of the participants in the meetings, I refer to the clinic simply as the Center (a term the women themselves used), and I have changed the names of the women who participated.

2. Published in the *Bulletin of International Nursing,* May 1985. All translations are my own unless otherwise noted.

INTRODUCTION

1. All clients' names appearing in the book are pseudonyms.

2. The number of housewives in the United States declined from 77 percent in 1955 to 22 percent in 1999 (Yamada 2001: 57).

3. The law was revised in 1997 to allow the government to take steps toward enforcing the new laws; the revision also did away with legal "protections" for women, including restrictions on overtime and the prohibition of night work.

4. Women earn on average roughly 67 percent of what men earn over the course of their careers (Ministry of Health, Labor, and Welfare, Hataraku Josei no Jitsujō, www.mhlw.go.jp, 2005).

5. These priorities are reflected in women's working trajectories over the life course, in which many leave the workforce during the early child-rearing years in order to be with their families full-time. Japa-

nese women's labor patterns over a lifetime conform to what is commonly called an M-curve: they enter the labor force upon graduation from high school or college, work as secretaries or "office ladies" until marriage, quit work to raise children, and then eventually returni in midlife to a low-skill or part-time position in the service sector or on the assembly line.

6. In keeping with this research, other scholars noted that, historically, dominant strands of Japanese women's activism have taken the form of activities that supplement and extend the values of the home, such as consumer activism, "Quality of Life" co-ops, and environmental protection and resource conservation (LeBlanc 1999; Lewis 1978). In the late 1970s, Lewis (1978) noted that women used their credentials as housewives to gain access to centers of power in various social movements, including consumer protection, environmentalism, and antinuclear protest. More recently, in a study of Japanese political women, Robin LeBlanc has suggested that it is through their daily lives as housewives that many women become involved in the world of politics, including neighborhood improvement campaigns, buyers' cooperatives, and local government—though they may not define themselves as political (79).

7. Studies of Co-Dependents Anonymous (CoDA) groups, which formed around the 1980s version of the codependency idea, suggest that members often resolve such tensions by simply "divesting themselves of relationships in which conventional social roles take precedence over the interest of the true self" (Rice 1996). In the words of one CoDA member, "I'm enough. Everyday, I'm enough. And there's so much freedom in that" (Rice 1996: 167).

8. In AA discourse, seeking the "cause" of one's drinking or dwelling on the past is regarded as another form of disavowing responsibility for one's drinking. As Rice puts it, "The disease model requires no great 'insights' and points no fingers. It merely calls for a tactical recognition of one's illness and the damage it has done, followed by a methodological agenda for the righting of wrongs and building life anew. According to original twelve-step truths, dwelling in the past, running it repeatedly through one's hands, is a symptom rather than a cause of the disease" (Rice 1996: 61).

9. The self-help concept that formed the basis of the AA conceptual apparatus emerged in the context of the Great Depression and New Deal, and recognized and grappled with the tension in American social life between "self-determination" and "public responsibility," between rights and responsibilities (Delbanco and Delbanco 1995). In contrast, the concept of moral obligation that emerges from the codependency literature of the 1980s is simply to look out for number one: "to be one's own principal priority" (Rice: 161).

10. Christopher Lasch remarked that not only did the movement encourage individuals to withdraw from social-political involvement into the realm of "the private," but it furthermore "debased" the realm of the private by encouraging individuals to flee from and trivialize social commitment, to regard enduring relationships to others with caution and skepticism in the endeavor to "live for the moment" (1978: 64–65).

11. Japanese clinicians working in the alcoholism field in the late 1970s recognized a type they called "the alcoholic wife" *(arukōru no tsuma)*; the profile of the mean, cold, or even frigid alcoholic wife who drove her husband to drink, popular in the United States in the 1940s and 1950s, also gained some credibility in Japan. However, with the introduction of Jackson's theories of family dynamics, ideas shifted.

12. ASK (Arukōru Yakubutsu Mondai Zenkoku Shimin Kyōkai), a citizens' group with a national base, is broadly concerned with alcoholism and substance abuse problems. The group circulates a magazine and, through its web site and other publicity, concerns itself with educating the public on matters of addiction.

13. The idea of the good wife and wise mother was a radical departure from what had come before. For most middle-class urban families and farm families (as well as poorer urban families), child care had often been provided by other children in the neighborhood, older siblings, or young women who were hired hands. Women had prioritized income-earning activities over household chores and domestic cleanliness (Tamanoi 1991). Nor had domestic work such as child-rearing and housekeeping been explicitly gendered. Historically, working-class and farm women had been assisted by children and men in domestic tasks such as cleaning and cooking; child care

was carried out by older children in the community or extended family (Tamanoi 1991; Uno 1993a, 1993b, 1997).

14. These leaders were inspired by the genteel treatment (as they perceived it) accorded to European women and the centrality of domesticity in West—although the concept of domesticity they ultimately promoted differed in significant ways from the European "cult of domesticity" (see Nolte and Hastings 1991; Folbre 1991).

15. In fact the 1950s and 1960s were the first time that many middle-class women were able to become full-time or "professional" housewives *(sengyō shufu)*. The postwar period has witnessed further consolidation of the gendered division of labor—evidenced by increasingly conservative attitudes toward women's roles in the family and workplace and increased women's economic dependence (Upham 1993).

16. *The Anatomy of Dependence* was reprinted in Japan in hardcover sixty-seven times in its first four years and has been reprinted in paperback 147 times since its initial publication in 1971 (Befu 1993: 109). The text remains in print both in Japanese and in English.

17. For further discussion of this shift in what constitutes political action and resistance and how our concept of resistance changes when we see power as infiltrating all aspects of everyday life and consciousness (not merely held in the hands of a few centralized figures of authority), see also Abu-Lughod 1990; Comaroff 1985; de Certeau 1984; Foucault 1979; and Diamond and Quinby 1988.

18. In a parallel argument concerning the interpretation of subjects' bodily complaints, Arthur Kleinman has argued that it is important to consider the ways in which people make use of the language available to them to enact social protest. He suggests that anthropologists run the risk of repeating the error of medicalization—imposing our own culturally rooted categories on the complexity and uncertainness of human problems—when we leap to assume that illness masks social protest. Kleinman's chief critique targets the language of medicine, which often obscures cultural particularities. Yet he also points to a tension in the critique of medicalization, which assumes that if it weren't for the medicalization of human problems, these problems would emerge as social protest in the forms we—those who

are trained in the traditions of liberal and Marxist thought—are most familiar with (Kleinman et al. 1995; Kleinman 1995; Kleinman and Kleinman 1993).

19. In Lydia Liu's exploration of the importation of discourses of individualism among May Fourth writers in China, she argues that although the writers sought to claim "modernity" and reject "tradition," historically influential discourses of nationalism and social collectivism "were never abandoned," and the privileging of the individual over society was never taken literally. However, discourses of individualism allowed Chinese writers to "open a new battlefront" in their struggle, in which they gradually came to rearticulate the meaning of both the individual and the national collectivity by seeing them as mutually compatible (the individual as citizen of the modern nation state) (Liu 1995: 95).

20. Comaroff and Comaroff talk about resistance to hegemony as a series of shifts that occur as subjects become aware of disjunctures between the "world as hegemonically constituted" and the world as apprehended through lived, daily experiences (Comaroff and Comaroff 1991)—the disjuncture between "commonsense" and "good sense" narratives of daily experience, in Gramsci's language (1971: 333).

21. One formal difference between these meetings and U.S. Al-Anon meetings is that neither the twelve steps nor the twelve traditions of recovery were recited. These were available in print at the Center but were rarely mentioned or discussed. To the best of my knowledge, none of the clients at the Center was formally involved in reading or practicing the twelve steps. This may be partly because of the notion of a "higher power," which has its roots in the Christian beginnings of AA.

CHAPTER 1. ALCOHOLISM AND CODEPENDENCY

1. Antabuse (also known as disulfiram) inhibits the enzyme that allows alcohol to be metabolized by the liver. If a person consumes alcohol while taking antabuse, he or she may experience palpitations, flushing, nausea, or severe headaches.

2. Stephen Smith (1988) also remarks on this phenomenon, noting that

"no matter how much a man drinks," as long as he continues to work he is not considered an alcoholic (184).

3. The phenomenon was explored by Hashimoto Meiko in a book entitled *Kichin Dorinkā* (Kitchen drinker, 1989) that explored housewives' alcoholism and the abuse of cooking sake and other alcohol by women at home.

4. While in 1985 there were only twenty alcohol treatment wards in hospitals in all of Japan and only five specialized clinics, by 1999 there were 76 such wards (3000 beds) (Global Status Report on Alcohol, WHO 1999).

5. Joan Jackson's description of the stages a wife or family goes through in managing alcoholism highlights the ways in which families structure themselves around alcoholism and the dramatic changes that must ensue to support the alcoholic's recovery. (Jackson's stages were key in shifting the belief that "wives of alcoholics" were cold and controlling, inviting their husbands' alcoholism, to showing how alcoholism itself shapes and overtakes family dynamics.) The first stage, denial, describes the way in which the family initially fights off change, adjusting its interpretations of what is happening in order to continue to maintain its usual modus vivendi. Fearing ostracism from the community, the family begins to withdraw socially in order to hide the alcoholic's unruly behavior. In the second stage, the family sets about "eliminating the problem." The wife nags her husband, threatens him, perhaps even threatening to leave, pampers him, or pours out his liquor. The family becomes increasingly isolated, focusing exclusively on managing the drinking; all family problems are attributed to the drinking; and husband and wife become increasingly alienated from one another. In the third phase, "disorganization," the family gives up trying to stop the alcoholic and gives up hiding the situation from the neighbors. In the fourth stage, the family attempts to "reorganize" despite the continuing problem. As Jackson notes, "The major characteristic of this stage is that the wife takes over." The alcoholic is either ignored or marginalized in the family, increasingly viewed as a "recalcitrant child" rather than the center of the home (1977: 8). The wife systematically fulfills her obligations to her children over her husband when these conflict. Bonds

between the wife and children grow tighter and exclude the father. As help is accepted from outside agencies, the wife gradually regains her strength and sense of worth. The family has reorganized itself to adapt to the crisis, although this reorganization may be accompanied by other crises, such as potential loss of income or violence on the part of the alcoholic. In the fifth stage, the wife begins efforts to escape the problem, often contemplating leaving the marriage. The sixth stage describes marriage after the alcoholic has attained sobriety and the problems that arise as the husband re-establishes his role as the breadwinner and attempts to reinstate himself as the head of the household.

6. According to Center records, the largest percentage of clients, 26.8 percent, were referred by physicians. The second largest share (23.7 percent) came from community health-care centers *(hokenjo);* other avenues that were becoming more frequent were the judicial system, children's welfare agencies, and friends, as the number of teenagers being referred for drug addictions was gradually increasing.

7. Margaret Lock has written, "While much contemporary medicalization acts to reduce psychosocial problems to the neutral terrain of the physical body, some of it may indeed serve to break down a little of the isolation that women experience in modern Japan. Hence medicalization may facilitate an ability to reinterpret the origins of distress as a social rather than a biological problem" (Lock 1987: 15).

8. In 2002 the government passed a law against domestic violence, provoking a broader consciousness of the issue.

9. Global Status Report on Alcohol. World Health Organization, Geneva, 1999.

CHAPTER 2. MOTHERHOOD,
NURTURANCE, AND "TOTAL CARE"
IN POSTWAR NATIONAL IDEOLOGY

1. Doi was an influential clinician who served as the chair of the Department of Psychiatry at Tokyo University for fifteen years and as head of the Japanese National Institute of Mental Health. As a psychiatrist, Doi wrestled with the problem of how to apply the West-

ern language of psychiatry to Japanese social experience. The convention among clinicians at the time had been to use German diagnostic categories to describe Japanese psychological and psychiatric problems. After commencing training in the United States, Doi became committed to finding a Japanese vocabulary for Japanese patients' experience. Thus Doi arrived at the problem of "culture" through the problem of psychiatry, and so began to grapple with the pivotal question that had characterized Japan's modernity: how to articulate Japan's cultural particularities through the universalizing Western vocabularies of self and modernity—how to be "modern" without being "Western."

2. Although such a model of family had been embraced by only a small minority of Japanese (chiefly samurai families), in the attempt to centralize its administration and instill a shared sense of national identity among its citizens, the Meiji government required all citizens to register with the local government as members of household structures.

3. Doi also cites Nishida Kitarō as well as Suzuki Daisetsu, the Zen thinker, whose writings were appropriated by nationalist ideologues. The culturalists sought to formulate a new vision of "humanism" resting on entirely Japanese values—to transcend the Western egotism that seemed to accompany capitalism (Najita and Harootunian 1998). Nishida resorted to Zen notions of human consciousness and the transcendence of the ego. These texts would have been central to college or *kōtō gakkō* curricula in the immediate prewar period, when Doi was educated. Doi cites Nishida and Suzuki's notions of Japanese indivisibility of subject and object and notions of self and other (77).

4. He explicitly makes this argument in such passages as this: "The people as a whole are nothing but one great and unified house, all stemming from an identical ancestor. Thus, the entire state is 'the house within the household,' and the fence that surrounds the latter is broadened conceptually to become the boundaries of the state. Within the borders of the state as a whole, there should be the same unreserved and inseparable union that is achieved within the house. The virtue that is called filial piety from the standpoint of the house

becomes loyalty from the standpoint of the state" (Watsuji 1961: 148).

5. In his analysis of the 1980 Ohira policy study report, *Bunka no Jidai,* Harry Harootunian (1989) points out that new discourses on Japanese culture that emerged in the context of postwar prosperity erased Japanese history—instead relying on inhering, timeless, and racialized cultural qualities forged in contrast to the West: "Yet clearly the new representation no longer conforms to the simple opposition between traditional and modern, seen as moments in an evolutionary narrative. Rather, it reveals the operation of a newer division between what the *Bunka no Jidai* text describes as the 'Japanized' view and the 'Westernized View,' now facing each other as absolutes standing outside of history, accountable only to an unchanging 'nature' (read as culture) and 'race'" (86).

6. Nishikawa has pointed out that the language of *katei* was invoked in the wartime agendas of nationalism and imperialism. *Shufu no Tomo* (A Housewife's Friend) created such slogans as *katei aikoku* (family patriotism) and urged family participation in wartime endeavors through participation in local neighborhood groups composed of families, *katei tonarigumi.* Yet the *katei* did not become subject to scrutiny for its complicity in Japan's militarist regime in the way that the institution of *ie* did. Hence it provided a language that could be easily recuperated in the postwar period to more democratic ends. Nishikawa writes:

> I was shocked to see how glibly the magazine *[Shufu no Tomo]* transformed its use of the term *katei* during the transition to postwar society. . . . [I]n its first postwar edition, [it] created a new slogan using the word *katei*—*Heiwa to katei kensetsu* (Peace and the building of the *katei*). At the beginning of the same issue, the following statement appears: "The women of the *katei* had great responsibilities during the war. The reason the conflict was able to go on for so long with meager national resources was that the *katei* expended all its energies to continue life during wartime. The women of the *katei* also have a large role to play in the building of peace in Japan." (*Shufu no Tomo* 29, no. 10 [Nov. 1945]: 3, cited in Nishikawa 1995: 30–31)

7. Exploring the question of why the Japanese government resisted mobilizing women to enter the workforce until relatively late in the war (in 1944 the government finally drafted single women into the workplace), Yoshiko Miyake has shown how women were constructed as a domestic analog to the soldier fighting in the fields through their role as reproducers of the citizenry (1991: 271). By the 1930s the draft and the urbanization of labor had already moved large numbers of men from the home. Miyake writes:

> Whereas the late Meiji government had strengthened the legal power of the father as household head and played up his role as rigid moral authority (following the definition in the Meiji Civil Code), the Showa version of family-state ideology, in an attempt to preserve the cohesion of the family system, focused on the image of fecundity and warmth of blood relations associated with mothers. (271)

Others have shown how women were able to create a seamless shift from wartime roles as patriots to postwar roles as pacifists and nurturing mothers. While during the war women sent soldiers to the front in the name of motherhood and the Japanese state, in the postwar period, images of home and family were used in the promotion of peace and democracy. In her analysis of the construction of war memory and Hiroshima, Lisa Yoneyama (1999) shows how women involved in postwar antinuclear movements linked home and motherhood to Japan's innocence and victimhood in the war. A monument, "Mother and Child in a Tempest," constructed after the war and placed at the entrance of Hiroshima's Peace Memorial Park in 1980, depicts a mother in socialist realist fashion, bending over a small child while hoisting another onto her back. The monument was built with funds raised by the Hirsoshima Women's Coalition. A narrative describing the monument's symbolism juxtaposes far-off male-initiated aggression with the daily life of mothers and children: "Just before the atom bomb attack, it was a usual calm morning in Hiroshima. . . . Despite the tense wartime atmosphere, mothers and children greeted the morning just like the morning before." The narrative culminates with mothers and children calling out for each other amid the destruction that ensued (Yoneyama 195).

8. Until that time, few women could afford to become full-time house-wives or to cultivate the domestic trappings of a middle-class lifestyle, although these ideals began to be promoted in the mass media in the early part of the twentieth century.

9. Such a culture had begun to take root among the urban upper class in the 1920s, as a growing number of office workers, government workers, and teachers moved to the residential outskirts of large metropolitan areas, and magazines such as *Shufu no Tomo* (A Housewife's Companion), first published in 1916, advocated the creation of a "modern" home through the rationalization of housework, scientific child-rearing, and an emphasis on husband-wife relations rather than parent and child (Nishikawa 1995: 22–23).

10. The pattern has been for companies to hire women almost exclusively in assembly line, clerical, and service capacities, with the expectation that women would leave work to start a family rather than demanding promotions and pay raises. Companies prefer to reserve upwardly mobile trajectories for men, on whom they can count to work long overtime hours and endure long-distance transfers. Women have historically served as a kind of economic "buffer" for companies, employable in times of prosperity and dispensable during downturns.

11. As Yoda (2000) notes, even young Prince Akihito (son of Hirohito, Japan's emperor from 1925 to 1989) and Princess Michiko, a commoner, emblemized the modern ideals of family, love, and romance. They met on a tennis court, and Japanese citizens eagerly followed their romance, marriage, and honeymoon, with young girls imitating the fashions of Michiko. Later they came to emblemize the ideal of the new family as Michiko insisted on breast-feeding her own children rather than handing them off to a wet nurse.

The shift that occurred over the next decades from the household lineage to the nuclear family was in reality more gradual than the shift in ideology. Multigenerational families endured in the postwar era in forms that defied statistical counting, such as two-generation apartments with adjoining units *(nisetai jūtaku)* so that two generations might live in proximity and share the labor of the household, even though they were officially counted as two independent households (Lock 1993b). In fact the nuclearization of the family had been going on for some time among the middle classes, beginning in the Meiji and becoming more pervasive in the Taishō period (1913–25).

12. The dramatic expansion of the middle class in the 1950s and 1960s was undergirded by the growing proportion of individuals attaining higher levels of education, including rising numbers of high school and college graduates. During these initial postwar decades, access to higher education proved remarkably egalitarian (Gordon 2000: 285–86), although this was later to change. As high school education became more universal, the cultural background and life experience of white-collar and blue-collar workers grew increasingly close (Gordon 2000; Rohlen 1973).

13. These ideas had already appeared in the 1920s in the context of growing urban professional and working classes, as motherly love began to be seen as a catalyst for social mobility. Magazines on child care began to appear, with articles like "Mother's Love How Great!" "The Evolution of Mother's Love," and "Training for Motherhood" (Ohinata 1995). Such articles emphasized the crucial nature of the training a child receives at home over the importance of education and social training. "If a mother neglects her child's education, the child will not grow up to be anything commendable or respectable," one article huffed (201). It is in this context, too, that breast-feeding comes to be seen as the sine qua non of motherhood itself: the vehicle through which a mother's love is passed on to her children, as described in articles such as "The Spirit of Motherly Love Flows through the Milk of a Mother's Breast" and "True Motherly Love Starts with the Breast."

14. Ohinata traces the discourse of "motherly love" and its importance in the child's education and development to the Taishō period, when urban, nuclear, working-class families grew in numbers. These women were chastised for delegating the labor of child-rearing to wet nurses and community facilities.

15. Since all males regardless of their social class were required to enlist, military ethics became the new universalism that replaced Tokugawa particularism, producing the "samuraization" of the male population across social classes (Tsurumi 1970: 81–85). Furthermore, the separation of military and civilian life was not seen as desirable, and

all males over twenty were considered either active soldiers or ex-soldiers (88–89).

By the prewar period, military education had permeated the public school system, beginning in Meiji and intensifying in the prewar period. Physical training and military training were historically joined; even after European calisthenics and physical education regimens were imported in early Meiji, former military officers with no training in physical education were often hired to supervise physical education, and the military arts were emphasized. Beginning in the 1920s, military officers were replaced with physical education teachers, but at this time active army officers conducted military training beginning in middle school (GHQ 1946: 33–35; 64–65). Similarly pedagogical methods generally emphasized book learning and authoritarian measures.

16. According to Ezra Vogel, the new middle class of the 1950s was explicitly critical of the hierarchical relations of loyalty and obedience that had characterized the prewar family and firm, dismissing these values as "feudalistic":

> Elders in the community who arbitrarily impose their will on community organizations would be considered feudalistic. Main family members in the country who make demands on the branch family in Mamachi are considered feudalistic. High status people who try to control some activities of low status people in the community are considered feudalistic. Too much interference by a work superior in the personal life of an employee would be considered feudalistic. (1963: 151)

17. See Kumazawa's (1996) discussion of "total quality control," which he sees as at times an insidious means to co-opt workers into their own regime of hyperproductivity.

18. Two examples show how such trade-offs were enacted, revealing how workers' needs were met while at the same time their autonomy was eroded. Andrew Gordon has shown how the promotional practices that eventually emerged were the product of a compromise between employees' demands for wages based on employee "needs" (age, fam-

ily demands, health needs, etc.) and employers' demands for wages and promotion based on employee competence and skill (the American model) (Andrew Gordon 1993). The eventual criterion that emerged, described as promotion based on "merit," defined *merit* neither as "skill" nor as seniority but rather as the employee's commitment to the company as seen in his diligence, effort, and loyalty. The "merit" system, while responding to employee desires for job stability, systematically rewarded workers who were willing to sacrifice personal needs and desires for the sake of the organization—thereby weeding out elements of resistance and contestation within the system (Andrew Gordon 1993; see also Kumazawa 1996).

In another example, Thomas Rohlen and Richard Pascale analyze negotiations between workers and management that took place in the context of the imminent bankruptcy of Tōyō Kigyō, manufacturer of the Mazda automobile, in 1975 (Pascale and Rohlen 1988). In the endeavor to cut costs while at the same time keeping workers on the payroll, the company proposed the "dispatched-worker program," dispatching thousands of mid-level Mazda employees to local (prefectural) Mazda dealers to help sell cars. Salaries would be paid in part by the retail dealer, with the balance, including bonus and benefits, paid by the company. The union approved the arrangement, under substantial pressure, after demanding assurances that (1) the program would be voluntary, (2) the workers would be guaranteed appropriate living conditions, and (3) their career would not be put in jeopardy if they failed to sell enough cars. The arrangement demonstrates both the commitment on the part of the company to keeping workers on the payroll and the difficult compromises made by workers. The company's flexibility in allocating its workers ultimately contributed to the recovery of the company.

CHAPTER 3. GOOD WIVES

1. One testimonial, published in the Al-Anon publication *Al Anon Faces Alcoholism* (1977), nicely illustrates this compromise. A woman describes how she learned to break free from the drinking dynamics, carving out a space where she could continue some of the activities that were important to her:

After our first baby son was born, I joined a bridge club. My husband never took me out, and we never entertained because he was always either drunk or hung over. And we were always too broke. I felt the need to go out; I wanted adult companionship, and looked forward to my Thursday evenings playing bridge; but my husband would stay out and get drunk on those nights, and since I had no one to stay with the baby, I would have to call at the last minute to apologize. Then I sat and stewed in my juice until my husband came home, whereupon I would unleash all my anger and frustration on him.

After I read the pamphlet and started coming to Al-Anon meetings, I realized how foolish I had been. A baby-sitter solved the problem very simply. I had always been afraid to get a baby-sitter before, either because we couldn't afford it or because I was ashamed to have her see my husband drunk. But since Al-Anon, I'm not afraid any more and when my husband doesn't come home, I just call the sitter and go out and have my much-needed diversion. Since he has to pay her, it automatically removes my excuse for resentment and helps to relieve his guilt. And having to pay, even in this small way, adds to the unpleasantness of his drinking episode, and adds to the pain he suffers as a result of his drinking. (1977: 92)

2. Some have argued that the notion of love that emerged in the Victorian middle class and bourgeoisie solved multiple social problems generated by the rise of industrialization. They have argued that the growing importance of love as a discourse solved the problem of a growing number of wayward and economically unstable men (as industrialization put family enterprises out of business), who could now be induced to settle into work for the sake of wife and family, and it solved the problem of economically dependent women, who, now seen as nonproductive beings who needed to be supported, found ways to prove their worth through beauty, sexuality, and seductiveness (Collier 1998)

3. As Nakane notes, productivity and cohesion were emphasized even over strict biological descent. Thus in a family with only daughters, the eldest daughter could bring her husband into the family line as an adopted son and the next male heir (Nakane 1977).

4. Lebra describes an instance in which the bond of love that developed between a young husband and wife caused considerable tension in the household and provoked the husband's family to attempt to throw her out (1984: 123).

5. In the 1980s and 1990s, when companies began to cut costs by ushering middle-management employees toward early retirement, unflattering nicknames for returning husbands circulated in the mass media. These names, such as "wet fallen leaves" *(nureochiba)* and "over-sized garbage" *(sodai gomi)*—a category of garbage collected once a month that includes old futons, umbrellas, and other non-recyclable and nonburnable waste—depicted men who were useless and unwelcome in the home.

6. At this point everyone roared with laughter because "Yo-chan" is the diminutive form of Yoshichiku and connotes a kind of affection that exists between two children. The idea of couples calling each other by their first names was inspired by the American custom. However, there are relatively few occasions when a Japanese person calls someone by his or her actual name without any suffix attached, so her choice was the only one that made sense, since he was probably called Yo-chan by his friends and family before he got married.

7. The notion is popularized in the expression known as *isshin denshin,* literally, "separate hearts communicating as one," often described in postwar literature on Japanese national identity as a distinctly Japanese feature.

8. Such practices have deep historical roots. The Imperial Rescript on Education *(Kyōiku Chokugo),* developed to educate elite young women in the Meiji period, emphasized the values of frugality, abstemiousness, and staid comportment. Women continue to be educated in these traditions today, including women in junior colleges training to be office ladies and good wives and mothers (McVeigh 1994; Lebra 1976: 40).

9. In the social casework department of a large Tokyo hospital where I observed family consultations, a young couple came in with marital troubles. Although I do not know what complex problems contributed to the couple's unhappiness, the central issue the husband broached to the counselor was his wife's inattentiveness. She left dirty

dishes in the sink, ignored tilted pictures on the wall, and let flowers stay in the vase after the petals had fallen. The young husband said, "As the flowers started to whither and fall, it kept bothering me that she didn't clean up the scattered petals. I suppose it would have been easier in the end if I just did it myself but what bothered is that she didn't notice *[ki ga tsukanai]*. . . . I feel that I'm quietly being 'damaged' by her behavior *[Kanojo no kōdō ni shizuka na damēji o ukete iru to omou]*." While to me these seemed like trivial, chauvinistic complaints, I was surprised that the social worker, ordinarily a progressive woman, seemed to sympathize with him. She chastised the young woman for becoming overly relaxed in her marriage and "letting herself go."

10. Lebra notes this pattern in several of the young couples she came to know in Shizumi. She describes one husband who liked to humiliate and verbally assault his wife in public. To avoid this embarrassment, the wife took great pains not to irritate him and made sure to shut all the windows of the house when he began yelling. Her mother, who lived nearby, also shared her shame (1984: 130).

11. Traditionally the Japanese dating system was based on the reign of the emperor, starting again at one with each new reign. The dating system was officially changed to the Western system after the war, though some continue to use the reign names. The Heisei period is the current period, which began in 1989.

12. Marxist feminism, drawing on the early work of Friedrich Engels, *The Origin of the Family, Private Property and the State,* sees gender inequality as primarily an expression of class inequality. Monogamy is an economic institution designed for men to pass on their wealth to future heirs; because it deprives women of social participation and participation in the political struggle for emancipation of the working class, it is seen as the inaugural subordinating institution for women (Engels 1972: 120, 128–29, cited in Jaggar 1988: 65).

13. Japan had its version of the "women's lib" *(ūman ribu)* movement in the 1970s, drawing inspiration from American liberal and radical feminism of the 1960 and 1970s. In the context of the *ūman ribu* movement, Japanese feminists criticized the role of housewife as destructive and demeaning to women, and encouraged women

to seek "self-realization," self-determination," and "emancipation" (Machiko Matsui 1990: 435). Tanaka Mitsu, a founder of the movement, criticized women's subordination to men and women's suppression of their own sexuality in the context of the patriarchal family. She argued that women had one of two choices in marriage: to be viewed by their husbands as a loving, maternal presence or else as merely a "depository" for their sexual desire *(seiyoku shōriki)*—but that equality was not an option (Tanaka 1992a: 202). Demonstrators near the Tokyo Ginza district in 1970 carried placards reading "What is femininity?" and "Wives are legal prostitutes" (Baldwin 1973: 237; see also Mitchell 1971: 52; Aoki 1997). Although the *ūman ribu* movement gained attention in the mass media and helped lay the foundation for the growth of women's studies in academia in the late 1970s, it remained strikingly remote from most women's daily lives.

CHAPTER 4. A SUCCESS STORY

1. The expression *tonde iru onna* ("flying woman") is used in contemporary Japanese to mean a woman who doesn't abide by social custom. The expression is a literal translation coming from the title of Erica Jong's book *Fear of Flying,* which has been translated into Japanese.

2. After marriage, a daughter became a member of her husband's family. In the Edō and Meiji periods, it was considered to be a "shame" on the family if the daughter had to return home after marrying, since this meant that she had somehow failed as a bride.

3. There is some evidence to suggest class and regional variations in the way young brides were treated, the ease of procuring a divorce, the extent to which they were segregated from male workers. Ueno (1987) for example, has argued that despite certain Edo period tracts on wifely behavior (such as *Onna Daigaku*), these constraining ideals were not always embraced. Furthermore, in upper-class families, husbands were less at liberty to mistreat their wives (who also were chosen from upper-class families). Regional variations in the ways that labor was organized also led to variation. Villages in northeastern Japan have traditionally been more household-oriented,

whereas southwestern villages were organized around age-group sets and children often lived away from their parents in a communal-lodging system.

CHAPTER 5. THE INESCAPABLE DISCOURSE OF MOTHERHOOD

1. The cloth books, which were displayed on the walls of the room, were a source of pride for the day care center workers, who pointed them out to me several times. They were, in fact, exceedingly crafts-manlike and compelling. They were made by a volunteer group, whose promotional sheet was passed out with the weekly song sheets and notices. The volunteer group donated their work to public day care centers, libraries, schools for disabled children, and to senior citizens' homes. The recruitment sheet for new members said the following:

    > We make not just cloth books but all kinds of toys and play gear, so that children's worlds of play will expand with no limits! We appreciate the softness, warmth, and kindness of the cloth as we incorporate our hearts into each stitch, each stitch. . . . There's only one mommy in the world and we want to give to children the cloth books and toys that were made by her.

2. The major Edo period (1600–1868) ethical text on the comportment of women, *Onna Daigaku* (The Greater Learning for Women), emphasized wifely duties (eschewing the company of men other than one's husband, attending to one's parents-in-law) while scarcely mentioning the role of motherhood. The inferior status of women at the time suggests that women (or at least mothers) may not have been have played a central role in child-rearing (Niwa 1993: 71–72). Article 10 of *Onna Daigaku* states, "A woman's infirmities include a lack of submission, ill temper, resentfulness, jealousy, slander of others, and stupidity. Seven or eight out of ten women are afflicted with these infirmities. Thus, women are inferior to men. They are not fit to raise children since they tend to be carried away by their love" (Ishikawa 1977: 54, cited in Niwa 1993: 72).

3. Niwa has written that the ideology of the good wife and wise mother allowed Meiji statesmen to meet the demands of two conflicting ideologies: conservative Confucionist interest in confining women to the home and modern demands of state-building and embracing the Western notion of gender equality (Niwa 1993: 75).

4. In her 1978 study of the Japanese consumer movement, Catherine Lewis noted that housewives agitating for better environmental and consumer protection gained access to corporate executives and politicians precisely by invoking their status as concerned mothers.

5. "Tough Love with Teens" (2002), available at www.ianr.unl.edu/pubs/family, a web site maintained by the Cooperative Extension, Institute of Agriculture and Natural Resources, University of Nebraska, Lincoln.

6. A survey conducted by the *Asahi Shinbun* in 1988 asked parents how long they felt their responsibility for their children continued: 32 percent answered "until they're adults," 21 percent answered "until they're married," and 16 percent answered "as long as a parent is alive." Only 4 percent answered "until they're done with required education" (*Asahi Shinbun Shasetsu,* Nov. 15, 1992).

7. John Bowlby described a strong mother-child attachment as the foundation that allows children to depart from the protection of the family and explore on their own; in their studies they videotaped mothers playing with their children and then watched how the child reacted when the mother left the room and returned again. Children who were upset but consolable when their mothers returned were deemed to have a healthy attachment; children who were either indifferent to their mothers returning or inconsolable were said to have frail attachments. They emphasized the continual presence of the mother during childrearing and blamed later developmental problems on insufficient maternal care. While the theory was eventually criticized in European and American psychological circles for overemphasizing the role of the mother, the critique failed to permeate Japanese child-rearing circles and is still very much part of conventional wisdom today (Ohinata 1995: 209).

8. For a brief period after the war, these tendencies fell out of fashion under the influence of Western child-rearing fashions. Japanese

mothers began reading Dr. Spock in translation; feeding times were strictly regulated, bottle-feeding and powdered milk became popular (partially due to economic exigencies), and children slept separately. Formula was advertised widely at the time, with ads featuring uncharacteristically fat babies. However, as Japan prospered economically, the trend reversed itself, and child-rearing manuals of the 1990s emphasize the importance of nursing and physical proximity with the child.

9. In their well-known study comparing American and Japanese patterns of mothering and socialization in the 1960s, Caudill and Schooler observe:

> In America the mother views her baby, at least potentially, as a separate and autonomous being who should learn to do and think for himself. . . . [S]o also does she think of herself as a separate person with her own needs and desires, which includes time away from her baby to pursue her own interests, and to be a wife to her husband as well as a mother to her baby. . . . [The Japanese mother] views her baby much more as an extension of herself, and psychologically the boundaries between them are blurred. Because of the great emphasis in Japan on the close attachment between mother and child, the mother is likely to feel that she knows what is best and that there is no particular need for him to tell her verbally what he wants because, after all, they are virtually one. (Caudill and Schooler 1973: 327, cited in Boocock 1999: 11)

10. The notion of *bosei* is relatively new in Japan, but its proponents describe it as an inhering maternal instinct, the culmination of an evolutionary process. The notion of *bosei* emerged in the 1920s under the influence of Western feminists. It emphasized the importance of mothers as the "first and foremost teachers of their children," and as "entirely responsible" for their children's fate. Women who did not bear children were seen as aberrant, and in turn, having a bad mother was seen as life's greatest misfortune (Niwa 1993: 76–77; Ohinata 1995: 200–203).

11. Sumiko Iwao makes this argument by describing the following incident:

In the city of Osaka a middle-aged man broke into a major bank and held a number of people hostage. . . . The technique used by the police to persuade him to give up was to ferret out the where-abouts of his aged mother and bring her all the way to Osaka from a small village in Shikoku, where she lived alone. As a mother, it was infuriating for me to watch the police bring forth a tiny gray-haired woman who was awed and frightened by the row of tele-vision cameras and microphones pointed at her and who could only bow deeply and apologize profusely to society watching on six channels. (Iwao 1993: 134)

CONCLUSION

1. The American Time-Use Survey reports that for all households (in-cluding households where women are at home), the average amount of time women focused on child care is 1.7 hours (and 2.7 for house-holds with children under age 6), marginally more than in homes where women work. But in this aggregate measure, women spend 6.4 hours a day providing "secondary" child care—that is, performing other tasks, such as shopping or housework, while in the company of their children. Thus the opportunity to spend time with one's chil-dren is far greater in these households (Bureau of Labor Statistics 2003, "First Results": 3).

2. There has been a steady rise in the number of women in their late sixties in the labor force in the past twenty years, while the number of older men in the labor force has declined. These women are enti-tled to little if any of their husbands' pension provisions despite their years of child-rearing service, and many remain in the workforce to retirement age or beyond in order to make ends meet.

3. The renewed trend among middle- and upper-middle-class Amer-ican women toward staying at home and the revised feminist notion that women should have the "choice" to become full-time mothers are perhaps important correctives to second-wave feminism's di-minishment of the home. But the fact remains that women who rely on their husbands to support them do not enjoy the same social and state-implemented financial support that Japanese housewives en-joy, and must continue to rely on their husbands' "love" for their sense of stability and security.

4. Civic and political movements in the United States often fall into this pattern by attributing such values as "nurturance," "communalism," "peace-loving," and "spirituality" to all women—for example antinuclear groups, pro-life groups and pro-choice groups, and New Age movements that seek to reclaim feminine spirituality. These agendas assume that women's contributions through the domestic sphere are motivated by deep differences between women and men; women contribute to the public good not as good citizens—adhering to values held up by all citizens—but rather by innately opposing these values. Since these movements cannot explain why all women would share these values, they assume shared values rooted in biological differences.

5. In one of these early debates, the "motherhood protection controversy" (which took place between 1915 and 1918), Hiratsuka Raichō, one of the most vociferous advocates of motherhood protection, argued that motherhood should be protected as a part of a larger national project:

> A mother is the source of lives. Women have a social and national presence beyond the individual through being a mother. Therefore, protecting a mother means not only women's well-being but also the whole society's well-being.
> . . . Children, whether you bear them or not, are not your possession but rather belong to the society and the nation.

The number and quality of children are related to the nation's development, progress, and destiny. The mother's task to bear and raise children is not just individual work but social and national work. This task is the social obligation assigned to women (*Fujin Kōron,* cited in Akaoka 1991).

6. Ueno Chizuko makes this point in discussing the appropriation of the "Take Back the Night Movement" by Japanese women. The movement misses the fact that for Japanese women, who are chiefly valued in their role as mothers, the chief site of violence may in fact be the home rather than the street (1997: 288).

7. This is the motivation behind a number of policies, known collectively as the "Angel Plan" *(Enzēru Puran),* currently being imple-

mented by four government agencies in order to create a more viable environment for women to work while having children (such as the expansion of public day care, the establishment of support centers for households with children, etc.)

8. The national Diet is now debating a bill, which seems certain to pass, to lower the spousal deduction ceiling to roughly $7,000. Women earning over that amount would be taxed at the usual rates, making it slightly more difficult for women to receive the full deduction.

9. Ironically, it is the more highly educated women who are most eligible for upwardly mobile marriage and thus, despite their education, are likely to end up as housewives. Conversely, middle-class or working class women who wish for a comfortable life must often continue working to help support the family (Yamada 2001: 56).

REFERENCES

Abu-Lughod, Lila. 1990. The Romance of Resistance: Tracing Transformations of Power through Bedouin Women. *American Ethnologist* 17 (1): 41–55.

———. 1995. A Tale of Two Pregnancies. In *Women Writing Culture,* ed. Ruth Behar and Deborah Gordon, 339–49. Berkeley: University of California Press.

Akaoka, Junko. 1991. The Myth of Japanese Working Mothers. Master's thesis, Eastern Michigan University.

Al-Anon. 1977. *Al-Anon Faces Alcoholism.* New York: Al-Anon Family Group Headquarters.

———. N.d. A Guide for the Family of the Alcoholic. New York: Al-Anon Family Groups.

Allison, Anne. 1991. Japanese Mothers and Obentōs: The Lunch-Box as Ideological State Apparatus. *Anthropological Quarterly* 64 (4): 195–208.

———. 1994. *Nightwork: Sexuality, Pleasure, and Corporate Masculinity in a Tokyo Hostess Club.* Chicago: University of Chicago Press.

———. 2000. *Permitted and Prohibited Desires: Mothers, Comics, and Censorship in Japan.* Berkeley: University of California Press.

Ames, Walter. 1981. *Police and Community in Japan.* Berkeley: University of California Press.

Aoki, Yayoi. 1997. Interview. In *Broken Silence: Voices of Japanese Feminism,* ed. Sandra Buckley, 3–17. Berkeley: University of California Press.

Aonuma, Yoshimatsu. 1972. The Japanese Corporation: Its Structure and Dynamics. *Wheel Extended* 2 (2): 3–12.

Appadurai, Arjun. 1991. Global Ethnoscapes: Notes and Queries for a Transnational Anthropology. In *Recapturing Anthropology: Working in the Present,* ed. Richard Fox, 191–210. Santa Fe, NM: School for American Research Press.

Asai, Michiko. 1990. Kindai Kazoku Gensō Kara no Kaihō o Mezashite [Toward a Liberation from Illusions of the Modern Family]. In *Feminizumu Ronsō: 70 Nendai kara 90 nendai e* [Feminist Debates: From the 1970s to the 1990s], ed. Y. Ehara, 87–117. Tokyo: Keisō Publishers.

Azuma, Hiroshi. 1984. Psychology in a Non-Western Country. *International Journal of Psychology* 19: 45–55.

Bachnik, Jane M., and Charles J. Quinn, eds. 1994. *Situated Meaning: Inside and Outside in Japanese Self, Society, and Language.* Princeton, N.J.: Princeton University Press.

Baldwin, Frank. 1973. The Idioms of Contemporary Japan V: *Ūman Ribu. The Japan Interpreter* 8 (2): 237–45.

Banton, R., P. Clifford, S. Frosh, J. Lousada, and J. Rosenthall. 1985. *The Politics of Mental Health.* London: Macmillan Publishers.

Beattie, Melody. 1987. *Codependent No More: How to Stop Controlling Others and Start Caring for Yourself.* New York: Harper Collins.

Beauchamp, Edward R., and James M. Vardaman, Jr. 1994. *Japanese Education since 1945: A Documentary Study.* New York: M. E. Sharpe.

Befu, Harumi. 1966. Corporate Emphasis and Patterns of Descent in the Japanese Family. In *Japanese Culture: Its Development and Characteristics,* ed. R. J. Smith and R. K. Beardsley. Chicago: Aldine Publishing.

Belkin, Lisa. 2003. The Opt-Out Revolution. *New York Times Magazine,* Oct. 26.

Bellah, Robert. 1985. *Habits of the Heart: Individualism and Commitment in American Life.* Berkeley: University of California Press.

Benedict, Ruth. 1974. *The Chrysanthemum and the Sword.* New York: Meridian.

Bernstein, Gail Lee. 1991. Introduction. In *Recreating Japanese Women, 1600–1945.* Berkeley: University of California Press.

Boocock, Sarane Spence. 1999. Social Prisms: An International Comparison of Childrearing Manuals. *International Journal of Japanese Sociology* 8 (Nov.): 5–33.

Borovoy, Amy. 1994. Good Wives and Mothers: The Production of Domesticity in a Global Economy. Ph.D. diss., Stanford University.

———. 2001a. Not a Doll's House: Public Uses of Domesticity in Japan. *U.S. Japan Women's Journal,* English Supplement no. 20.

———. 2001b. Recovering from Codependence in Japan. *American Ethnologist* 28 (1): 94–118.

———. 2002. Japan Studies and the Anthropology of the Self: Dialogues between Area Studies and Social Theory. Unpublished ms.

Bourdieu, Pierre. 1977. *Outline of a Theory of Practice.* Cambridge: Cambridge University Press.

Bradshaw, Jonathan, and Naomi Finch. 2002. *A Comparison of Child Benefit Packages in Twenty-two Countries.* Department for Work and Pensions Research Report No. 174. Leeds: CDS.

Braisted, William Reynolds, trans. 1976. *Meiroku Zasshi: Journal of the Japanese Enlightenment.* Tokyo: University of Tokyo Press.

Brinton, Mary C. 1993. *Women and the Economic Miracle: Gender and Work in Postwar Japan.* Berkeley: University of California Press.

Bryant, Taimie L. 1984. Marital Dissolution in Japan: Legal Obstacles and Their Impact. *Law in Japan* 17: 73–97.

Buckley, Sandra, and Vera Mackie. 1986. Women in the New Japanese State. In *Democracy in Contemporary Japan,* ed. Y. S. Gavan McCormack, 173–85. New York: M. E. Sharpe.

Bureau of Labor Statistics. 2004. American Time-Use Survey—First Results. Washington, DC: United States Department of Labor. Available at www.bls.gov.

Caudill, William A., and Carmi Schooler. 1973. Child Behavior and Child Rearing in Japan and the United States: An Interim Report. *Journal of Nervous and Mental Disease* 157 (5): 323–38.

Chatterjee, Partha. 1993. *The Nation and Its Fragments: Colonial and Postcolonial Histories.* Princeton, N.J.: Princeton University Press.

Chodorow, Nancy. 1991. *The Reproduction of Mothering: Psychoanalysis and the Sociology of Gender.* New Haven, Conn.: Yale University Press.

Christopher, Robert C. 1983. *The Japanese Mind.* New York: Fawcett Books.

Coles, Robert. 1980. Civility and Psychology. *Daedalus* 109 (3): 132–41.

Collier, Jane. 1974. Women in Politics. In *Woman, Culture, and Society,* ed. Michelle Zimbalist Rosaldo and Louise Lamphere, 88–96. Stanford, Calif.: Stanford University Press.

———. 1991. Negotiating Values: You Can't Have It Both Ways. In *Balancing Acts: Women and the Process of Social Change,* ed. P. L. Johnson, 163–77. Boulder, Colo.: Westview Press.

———. 1998. Love and Sex, Body and Soul, II. Course lecture in Civilizations, Ideas, and Values, Stanford University.

Comaroff, Jean. 1985. *Body of Power, Spirit of Resistance: The Culture and History of a South African People.* Chicago: University of Chicago Press.

Comaroff, Jean, and John Comaroff. 1991. *Of Revelation and Revolution: Christianity, Colonialism, and Consciousness in South Africa,* vol. 1. Chicago: University of Chicago Press.

Crittenden, Ann. 2002. *The Price of Motherhood: Why the Most Important Job in the World Is Still the Least Valued.* New York: Owl Press.

Cusumano, Michael. 1985. *The Japanese Automobile Industry*. Cambridge, Mass.: Council on East Asian Studies, Harvard University.

De Certeau, Michel. 1984. *The Practice of Everyday Life*. Berkeley: University of California Press.

Delaney, Carol. 1998. *Abraham On Trial: The Social Legacy of Biblical Myth*. Princeton, N.J.: Princeton University Press.

Delbanco, Andrew, and Thomas Delbanco. 1995. AA at the Crossroads. *New Yorker*, March 20, 49–63.

D'Emilio, John, and Estelle B. Freedman. 1997. *Intimate Matters: A History of Sexuality in America*. Chicago: University of Chicago Press.

Diamond, Irene, and Lee Quinby, eds. 1988. *Feminism and Foucault: Reflections on Resistance*. Boston: Northeastern University Press.

Dirks, Nicholas, Geoff Eley, and Sherry Ortner. 1994. *Culture/Power/History: A Reader in Contemporary Social Theory*. Princeton, N.J.: Princeton University Press.

Doi, Takeo. 1971. *Amae no kōzō*. Tokyo: Kōbundō.

———. 1973. *The Anatomy of Dependence*. New York: Kodansha International.

Dower, John W. 1986. *War without Mercy*. New York: Pantheon Books

———. 1999. *Embracing Defeat: Japan in the Wake of World War II*. New York: W. W. Norton and New Press.

Ebisaka, Takeshi. 1988. Men, Women, and Divorce. *Japan Echo* 14: 45–47.

Ehara, Yumiko. 1993. Japanese Feminism in the 1970s and 1980s. *U.S. Japan Women's Journal*, English Supplement, no. 4: 49–69.

Ehara, Yumiko, ed. 1990. *Feminizumu Ronsō: 70 Nendai kara 90 nendai e* [Feminist Debates: From the 70s to the 90s]. Tokyo: Keisō Shobō.

Ehrenreich, John. 1978. *The Cultural Crisis of Modern Medicine*. New York: Monthly Review Press.

Enchi, Fumiko. 1971. *The Waiting Years*. New York: Kodansha International.

Engels, Frederick. 1972. *The Origin of the Family, Private Property, and the State*. New York: International Publishers.

Erikson, Erik. 1963. *Childhood and Society*. New York: W. W. Norton and Company.

Etō, Jun. 1975. *Seijuku to Sōshitsu: Haha no Hōkai* [Maturity and Loss: The Destruction of the Mother]. Tokyo: Kodansha.

Evans, Sara. 1979. *Personal Politics: The Roots of Women's Liberation in the Civil Rights Movement and the New Left*. New York: Vintage Books.

Faiola, Anthony. 2004. Japanese Women Live, and Like It, on Their Own. *Washington Post*, August 31.

Firestone, Shulamith. 1970. *The Dialectic of Sex: The Case for Feminist Revolution.* New York: Morrow.

Folbre, Nancy. 1991. The Unproductive Housewife: Her Evolution in Nineteenth-Century Economic Thought. *Signs* 16 (3): 463–84.

Foucault, Michel. 1965. *Madness and Civilization: A History of Insanity in an Age of Reason.* New York: Vintage Books.

———. 1979. *Discipline and Punish: The Birth of the Prison.* New York: Vintage Books.

———. 1990. *The History of Sexuality,* volume 1. New York: Vintage Books.

Fraser, Nancy, and Linda Gordon. 1994. A Genealogy of Dependency: Tracing a Keyword of the U.S. Welfare State. *Signs* 19 (2): 309–36.

Friedan, Betty. 1963. *The Feminine Mystique.* New York: Dell Publishing.

Fukuda, K. 1982. *Ryōsai Kenbo o Osou Shufu Shōkōgun no Fukimi na Ryūkō* [Attack of the good wife and mother: The strange popularity of housewife syndrome]. *Shūkan Asahi* 87 (18): 141–43.

Garon, Sheldon. 1993. Women's Groups and the Japanese State: Contending Approaches to Political Integration, 1890–1945. *Journal of Japanese Studies* 19 (1): 5–41.

———. 1994. Rethinking Modernization and Modernity in Japanese History: A Focus on State-Society Relations. *Journal of Asian Studies* 53 (2): 346–66.

———. 1997. *Molding Japanese Minds: The State in Everday Life.* Princeton, N.J.: Princeton University Press.

———. 2000. Luxury Is the Enemy: Mobilizing Savings and Popularizing Thrift in Wartime Japan. *Journal of Japanese Studies* 26 (1): 41–78.

Gelb, Joyce. 1991. Tradition and Change in Japan: The Case of Equal Employment Opportunity Law. *U.S. Japan Women's Journal* 1: 51–77.

General Headquarters, Supreme Commander for the Allied Powers, Civil Information and Education Section, Education Division. 1952. *Postwar Developments in Japanese Education.* Tokyo.

Giddens, Anthony. 1991. *Modernity and Self-Identity.* Stanford, Calif.: Stanford University Press.

———. 1992. *The Transformation of Intimacy.* Stanford, Calif.: Stanford University Press.

———. 1999. *Global Status Report on Alcohol.* Geneva: World Health Organization.

Gordon, Andrew. 1993. Contests for the Workplace. In *Postwar Japan as History,* ed. Andrew Gordon, 373–94. Berkeley: University of California Press.

———. 1997. Managing the Japanese Household: The New Life Movement in Postwar Japan. *Social Politics* (summer): 245–83.

———. 1998. The Invention of Japanese-Style Labor Management. In *Mirror of Modernity: Invented Traditions of Modern Japan,* ed. Stephen Vlastos, 19–36. Berkeley: University of California Press.

———. 2000. Society and Politics from Transwar through Postwar Japan. In *Historical Perspectives on Contemporary East Asia,* ed. Merle Goldman and Andrew Gordon, 272–96. Cambridge, Mass.: Harvard University Press.

Gordon, Linda. 1992. Why Nineteenth-Century Feminists Did Not Support the "Birth Control" Pill and Twentieth-Century Feminists Do: Feminism, Reproduction, and the Family. In *Rethinking the Family: Some Feminist Questions,* ed. Barrie Thorne and Marilyn Yalom, 262–86. Boston: Northeastern University Press.

Gramsci, Antonio. 1971. *Selections from the Prison Notebooks.* Trans. Quintin Hoare and Geoffrey Nowell Smith. New York: International Publishers.

Haaken, Janice. 1990. A Critical Analysis of the Co-dependence Construct. *Psychiatry* 53: 396–406.

———. 1993. From Al-Anon to ACOA: Codependence and the Reconstruction of Caregiving. *Signs* 18 (2): 321–45.

Haley, John Owen. 1991. *Authority without Power: Law and the Japanese Paradox.* New York: Oxford University Press.

Hall, Robert King, ed. 1949. *Kokutai no Hongi* [Cardinal Principles of the National Entity of Japan]. Trans. John Owen Gauntlett. Cambridge, Mass.: Harvard University Press.

Hamabata, Mathews. 1985. *Crested Kimono: Power and Love in the Japanese Business Family.* New Haven, Conn.: Yale University Press.

Hamilton, V. Lee, and Joseph Sanders. 1992. *Everyday Justice: Responsibility and the Individual in Japan and the United States.* New Haven, Conn.: Yale University Press.

Hane, Mikiso. 1988. *Reflections on the Way to the Gallows: Rebel Women in Prewar Japan.* Berkeley: University of California Press.

Hara, Hiroko. 1994. Comments on "Studies about Women in Japan" Session. *The Fifth Annual Ph.D. Kenkyūkai Conference on Japan Studies* (June): 41–43.

Harootunian, H. D. 1989. Visible Discourses/Invisible Ideologies. In *Postmodernism and Japan,* ed. Masao Miyoshi and H. D. Harootunian, 63–92. Durham, N.C.: Duke University Press.

———. 1993. America's Japan/Japan's Japan. In *Japan and the World,* ed. Masao Miyoshi and H. D. Harootunian, 196–221. Durham, N.C.: Duke University Press.

Harvey, Paul A. S. 1995. Interpreting *Oshin*—War, History, and Women in Modern Japan. In *Women, Media, and Consumption in Japan,* ed. Lise Skov and Brian Moeran, 75–110. Honolulu: University of Hawai'i Press.

Hashimoto, Meiko. 1989. *Kichin Dorinkā: Muryoku kara no Kaifuku* [The Kitchen Drinker: Recovering from Powerlessness]. Tokyo: Aki Shobō.

———. 1995. Intoxicated Youth. *Japan Quarterly* 42 (2): 136–45.

Hendry, Joy. 1981. *Marriage in Changing Japan.* London: Croom Helm.

Higuchi, Yoshio. 1997. The Effects of Income Tax and Social Security Policy: Married Women in the Japanese Labor Supply. *U.S. Japan Women's Journal,* English Supplement, no. 13: 104–29.

Higuchi, Yoshio, and Ōta Kiyoshi, eds. 2004. *Joseitachi no Heisei Fukyō* [Women and Heisei Recession]. Tokyo: Nihon Keizai Shinbunsha.

Hobsbawm, Eric. 1996. *The Age of Extremes : A History of the World, 1914–1991.* New York: Vintage.

Hochschild, Arlie Russell. 1983. *The Managed Heart: Commercialization of Human Feeling.* Berkeley: University of California Press.

———. 1997. *The Time Bind: When Work Becomes Home and Home Becomes Work.* New York: Metropolitan Books.

———. 2003. *Commercialization of Intimate Life: Notes from Home and Work.* Berkeley: University of California Press.

Illich, Ivan. 1976. *Medical Nemesis.* New York: Pantheon Books.

Imamura, Anne. 1987. *Urban Japanese Housewives: At Home and in the Community.* Honolulu: University of Hawai'i Press.

Inoue Teruko, Ueno Chizuko, and Ehara Yumiko, eds. 1995. *Bosei* [Mother Instinct]. Tokyo: Iwanami Shoten.

Ishida, Hiroshi. 1993. *Social Mobility in Contemporary Japan: Educational Credentials, Class and the Labour Market in Cross-National Perspective.* Stanford, Calif.: Stanford University Press.

Ivy, Marilyn. 1995. *Discoures of the Vanishing: Modernity, Phantasm, Japan.* Chicago: Chicago University Press.

Iwao, Sumiko. 1991. The Quiet Revolution: Japanese Women Today. *Japan Foundation Newsletter* 19 (3): 1–9.

———. 1993. *The Japanese Woman: Traditional Image and Changing Reality.* New York: Free Press.

Jackson, J. K. 1954. The Adjustment of the Family to the Crisis of Alcoholism. *Quarterly Journal of Studies of Alcohol* 24: 562–86.

Jaggar, Alison. 1988. *Feminist Politics and Human Nature.* New York: Rowman and Littlefield Publishers.

Japan Statistical Yearbook. 1988. *Nihon Tōkei Kyōkai* [Japan Statistical Yearbook]. Tokyo: Mainichi Shinbunsha.

Johnson, Chalmers. 1982. *MITI and the Japanese Miracle: The Growth of Industrial Policy, 1925–1975.* Stanford, Calif.: Stanford University Press.

Kanō, Tsutomu. 1973. Why the Search for Identity. *Japan Interpreter* 8: 153–58.

Kanō, Mikiyo. 1995. *"Bosei" no Tanjō to Tennō Sei* [The Birth of "Mother Instinct" and the Emperor System]. In *Bosei* [Mother Instinct], ed. Inoue Teruko, Ueno Chizuko, and Ehara Yumiko, 56–61. Tokyo: Iwanami Shoten.

Katsura, Taisaku. 1983. *Daidokoro Shōkōgun* [Kitchen Syndrome]. Tokyo: San Maku.

Kawai, Hayao. 1976. *Bosei Shakai: Nihon no Byōri* [The Maternal Society: Japan's Pathology]. Tokyo: Chūō Kōron Sha.

Kawamura, Nozomu. 1989. The Transition of the Household System in Japan's Modernization. In *Constructs for Understanding Japan,* ed. Yoshio Sugimoto and Ross Mouer, 202–27. New York: Kegan Paul.

Kelly, William W. 2002. At the Limits of the New Middle-Class Japan: Beyond "Mainstream Consciousness." In *Social Contracts under Stress: The Middle Classes of America, Europe, and Japan at the Turn of the Century,* ed. Olivier Zunz, Leonard Schoppa, and Nobuhiro Hiwatari, 232–54. New York: Russell Sage Foundation.

Kelsky, Karen. 1994. Postcards from the Edge: The "Office Ladies" of Tokyo. *U.S. Japan Women's Journal,* English Supplement, no. 6: 3–26.

———. 2001. *Women on the Verge: Japanese Women, Western Dreams.* Durham, N.C.: Duke University Press.

Kiefer, Christie. 1984. The *Danchi Zoku* and the Evolution of Metropolitan Mind. In *Japan: The Paradox of Progress,* ed. Lewis Austin, 279–300. New Haven, Conn.: Yale University Press.

Kimura, Bin. 1972. *Hito to Hito no Aida: Seishin Byōrigakuteki Nihonron* [Between People: An Analysis of Japanese Mental Pathologies]. Tokyo: Kōbundō.

Kirita, Kiyohide. 1994. D. T. Suzuki on Society and the State. In *Rude Awakenings: Zen, the Kyoto School, and the Question of Nationalism,* ed. James W. Heisig and John C. Maraldo, 52–74. Honolulu: University of Hawai'i Press.

Kishida, Shu, and K. D. Butler. 1992. *Kurofune Gensō: Seishin Bunseki Kara Mita Nichibei Kankei* [Visions of the Black Ships: Japan-U.S. Relations from a Psychoanalytic Standpoint]. Tokyo: Seidosha.

Kleinman, Arthur. 1995. *Writing at the Margin: Discourse between Anthropology and Medicine.* Berkeley: University of California Press.

Kleinman, Arthur, and Joan Kleinman. 1993. Moral Transformation of Health and Suffering in Chinese Society. Paper prepared for the MacArthur Foundation Sponsored Meeting on Morality and Health, Santa Fe, NM, June 22–24.

Kleinman, Arthur, Wen-Zhi Wang, Shi-Chuo Li, Xue-Ming Cheng, Xiu-Ying Dai, Kun-Tun Li, and Joan Kleinman. 1995. The Social Course of Epilepsy: Chronic Illness as Social Experience in Interior China. *Social Science and Medicine* 40 (10): 1319–30.

Kondo, Dorine K. 1990. *Crafting Selves: Power, Gender, and Discourses of Identity in a Japanese Workplace.* Chicago: University of Chicago Press.

Koschmann, J. Victor. 1981–82. The Debate on Subjectivity in Postwar Japan: Foundations of Modernism as a Political Critique. *Pacific Affairs* 54 (4): 609–31.

———. 1993. Intellectuals and Politics. In *Postwar Japan as History,* ed. Andrew Gordon, 395–423. Berkeley: University of California Press.

Krestan, Jo-Ann, and Claudia Bepko. 1991. Codependency: The Social Reconstruction of Female Experience. In *Feminism and Addiction,* ed. Claudia Bepko, 49–66. New York: Haworth Press.

Kumazawa, Makoto. 1996. *Portraits of the Japanese Workplace: Labor Movements, Workers, and Managers.* Trans. Andrew Gordon and Mikiso Hane. Boulder, Colo: Westview Press.

Kyūtoku, Shigemori. 1980. *Bogenbyō* [Mother-caused illness]. Tokyo: Sanmaku Shuppan.

Lasch, Christopher. 1978. *The Culture of Narcissism.* New York: Norton.

LeBlanc, Robin. 1999. *Bicycle Citizens: The Political World of the Japanese Housewife.* Berkeley: University of California Press.

Lebra, Joyce, Joy Paulson, and Elizabeth Powers, eds. 1976. *Women in Changing Japan.* Stanford, Calif.: Stanford University Press.

Lebra, Takie Sugiyama. 1976. *Japanese Patterns of Behavior.* Honolulu: University of Hawai'i Press.

———. 1984. *Japanese Women: Constraint and Fulfillment.* Honolulu: Univ. of Hawai'i Press.

———. 1992. Self in Japanese Culture. In *Japanese Sense of Self,* ed. N. R. Rosenberger, 105–20. New York: Cambridge University Press.

LeTendre, Gerald. 2000. *Learning to Be Adolescent: Growing Up in U.S. and Japanese Middle Schools.* New Haven, CT: Yale University Press.

Lewis, Catherine. 1978. Women in the Consumer Movement. In *Proceedings of the Tokyo Symposium on Women,* 80–87. Tokyo: International Group for the Study of Women.

————. 1989. From Indulgence to Internalization: Social Control in the Early School Years. *Journal of Japanese Studies* 15 (1): 139–58.

Liu, Lydia. 1995. *Translingual Practice: Literature, National Culture, and Translated Modernity—China, 1900–1937*. Stanford, Calif.: Stanford University Press.

Lo, Jeannie. 1990. *Office Ladies and Factory Women*. New York: M. E. Sharpe.

Lock, Margaret. 1986. Plea for Acceptance: School Refusal Syndrome in Japan. *Social Science and Medicine* 23 (2): 99–112.

————. 1987. Protests of a Good Wife and Wise Mother: The Medicalization of Distress in Japan. In *Health, Illness, and Medical Care in Japan,* ed. E. Norbeck and M. Lock, 130–57. Honolulu: University of Hawai'i Press.

————. 1988. New Japanese Mythologies: Faltering Discipline and the Ailing Housewife. *American Ethnologist* 15 (1): 43–61.

————. 1990. Restoring Order to the House of Japan. *Wilson Quarterly* (Autumn): 42–49.

————. 1993a. *Encounters with Aging: Mythologies of Menopause in Japan and North America*. Berkeley: University of California Press.

————. 1993b. Ideology, Female Midlife, and the Greying of Japan. *Journal of Japanese Studies* 19 (1): 43–77.

Mackie, Vera. 1988. Feminist Politics in Japan. *New Left Review* 167: 53–76.

————. 2003. *Feminism in Modern Japan: Citizenship, Embodiment, and Sexuality.* Cambridge: Cambridge University Press.

Madoka, Yoriko. 1982. *Shufu Shōkōgun* [Housewife Syndrome]. Tokyo: Chikuma Bunko.

Mahmood, Saba. 2001. Feminist Theory, Embodiment, and the Docile Agent: Some Reflections on the Egyptian Islamic Revival. *Cultural Anthropology* 16 (2): 202–36.

Mäkelä, Klaus. 1996. *Alcoholics Anonymous as a Mutual-Help Movement*. Madison: University of Wisconsin Press.

Mani, Lata. 1998. *Contentious Traditions : The Debate on Sati in Colonial India*. Berkeley: University of California Press.

Marra, Robert J. 1996. Social Relations as Capital: The Story of Yuriko. In *Re-Imaging Japanese Women,* ed. A. E. Imamura, 104–16. Berkeley: University of California Press.

Matsuda, Michio. 1961. *Watashi wa Nisai* [I am Two Years Old]. Tokyo: Iwanami Shoten.

Matsui, Machiko. 1990. Evolution of the Feminist Movement in Japan. *NWSA Journal* 2 (3): 435–49.

Matsui, Yayori. 1975. Protest and the Japanese Woman. *Japan Quarterly* 22 (1): 32–39.

Matsushita, Kōnōsuke. 1984. *Not for Bread Alone: A Business Ethos, A Management Ethic.* Kyoto: PHP Institute.

Matthews, Glenna. 1987. *"Just a Housewife": The Rise and Fall of Domesticity in America.* New York: Oxford University Press.

McKinstry, John A., and Asako Nakajima McKinstry. 1991. *Jinsei Annai, "Life's Guide": Glimpses of Japan through a Popular Advice Column.* Armonk, N.Y.: M. E. Sharpe.

McLanahan, Sara. 2004. Diverging Destinies: How Children Are Faring under the Second Demographic Transition. *Demography* 41: 607–27.

McVeigh, Brian. 1994. Good Wives and Wise Mothers: Constructing Gender at a Japanese Women's Junior College. In *The Fifth Annual Ph.D. Kenkyukai Conference,* edited by Charles Weathers and Izumi Sato, 11–24. Tokyo: International House of Japan.

Millet, Kate. 1970. *Sexual Politics.* New York: Doubleday.

Minami, Hiroshi. 1974. *Shakai Fuan: Sono Nihonteki Kōzō* [The Structure of Japanese Social Anxiety]. Kyoto: PHP Kenkjjo.

Mitchell, Juliet. 1971. *Women's Estate.* New York: Vintage.

Miyake, Yoshiko. 1991. Doubling Expectations: Motherhood and Women's Factory Work under State Management in Japan in the 1930s and 1940s. In *Recreating Japanese Women, 1600–1945,* ed. Gail Lee Bernstein.

Miyamoto, Masao. 1994. *Straightjacket Society: An Insider's Irreverent View of Bureaucratic Japan.* New York: Kodansha International.

Mohanty, Chandra Talpade. 1991. Under Western Eyes: Feminist Scholarship and Colonial Discourses. In *Third World Women and the Politics of Feminism,* ed. Chandra Talpade Mohanty, Ann Russo, and Lourdes Torres, 51–80. Bloomington: Indiana University Press.

Molony, Kathleen Susan. 1980. One Woman Who Dared: Ichikawa Fusae and the Japanese Women's Suffrage Movement. Ph.D. diss., University of Michigan.

Morgan, Marabel. 1973. *The Total Woman.* New York: Pocket Books.

Morris-Suzuki, Tessa. 1998. *Re-inventing Japan: Time, Space, Nation.* New York: M. E. Sharpe.

Munakata, Tsunetsugu. 1986. Japanese Attitudes toward Mental Health and Mental Health Care. In *Japanese Culture and Behavior,* ed. T. S. Lebra and W. Lebra, 369–78. Honolulu: University of Hawai'i Press.

Murakami, Yasusuke. 1984. *Ie* Society as a Pattern of Civilization. *Journal of Japanese Studies* 10 (2): 281–367.

Najita, Tetsuo, and H. D. Harootunian. 1998. Japan's Revolt against the West. In *Modern Japanese Thought,* ed. Bob Tadashi Wakabayashi, 207–72. Cambridge: Cambridge University Press.

Nakane, Chie. 1967. *Kinship and Economic Organization in Rural Japan.* London: Athlone Press.

————. 1970. *Japanese Society.* Berkeley: University of California Press.

Narita, Ryūichi. 1995. Women and Views of Women within the Changing Hygiene Conditions of Late Nineteenth- and Early Twentieth-Century Japan. In *U.S.-Japan Women's Journal,* English Supplement, no. 8: 64–86.

National Cancer Center. 2001. *Cancer Statistics on Japan 2001.* Tokyo: Foundation for Promotion of Cancer Research (http://www.ncc.go.jp/en/statistics/ 2001/index.html).

Nishikawa, Yūko. 1995. The Changing Form of Dwellings and the Establishment of the *Katei* (Home) in Modern Japan. In *U.S.-Japan Women's Journal,* English Supplement, no. 8: 3–36.

Niwa, Akiko. 1993. The Formation of the Myth of Motherhood in Japan. Trans. Tomiko Yoda. *U.S. Japan Women's Journal,* English Supplement, no. 4: 70–82.

Nolte, Sharon H. 1987. Liberalism in Modern Japan: Ishibashi Tanzan and His Teachers. Berkeley: University of California Press.

Nolte, Sharon H., and Sally Ann Hastings. 1991. The Meiji State's Policy towards Women, 1890–1910. In *Recreating Japanese Women, 1600–1945,* ed. G. L. Bernstein, 151–75. Berkeley: University of California Press.

Norwood, Robin. 1985. *Women Who Love Too Much: When You Keep Wishing and Hoping He'll Change.* New York: St. Martin's Press.

Notehelfer, F. G. 1985. Review of *Flowers in Salt. Journal of Japanese Studies* 11 (1): 212–17.

Ochiai, Emiko. 1994. *The Japanese Family System in Transition: A Sociological Analysis of Family Change in Postwar Japan.* Tokyo: LCTB International Library Foundation.

Ohinata, Masami. 1995. The Mystique of Motherhood: A Key to Understanding Social Change and Family Problems in Japan. In *Japanese Women: New Perspectives on the Past, Present, and Future,* ed. Kumiko Fujimura-Fanselow and Atsuko Kameda, 199–211. New York: Feminist Press at the City University of New York

Ohnuki-Tierney, Emiko. 1984. *Illness and Culture in Contemporary Japan.* Cambridge: Cambridge University Press.

Okimoto, Daniel I., and Thomas P. Rohlen, eds. 1988. *Inside the Japanese System: Readings on Contemporary Society and Political Economy.* Stanford, Calif.: Stanford University Press.

Orrenstein, Peggy. 2001. Parasites in Prêt-à-Porter. *New York Times Magazine,* July 1, pp. 30–35.

Ōzawa, Ichirō. 1994. *Blueprint for New Japan: The Rethinking of Nation.* New York: Kodansha International.

Pascale, Richard, and Thomas P. Rohlen. 1988. The Mazda Turnaround. In *Inside the Japanese System,* ed. Daniel I. Okimoto and Thomas P. Rohlen, 149–69. Stanford, Calif.: Stanford University Press.

Peak, Lois. 1991. *Learning to Go to School in Japan: The Transition from Home to Preschool Life.* Berkeley: University of California Press.

Pyle, Kenneth. 1978. *The Making of Modern Japan.* Lexington, Mass.: D.C. Heath.

———. 1997. The World Historical Significance of Japan. In *A Vision of a New Liberalism? Critical Essays on Murakami's Anticlassical Analysis,* ed. K. Yamamura, 208–37. Stanford, Calif.: Stanford University Press.

Raymo, James M., Miho Iwasawa, and Larry Bumpass. 2004. Marital Dissolution in Japan: Recent Trends and Patterns. *Demographic Research* 11 (14): 396–420.

Renshaw, Jean R. 1999. *Kimono in the Boardroom: The Invisible Evolution of Japanese Women Managers.* Oxford: Oxford University Press.

Report on Local Community Mental Health Committee of Tokyo. 1981. Tokyo: Tokyo Metropolitan Comprehensive Mental Health Care Center Central District publication.

Reynolds, David. 1984. *Playing Ball on Running Water: Living Morita Psychotherapy, the Japanese Way to Building a Better Life.* New York: Quill.

Rice, John Steadman. 1996. *A Disease of One's Own: Psychotherapy, Addiction, and the Emergence of Co-dependency.* New Brunswick, N.J.: Transaction Publishers.

Rich, Adrienne. 1986. *Of Woman Born: Motherhood as Experience and Institution.* New York: W. W. Norton.

Robins-Mowry, Dorothy. 1983. *The Hidden Sun: Women of Modern Japan.* Boulder, Colo.: Westview Press.

Rohlen, Thomas P. 1974. *For Harmony and Strength: Japanese White-Collar Organization in Anthropological Perspective.* Berkeley: University of California Press.

———. 1983. *Japan's High Schools.* Berkeley: University of California Press.

———. 1989. Order in Japanese Society: Attachment, Authority, and Routine. *Journal of Japanese Studies* 15 (1): 1–40.

———. 1991. Outline Notes for a Paper Entitled: A Developmental Topography of Self and Society in Japan. Paper prepared for the Conference on Self and Society in India, China, and Japan, August 4–9, East-West Center, Honolulu, Hawai'i.

Rosaldo, Michelle Z. 1974. Woman, Culture, and Society: A Theoretical Overview. In *Woman, Culture, and Society*, ed. M. Z. Rosaldo and L. Lamphere, 17–42. Stanford, Calif.: Stanford University Press.

Rosaldo, Renato. 1989. *Culture and Truth: The Remaking of Social Analysis*. Boston: Beacon Press.

Rosenberger, Nancy. 1987 Productivity, Sexuality, and Ideologies of Menopausal Problems in Japan. In *Health, Illness, and Medical Care in Japan*, ed. M. Lock and E. Norbeck, 158–88. Honolulu: University of Hawai'i Press.

Rouse, Carolyn. 2004. *Engaged Surrender: African American Women and Islam*. Berkeley: University of California Press.

Saitō, Satoru. 1989. *Kazoku Izonshō* [Family Addiction]. Tokyo: Seishin Publishers.

———. 1998. *Kazoku no Yami o Saguru: Gendai no Oyako Kankei* [Exploring the Darkness of Families: Contemporary Parent-Child Relations]. Tokyo: NHK.

Saitō, Satoru, Pete Steinglass, and Marc A. Schuckit. 1992. *Alcoholism and the Family*. New York: Brunner/Mazel.

Saitō, Yoshiko. 1992. *Kodomo no Kimochi ga Wakaru Oya ni Naritai* [Becoming a Parent Who Understands Kids' Feelings]. Lecture for mothers at Chigasaki Dōmei Kyōkai, Chigasaki, Japan, October 15.

Sakai, Naoki. 1989. Modernity and Its Critique: The Problem of Universalism and Particularism. In *Postmodernism and Japan*, ed. M. Miyoshi and H. D. Harootunian, 93–122. Durham, N.C.: Duke University Press.

Sakamoto, Kazue. 1997. *Kazoku Imēji no Tanjō: Nihon Eiga ni Miru Hōmu Dorama no Keisei* (The Birth of the Family Image: The Development of the Home Drama in Japanese Movies). Tokyo: Shinyōsha.

Sakuta Keiichi. 1978. The Controversy over Community and Autonomy. In *Authority and the Individual in Japan: Citizen Protest in Historical Perspective*, ed. J. Victor Koschmann, 220–49. Tokyo: University of Tokyo Press.

Salome, Lou. 1985 [1892]. *Ibsen's Heroines*. Ed. and trans. Siegfried Mandel. New York: Limelight Editions.

Sasagawa, Ayumi. 2002. The Social World of University-Educated Mothers in a Japanese Suburb. Paper presented at the Anthropology of Japan in Japan Fall Workshop, Sophia University, Ichigaya Campus, November 2.

Schooler, Carmi, and William A. Caudill. 1988. Childrearing and Personality Formation. In *Inside the Japanese System: Readings on Contemporary Society and Political Economy*, ed. D. I. Okimoto and T. P. Rohlen, 15–19. Stanford, Calif.: Stanford University Press.

Scott, James C. 1987a. Resistance without Protest and without Organization: Peasant Opposition to the Islamic *Zakat* and the Christian Tithe. *Comparative Study of Society and History* 29 (3): 417–52.

————. 1987b. *Weapons of the Weak: Everyday Forms of Peasant Resistance.* New Haven, Conn.: Yale University Press.

Sechiyama, Kaku. 2000. *Shufu Hogo Seisaku no Daitenkan o: Jidō Teate Giron o Kikkake ni Shite. Ronza* vol. 11: 134–45.

Sennett, Richard. 1978. *The Fall of Public Man.* New York: W. W. Norton.

Sievers, Sharon L. 1983. *Flowers in Salt: The Beginnings of Feminist Consciousness in Modern Japan.* Stanford, Calif.: Stanford University Press.

Smith, R. J., and Ella Wiswell. 1982. *Women of Suyemura.* Chicago: Chicago University Press.

Smith, Robert J. 1961. The Japanese Rural Community: Norms, Sanctions, and Ostracism. *American Anthropologist* 63: 522–33.

Smith, Stephen. 1988. Drinking and Sobriety in Japan. Ph.D. diss., Columbia University.

Snitow, Ann. 1992. Feminism and Motherhood: An American Reading. *Feminist Review* 40: 32–51.

Statistical Research and Training Institute. 2003. *Statistical Handbook of Japan.* Tokyo: Ministry of Internal Affairs and Communications, Statistics Bureau.

Stracher, Cameron. 2000. Family Friendly Makes More Work Possible. *New York Times,* September 2.

Takemura, Michio, and Yūko Endō. 1992. Therapeutic Effects of Counseling on Wives of Alcoholics. In *Alcoholism and the Family,* ed. S. Satoru, P. Steinglass, and M. A. Schuckit, 254–65. New York: Brunner/Mazel.

Tamanoi, Mariko Asano. 1991. Songs as Weapons: The Culture and History of *Komori* (Nursemaids) in Modern Japan. *Journal of Japanese Studies* 50 (4): 793–816.

Tanaka, Mitsu. 1992a [1970]. Benjo Kara no Kaihō [Liberation from the Toilet]. In *Shiryō Nihon Ūman Ribu Shi I* [A History of Japanese Women's Lib in Documents, Vol. I], ed. Mizoguchi Akiyo, Saeki Yoko, and Miki Soko, 201–207. Tokyo: Shokadō.

————. 1992b. Feminism and the Family: Two Decades of Thought. In *Rethinking the Family: Some Feminist Questions,* ed. B. Thorne and M. Yalom, 3–30. Boston: Northeastern University Press.

Taussig, Michael. 1980. Reification and the Consciousness of the Patient. *Social Science and Medicine* 14B: 3–13.

Tobin, Joseph. 1992a. Japanese Preschools and the Pedagogy of Selfhood. In *Japanese Sense of Self,* ed. N. R. Rosenberger, 21–39. New York: Cambridge University Press.

————. 1992b. Re-Made in Japan: Everyday Life and Consumer Taste in a Changing Society. New Haven, CT: Yale University Press.

Tokyo Broadcasting System. 1993. *Soko mo Shiritai . . .* [Let's Find Out about . . .]. Tokyo Broadcasting System, January 26.

Tsurumi, Kazuko. 1970. Social Change and the Individual: Japan before and after Defeat in World War II. Princeton, N.J.: Princeton University Press.

U.S. Bureau of Labor Statistics, Department of Labor. 2004. *American Time-Use Survey Summary.* http:www.bls.gov/news.release/atus.nro.htm.

Ueno Chizuko. 1987. The Position of Japanese Women Reconsidered. *Current Anthropology* 28 (4): 75–84.

———. 1988. The Japanese Women's Movement: The Counter-values to Industrialism. In *The Japanese Trajectory: Modernization and Beyond,* ed. G. McCormick and Y. Sugimoto, 167–85. New York: Cambridge University Press.

———. 1996. Collapse of "Japanese Mothers." *U.S. Japan Women's Journal,* English Supplement, no. 10: 3–19.

———. 1997. Are the Japanese Feminine? Some Problems of Japanese Feminism in Its Cultural Context. In *Broken Silence: Voices of Japanese Feminism,* ed. Sandra Buckley, 293–301. Berkeley: University of California Press.

———. 1998. The Declining Birthrate: Whose Problem? *Review of Population and Social Policy,* no. 7: 103–28.

Uesaki, Hiroko. 2003. *Mama Hyakunin ni Kikimashita. Dōshite Futarime ō Umanai No?* [One Hundred Women on Why They Won't Bear a Second Child]. *Chūō Kōron* 2: 172–78.

Uno, Kathleen. 1993a. The Death of "Good Wife, Wise Mother"? In *Postwar Japan as History,* ed. A. Gordon, 293–324. Berkeley: University of California Press.

———. 1993b. One Day at a Time: Work and Domestic Activities of Urban Lower-Class Women in Early Twentieth Century Japan. In *Japanese Women Working,* ed. J. Hunter, 37–68. New York: Routledge.

———. 1997. Womanhood, War, and Empire: Transmutations of Ryōsai Kenbo in the Taishō Era. *Modern Japan Seminar,* Columbia University, 1997.

———. 1999. *Passages to Modernity: Motherhood, Childhood, and Social Reform in Early Twentieth Century Japan.* Honolulu: University of Hawai'i Press.

Upham, Frank. 1987. *Law and Social Change in Postwar Japan.* Cambridge, Mass.: Harvard University Press.

———. 1993. Unplaced Persons and Movements for Place. In *Postwar Japan as History,* ed. Andrew Gordon, 325–46. Berkeley: University of California Press.

Van Wolferen, Karel. 1989. *The Enigma of Japanese Power.* New York: Alfred Knopf.

Vogel, Ezra. 1963. *Japan's New Middle Class.* Berkeley: University of California Press.

Vogel, Suzanne H. 1978. The Professional Housewife. In *Proceedings of the Tokyo*

Symposium on Women, ed. Merry White and Barbara Moloney. Tokyo: International Group for the Study of Women.

———. 1988. *Professional Housewife: The Career of Urban Middle Class Japanese Women.* Cambridge, Mass.: Institute for Independent Study, Radcliffe College.

Wagatsuma, Hiroshi. 1977. Some Aspects of the Contemporary Japanese Family: Once Confucian, Now Fatherless? *Daedalus* 106 (2): 181–210.

Watsuji Tetsurō. 1961. *A Climate.* Trans. Geoffrey Bownas. Tokyo: Ministry of Education.

Watt, Ian. 1983. *The Rise of the Novel.* Berkeley: University of California Press.

Weiner, Michael. 1995. Discourses of Race, Nation, and Empire in Pre-1945 Japan. *Ethnic and Racial Studies* 18 (3): 433–56.

Wetzel, Patricia J. 1994. A Movable Self: The Linguistic Indexing of *Uchi* and *Soto.* In *Situated Meanings: Inside and Outside in Japanese Self, Society, and Language,* ed. J. M. Bachnik and C. J. Quinn Jr., 73–87. Princeton, N.J.: Princeton University Press.

White, Merry. 1987. The Virtue of Japanese Mothers: Cultural Definitions of Women's Lives. *Daedalus* 116 (3): 149–63.

———. 1992. Home Truths: Women and Social Change in Japan. *Daedalus* 121 (4): 61–82.

———. 1994. *The Material Child: Coming of Age in Japan and America.* Berkeley: University of California Press.

———. 2002. *Perfectly Japanese: Making Families in an Era of Upheaval.* Berkeley: University of California Press.

Williams, Raymond. 1977. *Marxism and Literature.* New York: Oxford University Press.

———. 1980. *Problems in Materialism and Culture.* London: Verso.

World Health Organization. 1999. Global Status Report on Alcohol. Geneva: World Health Organization, Department of Mental Health and Substance Abuse.

Yamada, Masahiro. 2001. The Housewife: A Dying Breed? *Japan Echo* 28 (2): 54–58.

Yamamura, Kenmei. 1971. *Nihonjin to Haha: Bunka to Shite no Haha no Gainen ni Tsuite no Kenkyū* [The Japanese Mother: Research on Cultural Images of Motherhood]. Tokyo: Tōyōkan Shuppansha.

Yanagisako, Sylvia. 1987. Mixed Metaphors: Native and Anthropological Models of Gender and Kinship Domains. In *Gender and Kinship: Essays Towards a Unified Analysis,* ed. J. F. Collier and S. J. Yanagisako, 86–118. Stanford, Calif.: Stanford University Press.

Yoda, Tomiko. 2000. The Rise and Fall of Maternal Society: Gender, Labor, and Capital in Contemporary Japan. *South Atlantic Quarterly* 99 (4): 865–902.

Yoneyama, Lisa. 1999. *Hiroshima Traces: Time, Space, and the Dialectics of Memory.* Berkeley: University of California Press.

York, Phyllis, David York, and Ted Wachtel. 1985. *Tough Love.* New York: Bantam.

Yoshizumi, Kyōko. 1995. Marriage and Family: Past and Present. In *Japanese Women: New Perspectives on the Past, Present, and Future,* ed. Kumiko Fujimura-Fanselow and Atsuko Kameda, 183–97. New York: Feminist Press at the City University of New York.

Zaretsky, Eli. 1976. *Capitalism, the Family, and Personal Life.* New York: Harper and Row.

Abu-Lughod, Lila, 162

abuse: nurturance and, 3, 155; of parents, 155, 160; perception of, 103. *See also* domestic violence; substance abuse

ACOA (Adult Children of Alcoholics), 12

activism: consumer, 178n6; environmental, 9, 178n6, 196n4; by Japanese women, 9, 16, 144, 178n6

addiction: discourses of, 27; in Japanese society, 56–57

adoption *(yōshi)*, 134

agency, Western idea of, 27

aidagara (relationality), 71

Akihito, Prince, 187n11

Al-Anon, 9–13; on caregivers, 33; versus CoDA, 12; compromise in, 86, 190n1; enabling in, 10; interventions in, 91; Japanese, 14, 39, 181n21; meeting format of, 34; methods of, 86; view of marital relationships, 92–93

Al Anon Faces Alcoholism (1977), 190n1

alcohol dependency syndrome *(arukōru izonshō)*, 52

alcoholics: families of, 10, 37–50, 58, 91–95, 183n5; female, 51, 182n3; hospitalization of, 126–27, 128; salarymen, 56. *See also* husbands, alcoholic

Alcoholics Anonymous, 10; on cause of drinking, 144, 178n8; Christian beginnings of, 181n20; versus CoDA, 12; meeting format of, 34; self-help in, 179n9

Alcoholics Anonymous, Japanese, 14, 59

alcoholics' wives, Japanese: anger of, 131; blame for drinking, 64; boundaries for, 86–87; divorce for, 87, 131; enabling by, 64–65; endurance by, 116–17; entitlement of, 116, 129–32, 164; humiliation of, 193n10; loss of identity, 62;

alcoholics' wives, Japanese *(continued)*
management of disease, 33, 40,
44, 52, 53, 91–93, 105–6, 115, 125–
32, 182n5; narratives of, 42–44,
51, 61–62, 65–66, 93–94, 99–102,
104–6, 108–11, 114, 118–32, 191n1;
psychosomatic symptoms of, 61;
recovery of, 133; revenge by, 129–
32; self-care by, 133; self-expression
by, 53, 133; seminars for, 86–87;
stereotypes of, 179n11, 182n5; strategies of, 129–32; support groups
for, xii–xiii, 129. *See also* housewives, Japanese; women, Japanese
alcoholism: American view of, 51–
53; awareness of, 45, 126; blame
for, 64; diagnosis of, 42, 43, 44,
50, 126; disease model of, 51–54,
178n8; education concerning, 44,
103; effect of paint thinner on, 42,
125; and gender division of labor,
51; housewives', 182n3; interventions for, 86–87, 91; in Japanese
daily life, 45–49, 56; management
of, 52, 103, 182n5; management
within families, 10, 91–95; open-
ness concerning, 104–5, 107; and
social functioning, 50–51; spiritual transformation following, 53;
toleration of, 44, 45–46; treatment
of, 52, 55, 58, 59, 126–28, 183n6. *See
also* drinking; husbands, alcoholic
alcohol treatment programs, 182n4;
family inpatient units in, 58; refer-
rals to, 183n6; in Tokyo, 55
alimony, Japanese law on, 163
Allison, Anne, 46, 90, 144–45;
"Transgressions of the Everyday,"
150
amae (passive dependence), 21–24;
children and, 69, 142; in codepen-

dency, 68; in corporations, 72; as
everyday sentiment, 72; in gendered division of labor, 76; and
motherly love, 159; in national
identity, 68; social conflict in, 80;
women's questioning of, 84
American Time-Use Survey, 198n1
ancestors, in Japanese family, 69
Angel Plan *(Enzēru Puran)*, 199n7
antabuse (disulfiram), 44, 52, 127, 181n1
antinuclear movement, Japanese:
women in, 144, 178n6, 186n7
apartment complexes *(danchi)*, 73
around-the-body care, 20, 98
Asai, Michiko: "Toward a Liberation
for the Myth of the Modern
Family," 171
ASK (Arukōru Yakubutsu Mondai
Zenkoku Shimin Kyōkau), 14,
179n12
assertiveness training *(jiko shuchō)*, 9
attachment theory, 150
attentiveness, in Japanese culture, 98,
192n9
authoritarianism, military, 73, 80,
119, 132
authority: centralized, 81; of housewives, 135; in Japanese daily life,
80–85
autonomy: of Japanese children,
33–34, 148, 159; in marriage, 107;
and self-realization, 27; Western,
33, 68, 162, 168, 170; women's, 24;
of workers, 189n18

Bachnik, Jane M., 62
battered women. *See* domestic
violence
Beattie, Melody: *Codependent
No More*, 10–11
Bepko, Claudia, 12

birth, out-of-wedlock, 162
Bombeck, Erma, 147–48
bosei, concept of, 197n10. *See also* love, motherly; maternalism; motherly nature
Bowlby, John, 150, 196n8
breast-feeding, 79, 188n13
brides, Japanese, 194n2; self-sacrificing, 123–25, 128–29, 134, 135; variations in treatment of, 194n3

capital, human, 169; Japanese children as, 144
capitalism: American-style, xi; in postwar Japan, 4
caregivers: Al-Anon on, 33; beautification of, 72–73; recovery for, 60
Caudill, William A., 197n9
child abuse, and alcohol use, 49–50
childbirth classes, 146
child-rearing, Japanese: advisors in, 137; *amae* in, 69, 142; versus American, 197n9; apathy toward, xiii; boundaries in, 154–59; as capital cultivation, 144; community values in, 140; delegation of, 188n14; difficulties of, 140; discipline in, 78; enjoyment of, 141–42; husbands' roles in, 123; in Japanese society, 8, 16–17; magazines on, 188n13; manuals for, 196n7; in Meiji period, 143; as national work, 199n5; nutrition education in, 140–41; permissiveness in, 146; pre-Meiji, 179n13; as public service, 105; rhythm in, 137, 139; scientific, 77, 187n9; seminars on, 78, 137–41, 150; socialization in, 138–39; tough love in, 33, 34, 142, 147–52, 159–60; by urban women, 75. *See also* nurturance

child-rearing, Western, 162–63, 165; influence in Japan, 196n7; versus Japanese, 197n9; state resources for, 170; time spent on, 198n1
children, Japanese: in *amae* relationships, 69, 142; autonomy of, 33–34, 148, 159; as capital, 144; centrality in family, 170; chores for, 149; dependency of, 149–50, 160; domestic violence by, 155, 160; in family status, 144; health-care coverage for, 146, 170; as household property, 148; intervention on behalf of, 152–53; intimacy with mothers, 142, 150–52, 155, 197nn8–9; mothers' investment in, 77; passivity of, 79; responsibility of, 160; social development of, 138–39; state care of, 166–67; substance abuse by, vii, 141, 155; weekly allowances *(okozukai)* of, 148; working-class, 167. *See also* teenagers, Japanese
Civil Code, Meiji, 186n7
co-alcoholism. *See* codependency
codependency, 14–15; of alcoholic husbands, 1, 51; *amae* in, 68; American, 9–13; changing, 102–5; complacency concerning, 3; *enryo* in, 100–101; versus interdependence, 11; Japanese discourse on, 13; Japanese perception of, 63–65; in Japanese therapeutic culture, 28; language of, 1, 24, 33, 85; male, 51; as norm, 66; nurturance and, 15, 24, 28, 84, 115; as pathology, 11; service in, 98–101; socialization in, 12–13, 64; as social product, 64
Co-Dependents Anonymous (CoDA), 11, 13, 178n7; versus AA, 12
Coles, Robert, 13

Comaroff, Jean and John, 32, 181n20
company men, Japanese, 38. *See also* corporations, Japanese
conformity, in Japanese society, viii
Confucianism, view of women in, 196n3
consciousness, false, 24–28
consciousness-raising groups, Japanese, xii, 8, 9, 54, 136
consumerism, in Japanese society, 29, 73, 173
consumer issues, Japanese women and, 9, 178n6, 196n4
cooking, home-style, 140
cooking sake, 182n3
corporations, Japanese: *amae* sentiments in, 72; commitment to, 83; democracy in, 81; exploitative practices by, 82–83; as family, 22, 81–82, 84; inculcation of values, 37; loyalty to, 190n18; marriage bonuses of, 74; negotiation with workers, 190n18; overtime in, 83; paternalism in, 83; personal relationships in, 67; postwar ideology of, 83; promotional practices of, 189n18; resistance within, 190n18; subordination of family to, 2; subsidization of family, 74; as total providers, 81–82; use of alcohol in, 2, 46–47, 56; women in, 4, 187n10
counseling services, Japanese, xiii, 8; on gender roles, 31
counselors, Japanese: training of, 31
crime, juvenile: women's management of, 81
Crittendon, Ann: *The Price of Motherhood*, 169
culture, Japanese: alcoholism treat-

ment in, 59, 91; alcohol use in, 45–49, 86; *amae* relationships in, 21–24; American influence on, 28–29; attentiveness in, 98, 192n9; codependency in, 13, 14–15, 28, 63–65; cuteness in, 146; effect of postwar prosperity on, 185n5; fissures in, xi–xii; hierarchical relations in, 23, 71; humanism in, 184n3; love in, 70, 87–91; motherhood in, 75–77; nurturance in, 76, 80, 146; relationality in, 71; therapeutic, 28; toleration of alcoholism, 44, 45–46; Western feminist view of, 25. *See also* Japaneseness
culture, transnational, 28–32
culture, Western: Japanese borrowing of, 28–32, 132

Danshukai (group for cessation of drinking), 14, 58–59, 127
dating system, Japanese, 193n11
day care centers, Japanese, 137, 146; paternalism in, 167; state-subsidized, 166, 167, 170, 173, 200n7
democracy, in postwar Japan, ix, 117, 132
dependence: children's, 149–50, 160; infantile, 67, 99–100, 170; in Japanese society, 67–80; of Japanese women, 168; language of, 84; origins of, 69; passive, 21–24; pleasurable, 72; Western feminism on, 170. *See also amae;* codependency
divorce, American, 165
divorce, Japanese, 38, 194n3; for alcoholics' wives, 87, 131; disadvantages of, 106–7; effect of

education on, 164–65; hardship following, 163; within the home (*kateinai rikon*), 91–95, 161; increase in, 164; motherhood following, 164; preparation for, 163–64

Divorce with a Smile Bureau, xii, 163

Doi Takeo: on *amae*, 76; *The Anatomy of Dependence*, 21–22, 67–69, 71–72, 76, 84, 100, 180n16, 184nn3–4; career of, 183n1; on filial piety, 184n3; on wartime leaders, 72

domesticity: culture of, 187n9; matricentric, 76, 83–84; as public service, 5; validation from, 33, 162; Western, 169, 180n14; women's empowerment through, 105–14, 136

domestic sphere: American women's contribution to, 199n4; importance of, ix; in women's activism, 9

domestic violence, 199n6; alcohol-related, 49, 58, 117, 126; battered women shelters for, 58; by children, 155, 160; Japanese perception of, 103–4; laws against, 183n8

drinking: AA discourse on, 144, 178n6; after-hours, 90, 125; corporate-sponsored, 2, 46–47, 56; legal age for, 45; role in nurturance, 45. *See also* alcoholism

drinking gatherings (*nomikai*), 45, 46–47

drug abuse. *See* substance abuse

economy, postwar Japanese, vii, 4, 73; deflation in, 175; effect on culture, 185n5; global competition in, 176; housewives' role in, 8, 20, 74–76, 162, 174; motherhood in, 145; slowdown in, 174; women in, 18

Edō period: brides during, 194n2; motherhood in, 143; wives during, 194n3, 195n2

education, Japanese: for alcoholics' wives, 86–87; concerning alcoholism, 44, 103; decentralized authority in, 81; effect on divorce rate, 164–65; gender equality in, 166; higher, 188n12; during Meiji period, 192n8; military, 189n15; morality in, 37; postwar, 80, 83; role of motherhood in, 144–45; standardized exam system, 142, 144, 149

egotism, Western, 184n3

Ehara, Yumiko: *Feminizumu Ronsō*, 170–71

eldercare, by housewives, xiii

electronics industry, Japanese, viii

emperor, Japanese: as father figure, 71

Engels, Friedrich: *The Origin of the Family*, 193n12

enryo (showing reserve), 100–101

environmental issues, Japanese women and, 9, 178n6, 196n4

Equal Employment Opportunity Law (Japan), xii, 5, 177n3

Erikson, Erik, 78

false consciousness, in Japanese feminism, 24–28

families, Japanese, vii; adult children in, 149, 196n6; of alcoholics, 10, 37–50, 58, 91–95, 183n5; ancestors in, 69; "apartment-house tribes," 73; brides in, 123–25, 128–29, 134, 135; centrality in society, 68–71,

families, Japanese (continued)
184n4; child-centric, 170; commitment to, ix; consumerism in, 73; corporate subsidization of, 74; discourse of, 30; effect of climate on, 70; elder sons in, 123–24, 133; husbands' role in, 47–50, 90; interdependence in, 72; law governing, 88; management of alcoholism in, 10, 91–95; marital communication within, 94; marital relations in, 70, 91–95, 187n9; as marker for Japaneseness, 69–70; medicalization of problems, 57–58; in Meiji period, 69, 188n11; modernity in, 74; mother-child relationships in, 68–70, 78–79, 142, 150–52, 155, 197nn8–9; multigenerational, 187n11; mutualism in, 72; patriarchal, 69, 72; political economy of, 174; popular movies on, 75; postwar ideology of, 83; power relationships in, 80; prewar, 36, 69, 71, 72–73, 117, 189n16; as prototype for national unity, 69, 72; regional variations in, 194n3; role of state in, 145–46, 176; samurai, 184n2; selflessness in, 69, 70; separate residences within, 92; social status of, 144; stem, 88, 133–35; subordination to corporations, 2, 74; of substance abusers, 1, 156–58; during Taishō period, 188n11; telepathy within, 76, 95–96, 192n7; upper-class, 194n3; working-class, 188n14; during World War II, 185n6. See also ie (traditional household)
families, Western, 87–88
family-home (katei), 73, 185n6

family meetings. See support groups, Japanese
family registry (koseki), 69, 133, 184n2; dismantling of, 73
femininity, Japanese, xiv, 194n13
feminism, Japanese, 4–9; false consciousness in, 24–28; housewife, 20, 143–44; motherhood in, 144; in public health centers, 57–58; self-determination in, 194n13
feminism, Western, xiii; academic, 9, 26, 31; on dependency work, 170; influence on bosei, 197n10; Japanese women and, xiv, 107, 113–14; Marxist, 171; radical, 113–14, 171; second-wave, 166, 168, 172, 198n3; self-determination in, 29; and third world women, 26; view of Japanese culture, 25
Feminist Therapy Mado, xii
fertility rate, Japanese: decline in, 173, 174
Friedan, Betty: The Feminine Mystique, 6–7
Fukazawa, Satoko, xiii–xiv
Fumiko, Enchi: Onnazaka, 18–19
fundamentalism, among Islamic women, 26–27

gambling, by husbands, xiii
ganguro (black-face) girls, 176
gender, in Japanese society, 3, 30, 105. See also labor, gendered division of
gender equality, 24, 162; in Japanese education, 166; in Japanese society, 8, 171; Marxist view of, 193n12; Western, 196n3; in workplace, 165, 166, 168
gender roles: Japanese counselors on, 31; Japanese women's view of, 25,

27–28; pre-Meiji, 179n13; resistance to, 27–28; traditional constructions of, 136; in treatment of alcoholism, 59

generations, vertical ties between, 88, 187n11

Gordon, Andrew, 20, 189n18

grandparents, traditional role of, 158

Group for the Promotion of Co-education in Home Economics (*Kateika no Danjo Kyōshū o Susumeru Kai*), 9

Haaken, Janice, 11

Hakuhodo Life Institute, 36

Harootunian, Harry: *Bunka no Jidai*, 185n5

Harvey, Paul A., 17–18

Hashimoto, Meiko: *Kichin Dorinkā*, 182n3

health-care centers, Japanese, xii, 54–55, 57–58; community, 108, 126, 146, 183n6

health-care system, Japanese: children in, 146, 170; state-managed, 31, 167

health insurance, Japanese, 173

hegemony, resistance to, 181n20

Heisei period (1989–), 193n11

hierarchy, in Japanese culture, 23, 71

Hiratsuka, Raichō, 199n5

Hiroshima Women's Coalition, 186n7

home: in Japanese industry, 8; as microcosm of nation, 15; in postwar society, 20–21; as production unit, 133; role in public productivity, 21; as sphere of productivity, 168; Victorian idea of, 168

home economics (*kateika*), 73

hospitality, Japanese, 76

households, Japanese: housewives' management of, 38, 65–66, 75, 87, 96, 105–6, 113, 161; postwar, 187n11; rural, 194n3; in stem-family system, 134; under Tokugawa government, 133. See also *ie* (traditional household)

housewife syndrome, 55

housewife welfare (*shufu hogo seidō*), 74, 173

housewives, American, 6–7; child-rearing by, 162–63, 165; full-time, 198n3; number of, 4, 177n2

housewives, Japanese: activities of, 54–55; adult children of, 149, 196n6; alcoholism of, 51, 182n3; alimony for, 163; authority of, 135; brides, 123–25, 128–29, 134, 135; change effected by, 102–5; community support for, 106–7, 108; cooperation with state, 19; declining viability of, 172–76; desexualization of, 90–91; economic stability for, 107, 108; during Edō period, 194n3, 195n2; eldercare by, xiii; full-time, 4, 187n8; gender equality of, 106–7, 108; holidays of, 92; isolation of, 54–55, 183n7; Japanese feminists on, 193n13; management of household, 38, 65–66, 75, 87, 96, 105–6, 113, 161; of Meiji period, 143; in national health insurance, 173; pathologizing of, 56–57; piecework by, 106; political activism of, 178n6; prewar, 15, 35, 143; privileges of, 107–8, 114; professional (*sengyō shufu*), 19, 180n15; questioning of roles, 3; relations with husbands, 91–95; resistance by,

housewives, Japanese *(continued)*
98–100, 115; resources of, 113;
retirement benefits for, 75, 173;
rights of, 117; role in postwar economy, 8, 20, 74–76, 162, 174; self-reflection by, 116; separated, 38,
108–11; social validation of, 33,
162; spousal tax deductions for,
74–75, 173, 200n9; state subsidization of, 111; support groups for,
xii–xiii, 129; wicked, 99. *See also*
alcoholics' wives, Japanese; service
wives; women, Japanese
housework: as public service, 105;
rationalization of, 187n9; state
training for, 20
husbands, alcoholic, vii; American,
10; codependency of, 1, 51; deaths
of, 39; in family life, 47–50, 90;
humiliation of wives, 193n10;
pathology of, 118; recovery of, 53,
183n5; wives' management of, 33,
40, 44, 52, 53, 91–93, 105–6, 115,
125–32, 182n5. *See also* alcoholics'
wives, Japanese
husbands, Japanese: gambling by,
xiii; infantility of, 99–100; marginalization of, 75; in parent-child
relationships, 93; philandering,
xiii; relations with wives, 91–95;
retired, 192n5; role in family,
47–50, 90

Ibsen, Henrik: *A Doll's House*, 106
identity, Japanese: *amae* in, 68; *ishin
denshin* in, 192n7; motherhood in,
152; nurturance in, 15–19. *See also*
Japaneseness
ie (traditional household), xiii, 36;
continuation of, 134–35; in Meiji
period, 69, 186n7; symbolism of,

69; in wartime, 185n6. *See also*
families, Japanese; households,
Japanese
Imperial Rescript on Education
(*Kyōiku Chokugo*), 192n8
independence: of American women,
xiv; of parents from children,
33–34
individualism, Western, xi, 23, 70,
71; alcoholics' wives and, 133; discourse of, 30; Japanese ambivalence toward, xiv
industrialization, discourse of love
following, 191n2
industry, Japanese: role of home in,
8. *See also* corporations, Japanese
infant formula, 196n7
interdependence, versus codependence, 11
internationalization, in postwar
Japan, ix
introspection, intensive (*jibun o
mitsumeru*), 35
Iwao, Sumiko, 95, 197n11

Jackson, Joan, 179n11, 182n5
Japan: American scholarship on,
xi; bombing of, 119; Civil Code,
88; Edō period, 143, 194n2, 195n2;
Equal Employment Opportunity
Law, xii, 5, 177n3; Meiji period,
69, 79, 133, 143, 184n2, 186n7,
188n11, 189n15, 194n2; Ministry of
Education, 80; Pension Fund Law,
75; Public Housing Corporation,
73; Shōwa era, 36, 186n7; Western
stereotypes of, 29; during World
War II, ix, 119, 185n6, 186n7. *See
also* state, Japanese
Japan, postwar: alcohol treatment
centers in, 55, 58, 182n4; alimony

laws in, 163; American consumer goods in, 29; Americanization in, ix, 117, 132–33; American occupation of, 36, 37, 117, 120–21, 132–33; anonymity in, 54; capitalist modernity of, 4; codependency in, 13, 14–15, 28, 63–65; conformity in, viii; constitution of, 28, 36, 88; consumerism in, 29, 73, 173; democratization in, ix, 117, 132; education in, 80, 83; family court in, 73; family wage in, 172; feminism in, 4–9, 20, 24–28, 57–58, 143–44, 194n13; gendered division of labor in, 51, 74, 76, 79, 88–90, 144, 161–62, 172, 180n15; health-care centers in, xii, 54–55, 57–58; hierarchical relations in, 23; infantalization of citizens, 170; during Kennedy years, 132; law enforcement in, 81; legal drinking age in, 45; lifetime employment in, 172; as maternal society, 21; motherhood in, 20–21, 75–77, 144; multigenerational families in, 187n11; national health insurance in, 173; nurturance in, 15–19, 32; public health centers in, 55, 57–58; separation of spheres in, 4; social control in, 81; socialization in, 12–13, 37–38, 138–39; spousal deduction law, 74–75, 173, 200n9; stresses of, 2. See also economy, postwar Japanese

Japan, prewar: exculpation of leaders, 72; families in, 36, 69, 71, 72–73, 117, 189n16; military authoritarianism of, 73, 80, 119, 132; military education during, 189n15; nationalism in, ix, 35–36, 185n6

Japaneseness *(Nihonjinron)*, 37; family in, 69–70; homogeneity in, 96; *ishin denshin* in, 192n7; postwar ideas of, 3; stereotypes of, 29; theories of, 67. *See also* culture, Japanese; identity, Japanese

Japan Inc., image of, xi

Jong, Erica: *Fear of Flying*, 194n1

Kanō, Mikiyō, 79

Kateika no Danjo Kyōshū o Susumeru Kai (women's group), 166

kekkon (marriage), 88

Kelsky, Karen, 174; *Women on the Verge*, 28–29

ki (animating spirit), 98

kinship, Chinese, 134

kinship system, Japanese: daughters in, 133–34; elder sons in, 123–24, 133; in Meiji period, 133, 184n2; stem-family in, 88, 133–35, 192n4

Kleinman, Arthur, 180n18

Kokutai no Hongi (Cardinal Principles of the National Entity of Japan, 1937), 69, 71

Kondo, Dorinne, 84

Krestan, Jo-Ann, 12

Kumazawa Makoto, 189n17

kumi (neighborhood organizations), 133

labor: reproductive, 24; in service sector, 97–98

labor, gendered division of, 51, 74, 88–90, 144, 180n15; *amae* in, 76; under Japanese state, 172; in marriage, 161–62; Meiji women and, 79

labor exchanges, rural, 133

labor force, Japanese: autonomy of workers in, 189n18; blue-collar, 188n12; gender equality in, 165,

labor force, Japanese *(continued)*
166, 168; hyperproductivity in,
189n17; mothers in, 153, 165–66,
175; older men in, 198n2; women
in, 74, 164, 173, 174, 177n5,
187n10, 198n2
Laing, R. D., 12
Lasch, Christopher, 179n10
LeBlanc, Robin, 178n6; bicycle
citizens, 5
Lebra, Takie, 20, 95, 98, 192n4,
193n10
lending, black-market, 148
Lewis, Catherine, 178n6, 196n4
liberation psychotherapies, 12, 13;
social commitment in, 179n10
Liu, Lydia, 181n19
Lock, Margaret, 36, 55, 183n7
love: in Japanese culture, 70, 87–
91; motherly *(boseiai)*, 151, 159,
188nn13–14; in stem-family
system, 88, 192n4; Victorian
ideal of, 88, 191n2
love marriages *(ren'ai kekkon)*, 88,
122–23
lunch boxes *(obentō)*, 145

Madoka, Yoriko, 163
Mahmood, Saba, 26–27
management, Japanese-style *(Nihon
shugi keiei)*, 81–82
manageriality, in Japanese society,
22–23
marital relationships: Al-Anon's view
of, 92–93; change within, 102–5;
communication in, 96–97; conflict in, 96–97; intimacy in, 95;
in Japanese families, 70, 91–95,
187n9; resistance in, 98–100, 115;
service *(sābisu)* in, 97–101

marriage, American: Japanese
women on, xiv; naïveté in, 161
marriage, Japanese: autonomy in,
107; ceremonies, 134; conservatism concerning, 110; corporate
bonuses for, 74; delayed, 175; in
Edō period, 194n2; endurance
in, 44; gender division of labor
in, 161–62; for love, 88, 122–23;
loveless, 161; media influence on,
88; political economy of, 174; post-
ponement of, 96–97; postwar, 88–
89; prewar, 117; reform under
occupation, 133; romance in, 107;
security in, 161; spheres of labor
in, 88, 94–95; women's empowerment through, 105–14, 136
Maslow, Abraham, 12
maternalism *(boseishugi)*, in Japanese
society, 23, 75, 80. *See also*
nurturance
Matsuda Michio: *I Am Two Years
Old*, 77–78
Matsushita Kōnōsuke: *Not for Bread
Alone*, 82
medicalization, 180n18; of women's
issues, xii, 57–58, 183n7
Meiji period (1868–1912): child-
rearing in, 143; Civil Code, 186n7;
family in, 69, 188n11; home
during, 79; households of, 69,
186n7; kinship system in, 133,
184n2; military education during,
189n15; motherhood in, 143
Meiji women, 15–18; brides, 194n2;
education of, 192n8; and gendered
division of labor, 79; legacy of,
19–24; mothers-in-law, 124–25;
political rights of, 143; role in
state-building, 196n3

men, Japanese: feminization of, 166; samuraization of, 188n15. *See also* husbands, alcoholic; husbands, Japanese

menstruation, paid leave during, 170

mental health care, in Tokyo, 54–55

Michiko, Princess, 187n11

middle-class, Japanese: advancement of, 56; expansion of, 76, 188n12; motherhood in, 81; of 1950s, 189n16; postwar growth in, 73, 79; urban, 75–76; women, 5, 7, 9, 19–20, 37, 54–55, 74, 84, 89, 172–74

middle-class consciousness *(chūryū ishiki)*, 37

military, Japanese: authoritarianism of, 73, 80, 119, 132; devaluation of, 80; socialization in, 188n15

minorities, counter-hegemonic discourses among, 31

Miyamoto, Musashi: *The Book of Five Rings*, viii

modernity: ideologies of, 28; for Japanese women, 4; Western idea of, 68, 184n1

Mohanty, Chandra Talpade: "Under Western Eyes," 26

monogamy, Marxist view of, 193n12

Montague, Ashley, 78, 150

Morita therapy, 60

mother-child relationships, Japanese, 196nn7–8; in alcoholic families, 183n5; centrality for family, 68–70; intimacy in, 142, 150–52, 155, 197nn8–9; skinship in, 78–79, 150, 153; as template for social relationships, 79

motherhood, Japanese: abuse of, 155; boundary-setting by, 154–59;

centrality for women, 161, 168; communalism in, 140; culture of nurturance in, 146; discourse of, 141–42, 150, 171, 175; in Edō era, 143; empowerment through, 172; fantasy of, 171; following divorce, 164; idealization of, 176; intimacy in, 150–52, 155, 197nn8–9; in middle-class society, 81; narratives of, 154, 155, 156–60; and nationalism, 143; in postwar society, 20–21, 75–77, 144; privacy for, 154; as public service, 5; rights of, 154; role in education, 144–45; state support for, 143, 145–46, 162, 169; during Taishō period, 188n14; values of, 76; as womanhood, 143–47, 171

motherhood protection controversy, 199n5

motherly nature *(bosei gensō)*, 151, 171

mothers, American, 162–63; full-time, 169, 198n3; working, 165–66, 169

mothers, Japanese: abuse of, 155, 160; activism of, 144; as agents of patriarchy, 172; intimacy with children, 142, 150–52, 155, 197nn8–9; nurturing, 152; performative space for, 139; responsibility for children, 152–54, 169, 196n6; social services for, 146; of substance abusers, 33, 34, 40, 156–58; working, 153, 165–66, 175

mothers-in-law, Japanese, xiii, 124–25; in stem-family system, 135

mutualism, in Japanese family, 72

Naikan therapy, 60

Nakane Chie, 67, 191n3

Nar-Anon, 39

nationalism, Japanese: prewar, ix, 35–36, 185n6; role of motherhood in, 143

nationhood, Japanese discourse on, 30

New Age movements, 199n4

New Housewives Association *(Shin Nihon Fujin no Kai)*, 111

New Japan Women's League, 143–44

New Year's gifts *(otoshidama)*, 148

NHK (public broadcasting), 17

Nihonjinron. See Japaneseness

Nishida Kitarō, 184n3

Nishikawa, Yūko, 185n6

Niwa, Akiko, 196n3

nurturance, 72; and abuse, 3, 155; American, 169, 199n4; in American political movements, 199n4; and codependency, 15, 24, 28, 84, 115; culture of, 76, 80, 146; domineering, 152; and economic growth, 145; language of, 76, 84, 114; maternal, 23, 67, 77, 79, 145; in postwar identity, 15–19; renunciation of, 149–50; role of drinking in, 45; and self-sacrifice, 160, 172; validation by society, 22, 32

Oedipus complex, 149–50

office ladies, 174–75, 177n5

Ohinata, Masami, 188n14

Oku Mumeo, 144

Onna Daigaku (Greater Learning for Women, tract), 194n3, 195n2

"The Opt-Out Revolution" *(New York Times)*, 165

Oshin (television drama), 17–18

paint thinner: abuse of, 1, 142, 154; effect on alcoholism, 42, 125

parent-child relationships, 71–72; husbands in, 93

parents, Japanese: abuse of, 155, 160; responsibility for children, 152–54, 196n6; responsibility for substance abuse, 156–58; rights of, 34, 154; separation from, 148

Pascale, Richard, 190n18

paternalism: benevolent, 72, 83; in corporations, 83; in day-care system, 167; Meiji, 186n7

Peace Memorial Park (Hiroshima), 186n7

Perls, Fritz, 12

person-centered therapy, 12

personhood, liberal-humanist view of, 27

political protest, Marxian view of, 25

power, social, 25

pregnancy, paid leave during, 170

productivity: home and, 21, 168; Japanese commitment to, ix; in stem-family system, 134, 191n3

provincialism, American, viii

Psychiatric Research Institute (Tokyo), 91

psychiatry, Japanese, 60; adaptation of vocabulary, 184n1; Oedipal narrative in, 150

psychology, American, 2, 30, 133, 172; self-loathing in, 63

public broadcasting, Japanese, 17

public health centers, 55, 57–58

Public Housing Corporation (Japan), 73

Quality of Life co-ops, 178n6

Quinn, Charles J., 62

recovery: of alcoholic husbands, 53, 183n5; for caregivers, 60

recovery movement, American, 57, 103, 141

resistance: changing concepts of, 180n17; within corporations, 190n18; to gender roles, 27–28; to hegemony, 181n20; in marital relationships, 98–100, 115; theories of, 26

Rice, John Steadman, 178n8

rights: American discourse on, 33; housewives', 117; of parents, 34, 154; workers', 83

Rogers, Carl: person-centered theory of, 12

Rohlen, Thomas, 190n18

Ronza (magazine), 173

ryōsai kenbo. See Meiji women

Saitō, Saturu, 14, 93, 159; on domestic violence, 104; group meetings under, 60; *Kazoku Izon Shō*, 56; social criticism of, 55–57

samurai families, 184n2

Schaef, Anne Wilson, 12

Schooler, Carmi, 197n9

school-refusal syndrome, 139

Scott, James, 26

Sechiyama, Kaku, 173

self: cultural constructions of, 62; in Japanese grammar, 62–63; Japanese understanding of, 30; Western idea of, 184n1

self-actualization, 12, 13; home-centered, 168

self-determination, 9; Japanese feminists on, 194n13; Western, 170, 179n9; in Western feminism, 29

self-expression, 9; by alcoholics' wives, 53, 133; in liberation psychotherapy, 13

self-realization, liberal notion of, 27

self-reflection *(hansei)*: healing through, 60; housewives', 116

self-sacrifice: by Japanese women, 24, 57, 64, 84–85, 123–25, 128–29, 134, 171; and nurturance, 160, 172

separation, marital, 38, 108–11, 132; contemplation of, 135

service *(sābisu)*, in marital relationships, 97–101, 116

service wives, 43, 97–99, 116

sex, premarital, 153–54

sexual harassment, lawsuits concerning, 5

Shōwa era (Japan), 36; family-state ideology of, 186n7

Shōwans, single-digit, 37

Shufo no Tomo (magazine), 185n6, 187n9

singles, "parasite," 174, 175

skinship *(sukinshippu)*, 78–79, 150, 153

Smith, Stephen, 50, 181n2

social alignment *(shakai teki dōchō)*, 56

social criticism: Japanese discourse of, 28–32; Marxist, 26; Saitō's, 55–57

socialization: in child-rearing, 138–39; in codependency, 12–13, 64; postwar, 37–38

social mobility, role of motherly love in, 188n13

society, American: public responsibility in, 179n9; self-loathing in, 63

society, Japanese: addiction in, 56–57; aging of, 173; centrality of family to, 68–71, 184n4; child-rearing in, 16–17; codependency in, 3; conflict within, xii; conformity in, viii; conservatism of, 54; consumerism in, 29, 73, 173; cultural borrowing by, 28–32; dependence in, 67–80; gender constructions in, 3, 105; gender

society, Japanese *(continued)*
equality in, 8, 171; group orientation in, viii; home in, 20–21; homogeneity in, 37–38; housewife syndrome in, 55; manageriality in, 22–23; maternalism in, 23, 75, 80; "pedigree society" *(gakureki shakai)* in, 144; postwar reorganization of, 28, 80; postwar stresses in, 2; power relationships in, 79; work ethic in, 2; work regimens of, ix

Soko mo Shiritai (television series), 47

soldiers: American, 120–21, 132; Japanese, 186, 189

solitude, American, xiv

sons, elder, 123–24, 133

spirituality, feminine, 199n4

Spock, Dr. Benjamin, 77; translations of, 78, 196n7

spouses, Japanese: friendship between, 20; nicknames between, 93–94, 192n6. *See also* marital relationships

state, Japanese: children under, 166–67; domestic training by, 20; gendered division of labor under, 172; housewives' cooperation with, 19; health care in, xii, 31, 54–55, 57–58, 167, 173; management of family life, 145–46; Meiji women in, 196n3; as national family, 69; shared values under, 37; social management by, 22–23; subsidization of day care, 166, 167, 170; subsidization of housewives, 111; support of families, 176; support of motherhood, 143, 145–46, 162, 169

stem-family system, 88, 133–35; love in, 88, 192n4; mothers-in-law in,

135; productivity in, 134, 191n3; women in, 134

St. Luke's Hospital (Tokyo), Medical Social Casework Department, xiii

subject, indivisibility from object, 184n3

substance abuse: caretakers in, 60; children's, vii, 141, 155; in Japanese society, 56; parents' responsibility for, 156–58; of stimulants, 157–58; in United States, 33

substance abusers, families of, 1, 156–58

substance abusers, teenage, 142–43; mothers of, 33, 34, 40, 156–58

support groups, Japanese: for housewives, xii–xiii, 129; nonhierarchical, 58; on revaluing of home, 166; for substance abuse families, 1; in therapeutic practice, 60–61

Suzuki Daisetsu, 184n3

Taishō period (1913–25): family during, 188n11; motherhood during, 188n14

Take Back the Night Movement, in Japan, 199n6

Tanaka Mitsu, 194n13

teenagers, Japanese: autonomy of, 148; debts of, 148–49, 152, 155–56; exams for, 142, 149; parents' responsibility for, 152–54; pregnant, 143; social life of, 142; tough love for, 33, 34, 147–52, 159–60. *See also* children, Japanese

teenagers, substance-abusing, 142–43; mothers of, 33, 34, 40, 156–58

telepathy *(ishin denshin)*, within families, 76, 95–96, 192n7

Tobin, Joseph: *Re-Made in Japan*, 29

Tokugawa government (1603–1868): household system under, 133; particularism of, 188n15

Tokyo: alcohol treatment programs in, 55; Feminist Therapy Center, xii; Matsuzawa Hospital, 57; mental health care in, vii, 54–55; Metropolitan Mental Health Center, 54; Psychiatric Research Institute, 91; public health centers of, 57; St. Luke's Hospital, xiii; during wartime, 119

Tokyo Lifeline, xii–xiii

total fertility rate, decline in, 73, 173

tough love (tafu rabu): in child-rearing, 33, 34, 147–52, 159–60; discourse of, 33, 34; rejection of, 159–60

"Tough Love with Teens" (2002), 196n4

tradition, Chinese rejection of, 181n19

Ueno, Chizuko, 134, 166, 172, 194n3; on domestic violence, 199n6

United States: codependency theory in, 9–13; divorce in, 165; domesticity in, 169; Japanese women's view of, 29; nurturance in, 169, 199n4; substance abuse in, 33; therapeutic society in, 12; view of alcoholism, 51–53

unity, national: family as prototype for, 69, 72

urbanization: effect on Japanese women, 33; postwar, 73

Victorian era: home during, 168; ideal of love, 88, 191n2

villages, Japanese: households in, 194n3; as social units, 133

Vogel, Ezra, 189n16

Vogel, Suzanne, 151

wages: family, 172; of Japanese women, 5, 177n4

Watsuji Tetsurō: Fūdo, 70–71, 72

wedding ceremonies, 134

West: autonomy in, 33, 68, 162, 168, 170; domesticity in, x, 169, 180n14; family model in, 87–88; as prototype for modernity, 68; self-centeredness of, 70. See also child-rearing, Western; feminism, Western; women, Western

Wetzel, Patricia J., 62

White, Merry: "The Virtue of Japanese Mothers," 7

widows, Japanese, 111, 112

women: Confucianist view of, 196n3; equal opportunity for, 24, 168, 171; Islamic, 26–27; spirituality of, 169; third-world, 26

women, American: contribution to domestic sphere, 199n4; independence of, xiv. See also housewives, American

women, Japanese: activism of, 9, 16, 144, 178n6; alcoholic, 51, 182n3; ambivalence toward individualism, xiv; under American occupation, 36, 37, 117, 120–21; in antinuclear movement, 144, 178n6, 186n7; battered, 58; civic participation of, xii; college-educated, 175; consumer activism of, 9, 178n6, 196n4; in corporations, 4, 187n10; desexualization of, 171; economic opportunities for, 164, 180n15; during Edō period, 194n3; effect of urbanization on, 33; and envi-

women, Japanese *(continued)*
ronmental issues, 9, 178n6, 196n4; exploitation of, 76; financial dependence of, 168; housewife trajectory of, 174; investment in children, 77; invisible labor of, 95–102; in labor force, 74, 164, 165–66, 173, 174, 175, 177n5, 187n10, 198n2; management of juvenile crime, 81; middle-class, 5, 7, 9, 19–20, 37, 54–55, 74, 84, 89, 172–74; modernity for, 4; as modernizers, 15–16; *National Geographic* essay on, 4; older, 198n2; oppositional strategies of, 32; as primary caregivers, 78; questioning of *amae*, 84; relations with physicians, 55; role in community, 5–6, 7, 38; role in workaholism, 56; rural, 179n13; self-change by, 34; self-reflection by, 3–4; self-sacrifice by, 24, 57, 64, 84–85, 123–25, 128–29, 134, 171; single, 174; single-digit Shōwans, 37; social participation of, 5–8, 84; status of, xii; in stem-family system, 134; teachers, 80; unconventional, 194n1; use of Western culture, 28–29, 30; view of America, 29; view of gender roles, 25, 27–28; view of romance, 114; volunteer work by, 54; wages of, 5, 177n4; wartime work of, 186n7; and Western feminism, xiv, 107, 113–14; working-class, 113, 134, 179n13. *See also* alcoholics' wives, Japanese; housewives, Japanese; Meiji women
women, Western, 88; images of, 6–7;

independence of, xiv; in workforce, 8
women's liberation *(ūman ribu)* movement, 193n13. *See also* feminism, Japanese
workaholism, women's role in, 56
work environment, humanization of, 46
workers. *See* labor force, Japanese
work ethic, in postwar society, 2
working-class, Japanese: children, 167; growth in, 188n14; women, 113, 134, 179n13
World Health Organization, 45
World War II: family participation in, 185n6; *ie* during, 185n6; memory of, 186n7; sacrifices during, ix; Tokyo during, 119; women's work during, 186n7

Yamamoto, Shegeo and Katsuko, ix–xi; children of, x
Yanagita Kunio, 134
Yoda, Tomiko, 75–76, 79–80; on matricentricity, 83–84
Yokohama Women's Forum, xii
yome (brides), 123–25, 128–29, 134, 135
yomeiri (marriage), 88
Yomiuri Daily News, "Life Guidance" column, 65–66
Yoneyama, Lisa, 186n7
York, Phyllis and David: *Toughlove*, 147
Yoshiko Miyake, 186n7
Yoshiro Mori, 170
youth assistants *(shōnen kyōjoin)*, 81

Zen: idea of consciousness, 184n3; in Japanese therapy, 60

Text:	11/14 Adobe Garamond
Display:	Gill Sans Book
Compositor:	Integrated Composition Systems
Printer and binder:	Maple-Vail Manufacturing Group
Indexer:	Roberta Engleman